TRANSFORMATION:

ASTROLOGY AS A SPIRITUAL PATH

Bruno and Louise Huber

HopeWell

Knutsford, England

Contents

Symbols and Abbreviations   vii

Forward   1

Chapter 1

Development and Evolution   3

Microcosm and Macrocosm   4
Eastern Theories of Development   4
Causality: The Law of Cause and Effect   6
The Course of Life in the Crosses   7
Karmic Problems in the Axes   7

Chapter 2

Dynamic Quadrants and The Dynamic House System   11

Quadrant Theory   11
The Static House System   12
The Dynamic House System   13

Dynamic Quadrants   14
The Four Dynamic Quadrants   16
Psychological Process: Thought – Energy – Form   17
Technique for Determining Sequences of Behaviour   19
The Nine Phases of the Behavioural Sequence   20
Rules for Interpreting the Sequence of Reflex Behaviour   24
Beginning and End of the Reflex Sequence   27
Circulating Planets   28
Planets at Beginning and End of Behavioural Sequence   30
Sequence of Planets = Sequence of Behaviour   30

Partnership Comparison   36
Team Selection   39
The Ego Planets in Teamwork   40

Chapter 3

Stress Planets   43

What are Stress Planets?   43
Behaviour   45
Compensations   45
Gauquelin Effect   46
Psychological Effect   48
Energy Exploitation   49
Compensation, Sublimation, Transformation   50
Transformation Meditation on Stress Planets   53

The Stress Planets in the Three Crosses   **55**
Stress Planets in the Cardinal Cross   56
Ego Powers before the AC, IC, DC, MC   57
Jupiter in the Stress Area AC, IC, DC, MC   59
Stress Planets in the Fixed Cross   63
Stress Planets in the Mutable Cross   72
The Age Point through the Stress Areas   **76**
Consultation and Critical Reflection   78

Chapter 4

The Influence of Heredity and Environment   **79**
The House Horoscope   79
Discovery of the House Horoscope   80
Application of the House Horoscope   84
Aspect and Aspect Pattern Colouring   85
Example Horoscope   87
The Personality Planets   90
The Moon Node Horoscope   91
Aspect Comparison   91
The Three Horoscopes   92
Unaspected Ego Planets   93
The Local Horoscope   **95**
Local Horoscope Description   96
The Age Point in the Local Horoscope   98
Discrepancy between Temperament and Environment in Signs and Houses   **99**
Differences Between Sign and House (Temperament and Behaviour)   101
House/Sign Combinations in the Crosses   102

Chapter 5

The Age Point and the Four Temperaments   **105**
Typology   **107**
Typology and the AP   108
I and You Temperaments   109
House/Sign Combination and the Temperaments   **110**
Fire Houses 1, 5, 9   111
Earth Houses 2, 6, 10   113
Air Houses 3, 7, 11   114
Water Houses 4, 8, 12   116
The Synthesis of Sign and House   **118**
Discrepancy Between Signs and Houses – Dynamic Calculations   120
The AP Through Plus and Minus Houses   121

Chapter 6

The Temperament Age Point   **125**
The Spiral of Development   127
1. Personality Development   129
2. Social Development   131
3. External Relationships   134
4. Inner Orientation   136
New Beginnings   139

Chapter 7

The Age Point in the Twelve Signs   **141**
AP at the "Zero Point"   141
AP in Aries   142
AP in Taurus   143
AP in Gemini   143
AP in Cancer   144
AP in Leo   145
AP in Virgo   145
AP in Libra   146
AP in Scorpio   147
AP in Sagittarius   147
AP in Capricorn   148
AP in Aquarius   149
AP in Pisces   149

Chapter 8

The Zodiac in Colour   **151**
The Colour Spectrum   151
Astrological Colours   153
Psychological Effect of Colours   154
The Colour Circle as a Life Clock   157

Chapter 9

The Moon Nodes   **161**
The Lunar Houses   162
The Shadow Function of the Moon Node Horoscope   162
The Moon Node Age Point   **163**
Encounter of the Two Age Points   165
The Horoscope of Jiddu Krishnamurti   166
The Age Point in Krishnamurti's Horoscope   170

The Integration Horoscope   177
The Threefold Personality   177
How the Integration Horoscope was Developed   179
Hints for Interpreting the Integration Horoscope   181
Aspects in the Integration Horoscope   181
Age Progression through Natal and Nodal Signs   187

Chapter 10

Low Point Experiences: Twelve Gates to the Spiritual Life

189

The Five Levels of the Horoscope   189
Cycles and Intermissions   191
Spiritual Meaning of Low Point Stations   192
The Circle in the Centre   194
Experiencing the Horoscope Through Meditation   **195**
Horoscope Meditation   199
Breathing Rhythms   200
Crises of Development and Awareness   **201**
The Three Crosses and the Transmutation of the Ego   **204**
The Cardinal Cross   206
The Fixed Cross   208
The Mutable Cross   212
Bibliography   **215**
Contacts and Resources   **217**

Symbols and Abbreviations

The Planets

Sun	☉	♂		Mars
Moon	☽	♃		Jupiter
Saturn	♄	♅		Uranus
Mercury	☿	♆		Neptune
Venus	♀	♇		Pluto
ascending Moon Node	☊			

The Signs

Aries	♈	♎		Libra
Taurus	♉	♏		Scorpio
Gemini	♊	♐		Sagittarius
Cancer	♋	♑		Capricorn
Leo	♌	♒		Aquarius
Virgo	♍	♓		Pisces

The Aspects

Green	Semi-sextile	Angle of 30°	⊼
	Quincunx	Angle of 150°	⊼
Blue	Sextile	Angle of 60°	✳
	Trine	Angle of 120°	△
Red	Square	Angle of 90°	□
	Opposition	Angle of 180°	☍
Orange	Conjunction	Angle of 0°	☌

Abbreviations

AC = Ascendant	HC	=	House Cusp
IC = Imum Coeli	LP	=	Low Point
DC = Descendant	BP	=	Balance Point
MC = Medium Coeli	MNH	=	Moon Node Horoscope
AP = Age Point	TAP	=	Temperament Age Point

Forward

Dear Reader

For many students of astrology, it has become a natural source of psychological self-help and spiritual orientation. For the past 30 years, the Astrological Psychology Institute (API) has taught an astrology that focuses on the individual's growth towards independence. During many years of research work, growing demand has also led us to develop new astrological methods for identifying the personal spiritual developmental path. Evolutionary ideas and esotericism will always lie at the heart of what we do. After working with Alice A. Bailey for three years to build up the Arcane School in Geneva, and then studying psychosynthesis with Roberto Assagioli in person in Florence, we wanted to incorporate this expanded understanding of man and his world into astrology.

Other astrological schools are also increasingly using the individual horoscope as a way to wholeness, to synthesis and spiritual development. This new direction in astrology aims to take into consideration the laws of spiritual growth, which have much more to do with evolutionary thoughts, with religion and meditation, than had originally been accepted. It is our intention to contribute to this new trend with this book.

By way of an overview, we start by listing the methods that are already used throughout the world in the API School, and which aid our spiritual and holistic development:

1. Seeing the aspect pattern as a whole: colour, shape, position, aspect figures.
2. Seeing aspect structures as the expression of life motivation: triangular, quadrangular, linear.
3. Three-dimensional horoscope interpretation: physical, emotional, mental.
4. Intensity curve: strong and weak points of the planets.
5. Integration of the threefold personality.
6. Influence of nature and nurture (House Horoscope).
7. The Family Model: Sun, Moon, Saturn.
8. Comparison of horoscopes for couples.
9. Dynamic Calculation method – motivation changes.
10. Stress Planets: compensation, sublimation, transformation.
11. Moon Node as point of opportunity for spiritual growth.

12. Moon Node Horoscope (shadow personality).
13. Integration Horoscope (personality and shadow).
14. The Life Clock in the horoscope (Age Progression).
15. The astrological colour wheel as a life progression.
16. The journey of initiation through the Low Point stations.
17. Upbringing as the source of character.
18. Spiritual Planets: transformation and initiation.
19. Esoteric Rulers: change of consciousness.
20. Ascendant Signs: seed thoughts/ goal development.
21. Working with three horoscopes: Basic, House and Moon Node Horoscopes.
22. Horoscope meditation.
23. Zodiac meditations.

We deal with only some of these methods in this book. As well as the representation of Dynamic Quadrants and the behavioural processes they reveal, we describe the compensative effect of Stress Planets and how this is transformed. We also deal with the psychological application of the House Horoscope, with the developmental potential that is discernible in the discrepancies between genetic disposition and behaviour. We also show how the Moon Node Horoscope can help here. The whole personality can only be identified by examining the interaction of the three horoscopes (Basic, House and Moon Node).

We also explore in more detail the spiritual significance of Age Progression, as was described earlier in our book *Astrology and the Spiritual Path*. Using the colour wheel enables a better understanding of our life journey; with the Low Point stations, we can establish whether any problems are due to a conflict between genetic disposition and behaviour, or to a transformation crisis of the personality. This distinction, as well as the knowledge that an acute crisis is also an evolutionary event, enables the person concerned to find harmony once again with nature's laws and with themselves.

We therefore hope that this book will give new insights and encouragement to further research as well as giving searchers hope on their spiritual journey. We would also now like to express our gratitude to all who have collaborated on the production of this book.

February 1996   Bruno and Louise Huber

Chapter 1

Development and Evolution

The idea of evolution is an integral part of astrological psychology. The latter is based on a fundamental psychological concept that views a man or woman holistically – as a human being linked both to the immediate environment and to the universe – and as a spiritual entity (individual) who can relate freely and consciously to either.

Taking the idea a stage further, it is postulated that an evolutionary plan runs throughout creation, and that the human soul or spirit has descended into matter from pure, celestial consciousness for the purpose of manifesting in physical form. But the time eventually comes to return to source. The journey back starts with a total inner reversal produced by a sense of the nullity and transience of physical life. Now it is clear, on looking at the spiritual development of individuals, that Age Progression [see *LifeClock* (14)] has to do with this journey back. It marks the various stages of evolution in the rhythmic course of life. This law of development is active throughout nature and produces a steady unfolding of the self as it germinates, ripens and dies.

A knowledge of this evolutionary theory gives us a better sense of time. By looking down a longer vista, we expand our consciousness and improve our understanding of the present. We gain a general view of our own life and of the evolutionary history of our race, and penetrate to the meaning behind everything. This developmental dynamic underlies all that happens to us and its aim is to make us complete and to correct any faults of personality we may have acquired. By making us complete, we mean to help each of us to become whole, undivided beings. From this standpoint, everything we experience as shown in the horoscope makes sense; everything has a symbolic meaning for our further development. That is the fundamental idea of astrological development theory.

We shall now endeavour to elucidate the above from various points of view, while also looking at the parallel idea of Age Progression as a dynamic element of development for the personality. Since our personal lives are embedded in a greater cosmic event, it will be wise to proceed from above to below, from bigger to smaller, in studying these patterns. We must first see the laws of development at work in a wider setting before we can understand their possible effects on our relatively insignificant human lives.

Microcosm and Macrocosm

As we all know, man/woman is the "microcosm in the macrocosm," a little copy of larger cosmic realities. Each of us is only a part – a minute part – of an immeasurable and all-embracing whole, the cosmic whole. The living energies penetrating ourselves and nature are the energies of a great Life, in which we live and move and have our being.

The relating of small to big, of humanity to the universe, and the consideration of all human problems from the standpoint of the one Life, gives a proper sense of proportion and direction, correct evaluation and judgment, and a deeper understanding of the connectedness of things.

The development changes taking place in nature and in human beings are always in the direction of balance and maturity. We can observe this everywhere: in biology, in the life of animals, in sociology, in human relationships; also in the universe, in the histories of the planets and the fixed stars, and even in the galaxies. Everything is governed by a wonderful order that keeps it in balance. Whenever the balance is disturbed, nature finds ways and means of restoring it. Often the remedy is surprisingly drastic, for reasons that are hard for us to understand.

Eastern Theories of Development

Karma and Reincarnation

The Hindu and Buddhist religions offer reincarnation and karmic law as an explanation of the balancing process. They assume that the life within us is imperishable, and that only the form or body is subject to physical laws and to death; while the spirit, soul, or self endures – repeatedly incarnating on earth according to the laws of evolution in order to acquire a complete experience of the universe. Their teaching is that each individual has been set an evolutionary goal impossible to reach in a single lifetime. Therefore numerous opportunities are given of getting closer to this goal in different lives. The rebirth or reincarnation from oriental religion involves a cyclic development that continues until the individual has reached the desired state of perfection and can manifest on earth as a fully functional child of the Deity.

The questions "Where do I come from?" "Why was I born?" "What is the purpose of my life?" "Why must I suffer like this?" "Why are the lives of others so much easier than mine?" are explained by the law of karma. This is the law of cause and effect, which invariably strives for balanced development. Nothing can be thought, wished or done by a person without being lodged in the great energy store of the cosmos ready to come home to roost one day. Hence different destinies – one person possesses everything he or she needs, while another is always fighting for physical survival.

According to eastern philosophy, the law of karma plays a double role: firstly, the individual is forced to pay debts accumulated in former lives; and, secondly, he or she develops further under the law of cause and effect and learns not to do certain things because of their unfortunate results. It is intelligence, discrimination, and decisiveness that are liberating here.

This fits in well with what we have gleaned from psychological astrology. People are compelled by the rough-and-tumble of life to develop abilities, many of which have been slumbering all unknown in the unconscious. We learn from experience to bring about an increasingly positive exchange between our inner being and the environment. By rousing our innermost nature to consciousness, we can release ourselves more and more from coercion by our stars, acting as these do through unconscious drives, faulty mental attitudes, groundless fears and paranoia, guilt feelings and delusions – or, in other words, through our karma.

But, when all is said and done, it does not matter what names we give to these active forces, provided we understand them and deal with them correctly. The very knowledge that problems arise from inherited factors, from transferring to the environment our connection with father and mother – or the knowledge that the causes of difficulties lie in karma – helps us to rid ourselves of these problems and difficulties or, at least, to adopt a different attitude towards them. What matters is to recognize the causal relations affecting us.

Causality: The Law of Cause and Effect

"Karma" in Age Progression

Age progression as a cyclic phenomenon has much to do with the law of cause and effect. "We reap what we sow." The Age Point (AP) enables us to see at a glance the native's whole life – past, present and future. It enables us to pinpoint the period in which a given error is committed, or some decision is made that later results in favourable or unfavourable circumstances.

We recognize what made us react in a certain way; whether, at the time, we did so consciously or unconsciously. As already mentioned, it does not matter if we view our impulses as due to predetermination, compulsion mechanisms, or karma. In any case, it seems that karmic law operates essentially in the unconscious. Our blind reactions arise chiefly out of our instinctual nature – the three basic drives: self-preservation (hunger, thirst), reproduction (sexuality) and self-assertion. The law of cause and effect is decisive in the realm of the drives and instincts. When we are functioning in this area, we are ruled by our drives. It is this response mechanism, which is automatically for or against a thing, that is always creating fresh karma in reprisal.

If, for example, someone sticks out a leg and trips us, we get angry and aggressive. Our automatic reaction is to pay him back in kind. Great self control is required to behave as if nothing had happened; but, if we immediately and blindly give way to a desire for revenge, we shall remain subject to the law of karma. Our action will come back to us like a boomerang. If, on the other hand, we succeed in not reacting or even in taking into consideration the motives of the person who tripped us, then we come to grips with the causes and help to efface the karma. Individual development aims at positive control both of oneself and of one's surroundings, and at freedom from compulsions and contingencies, from inner needs and desires. Here is where modern psychological and spiritual insights prove useful. They permit us to take stock of ourselves, to recognize both our potential and our limitations. Astrology gives similar assistance.

Thanks to age progression, astrological psychology allows continual self-observation, self-knowledge, and self-mastery. Finally, an understanding of the mechanisms underlying the way we function permits us to recognize trends in our mental and spiritual development, and also possible dangers and karmic repercussions.

In a horoscope, there are many factors that can indicate circumstances that are more or less forced on the native. We shall not enumerate them all here. However, the karmic components of the three crosses do deserve scrutiny, because the qualities of the crosses point to deep layers of human motivation. We now take a closer look at these.

The Course of Life in the Crosses
Cardinal, Fixed, Mutable

In considering the Age Point, we need to remember that more often than not the matters indicated relate to our environment and not to ourselves. They will thrust themselves on us unrelentingly until we have sorted them out. If we fail to do so while the AP is in the house where they first arise, they will return to haunt us afterward and will then be harder to remedy. Everything left undone must be tackled later with more effort and possibly less success.

For example, problems that were not solved in the 5th house recur in the 8th house, but in a more severe, acute and troublesome form. There are certain sets of problems that are strung together by the same cross. That is to say, similar problems or situations keep cropping up in the same cross as the corresponding stage of life is reached. If, owing to anxieties or taboos, we fail to experience true love in the fixed 5th house, the problem will arise again more sharply in the fixed 8th house. Frequently, our whole way of life and place in society are put at risk. Then if, in the 8th house, we do not come to terms with inner change, we shall have no chance of possessing true friends in the 11th house. It is instructive to look at this topic in relation to the axes. [See also *The Astrological Houses* (13).]

Karmic Problems in the Axes

In the cardinal cross, karmic problems arise from the I-You relationship of the 'encounter axis' (houses 1 and 7). In the 1st house, especially in the first 4 years, the infant experiences self-preservation and self-assertion drives only. This is the time of ego formation. Others do not yet consciously exist for the child. If, through external circumstances, lack of affection, or breaking of the will, the ego is

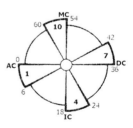

thrown back on itself, it hardens and becomes incapable of love. The ease with which we make contacts largely depends on the first years of life. If they are unhappy, we shall have to cope with partnership problems at ages 36-42, when the Age Point is traversing the 7th house. What is more, our I-problem or egocentricity will be activated when the Age Point passes through the 4th house between ages 18 and 24. Misguided behaviour in contacts and intimate relationships will bring painful experiences. We shall lack understanding and love from partner and friends until we learn to give love. In the 7th house we shall be involved in continual confrontation, struggle and strife with the You, until we achieve a harmonious balance between them and us. Whatever we have done to them has to be made good. Divorce is common at this stage of life.

In the other cardinal axis (houses 4 and 10), we usually reap in the 10th house, from ages 54 to 60, what we have sown in the 4th (and also in the 7th) house. If we have treated others fairly and squarely and have scrupulously discharged obligations and responsibilities, then we shall be accorded honour and recognition in the 10th house. But if we have refused to make terms with those who have something against us, or if we have gained a position by unjust means, then karma will catch up with us at this stage. We shall be hurled from our throne, firmly put in our place, or cold-shouldered.

In the fixed cross karma shows up in all fixed requirements or conditions. If, for example, when the Age Point was passing through the 2nd house (between ages 6 and 12), we felt unduly pressurized by those around us and built a defence system against them, we may be disappointed in love in the 5th house (between ages 24 and 30), because we make it 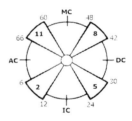 too hard for the You to get to us. If this problem is unsolved, or if our attitude hardens still further, the process of change taking place when the Age Point traverses the 8th house (between ages 42 and 48) will be intensified. The dying and becoming, the letting go of material security, the conquest of problems stemming from wrong behaviour in the periods of the 2nd and 5th houses require greater effort. Fate cracks down hard, especially at the Low Point of the 8th house (ages 45-46), or when the house cusp is crossed, or upon entry into the sign occupying the 8th house. Many of us then need to take a few blows to shake us out of our set ways and to breach the walls we have built around ourselves in a wrongly conceived scheme of self defence.

The other fixed-cross axis (houses 5 and 11) also has to do with the development of fixed patterns of behaviour. If, in the 5th house (between ages 24 and 30), we fight shy of love affairs because we fear bad experiences or because of moral inhibitions, we cannot experience the 5th house as it really is. Usually in the 8th house (ages 42-48) and even in the 11th house (ages 60-66), we get further opportunities to discover what we have missed. We may start flirting like teenagers! However, the lost opportunities will return only when true love is awakened as an energetic inner power. For, in the 8th house, where rigidity sets in all too easily and there is a danger that existence will become mere routine, love is a healing, life-giving element. But makeshift experiences, in which we merely buy love or friendship, will quickly disappear; leaving behind a bitter emptiness, which can lead to resignation or to a mental crisis in which life seems futile.

In the mutable cross karma involves questions of both material and spiritual existence. During the passage through the 9th house (ages 48-54), impressions from the 3rd house (ages 12-18) have a marked effect. Even if, at the earlier age, we allowed ourselves to be worsted by the environment, agreed to toe the party line and lost our ideals in time-serving, there is still a possibility in the 9th house of developing individuality and finding our own life-style; especially if our personal conceptions of the world, and our dreams, visions, and youthful ideals, remain alive in us.

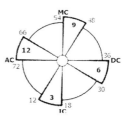

The other cross (houses 6 and 12) supplies a direct karmic relationship, too, for what we have achieved in the 6th house (ages 30-36) in terms of civic responsibility, sharing in the community, acceptance of obligations and involvement in social service will contribute to our inner peace in the 12th house (ages 66-72).

If we have served others and have been neighbourly, then assistance and further instruction can mean something to us in the 9th house, for in the 6th house we have prepared ourselves for them and can "come home" with a clear conscience in the 12th house. But if in the 6th house (ages 30-36) we shirked work, did not labour for our bread and lived at the expense of others, we cannot progress in the 9th house (ages 48-54). If we possess material wealth without ever having had to struggle for it, the question will arise in the 9th house and especially at the crisis of meaning at the Low Point (ages 51-52): "What can possibly require my attention? I have all I want for myself – what more should I do?" We stagnate, our souls wither, and we find no entry to the spiritual home in old age. Its door has been bolted by our own hands.

Chapter 2

Dynamic Quadrants
and
The Dynamic House System

In the following Koch houses are used exclusively. Placidus or other house systems are not suitable for dealing with the questions formulated.

Quadrant Theory

The dynamic quadrants are a new way of looking at the house system in which the usual classical quadrants which extend from one angular cusp to the next are not used, but instead are measured between the low points of the fixed houses. In traditional astrology it is usual for the house system to be tied to the angles of the charts. Thus the first quadrant starts at the AC and ends at the IC, and so on. The quadrants are therefore delimited by the cardinal points AC, IC, DC, MC, the so-called angles or cardinal points in the house system. The effect of the houses begins at the ascendant with a cardinal house, which is followed by a fixed and then a mutable house. The cross sequence (C-F-M) gives rise to a three-step sequence of development, which is ignited and set in motion through an impulse to action at the main angles (action as cause).

The Static House System

The four quadrants arise from the so-called "cross-hair" that divides the circle into four equal parts [see *The Astrological Houses*, page 54 (13)]. The upright-standing cross is anchored in the earth by the vertical axis; it therefore has a firmly established position that cannot be easily changed. From a psychological viewpoint this anchoring shows a rootedness in the family, the collective, and also a steadfastness and stasis.

The static house system built around the "cross-hair" is in general use in traditional astrology. This explains the rigid terms that have been given to the individual houses, such as 1st house: appearance; 2nd house: possession; and so on. The static thinking could clearly be expressed only in simple keywords, and stuck to these fixed terms for centuries. Modern man is not satisfied with these terms, on the contrary, they put him off astrology. Although psychological thought is ubiquitous today, in many cases formal deterministic statements are still made about the house system.

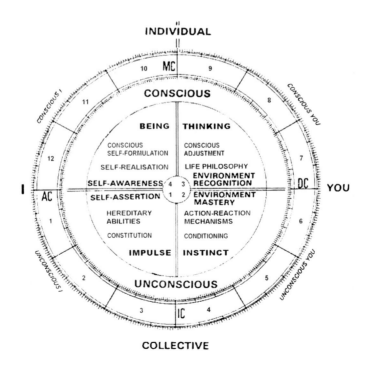

The Four Quadrants (Static)

The Dynamic House System

In our time many terms have been changed and extended through the realisations of psychology. As well as psychological questions, in astrology we also increasingly come up against spiritual considerations and ways of looking at problems. With the help of the horoscope we want not only to clear up psychological conflicts, but also to point to new ways of further development. The old methods are no longer sufficient for that. As soon as the spiritual comes into question, it has to do in principal with growth processes and not with static circumstances, and for this the dynamic house system is especially useful. Deciding which house system to use thus depends on which questions are introduced into astrology. If developmental considerations are to be central, then the preference is for the dynamic house system, in which the houses are measured from low point to low point. If we are asking about the conditions and static circumstances in an area of life, then we use the static house system.

Overall View

For an overall consideration of the horoscope and for a differentiated interpretation of planetary placements we take the static house system into account alongside the dynamic houses, albeit in the background. For interpretation of the radix chart we therefore use both systems. They can be seen as two superimposed levels and their combined effect produces interesting insights. To ascertain these effects we use the intensity curve [below; see also *The Astrological Houses* (13)]. In

The Intensity Curve

it, according to the static house system, the 9th house for example extends from the cusp of the 9th to the cusp of the 10th house. In the dynamic house system, the 9th house already begins to have an effect at the low point of the 8th and this continues to the cusp of the 10th. In the diagram on the previous page, the merging of the two house systems is illustrated by means of the zodiac signs which begin at the low points of the houses.

From this it is evident that the area between the low point and the next cusp always represents a dual path. A planet situated there has to deal with two house themes; it will be taxed with this two-fold demand and really stressed with the burden. For that reason we call it a *stress planet*. *Stress planets* are further covered in chapter 3.

Dynamic Quadrants

According to the law of the analogy "As in the small, so in the great", with the dynamic quadrants we broaden the theme of the intensity curve stated above to apply to an entire quadrant. The low points of the individual quadrants then correspond to the low points of the four fixed houses (2, 5, 8, 11). From there we proceed on the assumption that the low points of the fixed houses are special zero-points in the house system. Here our powers contract inwards; every drive comes to a standstill.

The mutable and cardinal houses frame each of the four main axes. At these dynamic poles of the cardinal axes (AC, IC, DC, MC) energies are at optimal effectiveness in life, at the low points of the fixed houses they are withdrawn inwards. It is known that at the low point of a house, the energies begin to concentrate and redirect themselves towards the next cusp. There they unfold and discharge themselves until the driving energies again succumb to the next low point. This rhythmic sequence with its high and low points also takes place in the quadrants.

A dynamic quadrant therefore extends from the low point of a fixed house to the low point of the next fixed house. In the middle of this stands the action-producing cardinal axis (which gives its name to the quadrant). With the dynamic quadrants therefore, we begin with a mutable house, which is followed by a cardinal and then a fixed house. This three-phase process begins with criticism of the existing and with planning of the new, according to the principle "think first and then act" (Thought, Energy, Form). We will return to that later. This division is dynamic and extremely informative when considering spiritual and psychological matters.

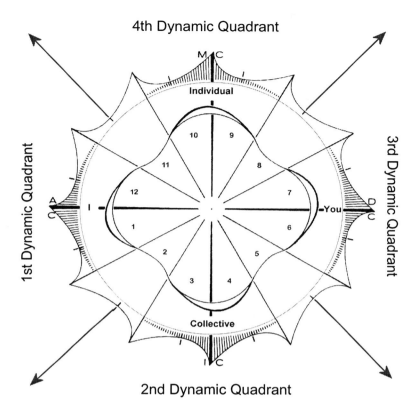

The Dynamic Quadrants

Low Points

The first dynamic quadrant therefore does not begin at the AC but at the low point of the 11th house. This point is chosen consciously, it corresponds to the creation maxim from classical antiquity "From thought comes the energy which brings forth form".

At the low point of the 11th house everything is in a state of rest, strength is being concentrated for a new start. Although there is not really any drive available, things run along accustomed lines. This state is not dead in the sense of an absence of movement, but everything functions automatically. There can be a long-established routine to which one adheres. In this process of moving along fixed lines there sometimes surface feelings of resignation and dissatisfaction with what has come to be and we begin in a sense to explore. The sequence of development begins with the mutable house in which emerge new thoughts and impulses which should guide us onwards.

Cardinal Points

As the previous diagram shows, the main axes stand in the middle of the dynamic quadrants, in between the other two house cusps. We know that cardinal impulses are set in motion at the main axes, so with that there exists the possibility to use planets in the area of the AC, IC, DC and MC successfully.

The Four Dynamic Quadrants

The dynamic quadrants characterise four fundamental modes of human behaviour. Planets situated there function in the environment according to the overriding theme. There follows a short description of their effect.

1st Dynamic Quadrant – the "I" Quadrant

(from LP of the 11th to LP of the 2nd house)

Planets in this area are interested in the development of personality; they concern themselves chiefly with the manifestation of the strength of the ego, in a positive as well as a negative way, in a mundane as well as a spiritual sense. Here is the really intimate area of a person, into which no-one may enter uninvited, where the ego must feel itself to be secure and strong.

2nd Dynamic Quadrant – the Collective Quadrant

(from LP of the 2nd to LP of the 5th house)

With planets situated here we tend to want to be involved, to belong and in the end to be the same as others. We feel ourselves to be a part of humanity and experience ourselves as a cell in a greater whole. We stick to collective standards and do what everyone else does or finds acceptable.

3rd Dynamic Quadrant – the "You" Quadrant

(from LP of the 5th to LP of the 8th house)

In this quadrant we are most strongly and intensively oriented towards the other, and thus to the environment. Planets in this area can pull themselves away from the environment only with difficulty. People with such placements thus also feel themselves to be under an obligation to the other. If they want to do something for themselves alone they possibly feel guilty. They must concern themselves with the other whether it happens to suit them or not. Also, if disputes or dependencies are involved, they remain reliant on others, on the environment.

4th Dynamic Quadrant – the Individual Quadrant

(from the LP of the 8th to the LP of the 11th house)

Here we experience our individuality in the world, as someone who is certain in himself what to do or to leave alone. We experience ourselves as an individual, like an isolated tower in the landscape. Indeed, we stand out from this landscape, although without it the tower would not stand anywhere. The landscape is the collective on which we are dependent (2nd dynamic quadrant). Besides, there are other towers who are likewise individualities. We have to come to an arrangement with them, even if we might feel them to be rivals.

Three-Step Process

In the dynamic quadrants we therefore ascertain to which degrees we are in interchange with the environment through individual planets. In this we have to take into account the qualities of the crosses. As already mentioned, we begin with the mutable house at the low point of the 11th, followed by the cardinal house at the low point of the 12th, then comes the fixed house beginning at the low point of the 1st. Three-step processes also start here according to quality of the crosses, but in this case it is an organic sequence, a three-stage creative process following the principle Thought (mutable) – Energy (cardinal) – Form (fixed), and not as in the static house sequence Energy (cardinal) – Form (fixed) – Thought (mutable).

Psychological Process: Thought – Energy – Form

A psychologically very productive application of the dynamic quadrants according to this law is the investigation of reflexively controlled sequences of behaviour, which we look at more closely below. Above all, these three phases should be considered in the context of coping with issues in everyday life and in the workplace. If it is clear to us that every deed starts with a thought, then a true creative process should have its prior intellectual fermentation, so that a clear goal can be set. Then it is a conscious act of creation that also produces better results and ultimately yields something useful. If we put the deed first, the consequences usually catch us up in a crisis (mutable phase at the end of the process), in which we find out why we have had no success and what we have done wrong. How often we have to make corrections, take things back and fix them, because we have acted prematurely. That costs time and money. For that reason it is better to proceed according to the dynamic houses. There we finds a natural sequence of development which follows the wise old principle "Think first and then act".

First there is a thought, the idea (mutable), then there arises the strength to realise this idea (cardinal), and then the emergent form comes to optimal use (fixed). In the mutable houses we have experiences, recognitions, and draw conclusions. In the cardinal houses we can work creatively out in the environment, use and enjoy the finished product in the fixed houses, and in the mutable houses the cycle begins anew. In this the dynamic quadrants follow completely the already-quoted ancient esoteric law of creation:

THOUGHT

ENERGY

FORM

These terms are the keywords for the sequence of the three crosses in the dynamic quadrants: mutable – cardinal – fixed. Every course of events in life, even the smallest, begins in reality with an instinctive awareness, a desire or a thought, however brief or fleeting it may be. These definitions correspond to the mutable cross. As long as we think that everything begins with an action, we have the classical arrangement of the quadrants cardinal – fixed – mutable; we do – we have – and then we think about the whole thing. That might well be the basis for the lesser or even negative view of the mutable houses in the past, as they are sometimes termed "falling or weak houses". Thinking about something afterwards is often not advantageous.

With the dynamic quadrants the correct framing of the question is therefore:

How do I begin a task in consciousness? (mutable phase)

How do I realise it? (cardinal)

What will I get out of it? (fixed)

Technique for Determining Sequences of Behaviour

We have developed a new method to be able to answer this question. In it the four quadrants with all the positions of the planets are placed one above the other so that each of the four houses in the same cross lie next to each other in four strata. Each stratum consists of 90° of the house system. The new arrangement of the planets which emerges from this is understood as the reflex sequence of the pattern of behaviour. In practical terms, if a person takes up a new issue or sequence of events then he begins with the planet which is furthest to the left (♃ in the example below). Thereupon follows in order the planet which is next to the right (♀ in the example). He proceeds in this manner along the whole row until he comes to the end with the planet at the extreme right (in this case ☊). The sequence of behaviour ends here. In this manner of consideration, it is unimportant that the planets in sequence from left to right may have their origin in different quadrants. This is naturally apparent from the four levels in the diagram but can be ignored initially.

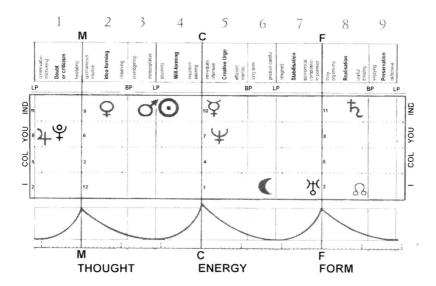

It is evident from practical observation that everyone puts into motion the same sequence of planets in dealing with everyday issues, large or small, in the way that they are arranged in the dynamic quadrants. It is thus an entirely personal action scheme or coping scheme – a pattern of behaviour learned in childhood as to how one deals with things and life situations.

The Formula

As a convenient formula, the dynamic quadrants contain everything needed for interpretation. The central area in which the individual planets are recorded is divided into four rows which correspond to the four dynamic quadrants. (see the small numbers which indicate the houses). They are labelled in the margins with names which correspond to the meaning of each of the cardinal points: I, Collective, You and Individual Quadrants. (All the planets within each quadrant are involved with the appropriate theme.) This permits a finer interpretation, because it is significant whether a planet is tied to "I" or "You", orientated to the collective or is individualistic in its action within a particular phase of a matter. However, the actual course of action works from left to right regardless of the quadrant to which planets belong.

Division of the Sequence

The space containing the planets is divided by vertical lines into nine phases of activity. The thicker lines represent house cusps, the thinner ones correspond to the balance and low points. Along the upper edge the phases are identified with keywords. Their sequence speaks for itself. In the bottom part, the course of the intensity curve through the quadrants is shown, and the three main phases are associated with the keywords given above (THOUGHT – ENERGY – FORM). The principal zones, shown in bold type, are: Doubt and Criticism, Idea Formation, Will Formation, Creative Process, Stabilisation, Realisation, Preservation.

The Nine Phases of the Behavioural Sequence

1. The Doubt and Criticism Phase

(Low point of the fixed house to cusp of the mutable house)

Arriving at the low points of the fixed houses, all his own drives are extinguished, he is finally in a state of rest and perhaps thinks that this might be final. However, immediately after the low point he is suddenly no longer so sure about that. That previously satisfying feeling of well-being develops cracks. He has everything so nicely ordered and solidly organised, and suddenly it's too good to be true.

In this phase consciousness (or at least subconsciousness) becomes critical. This naturally works variably with different types. It may be that he simply becomes disenchanted with the routine of such a completely organised life. But it can also be that he increasingly sees (possibly justifiable) faults in the existing situation. That may range from becoming aware of small blemishes, through sensitivity to injustices, to recognition of complete unsuitability. The results are doubt and criticism of the status quo that may indeed at first be dispelled by the fear of possible change or at least may be kept hidden. Anyone who has active or mobile planets in this vicinity, such as Mars, Mercury, Jupiter, Sun, Uranus etc. will not be able to keep their doubts concealed in the long run.

2. The Idea Formation Phase

(Cusp to balance point of the mutable house)

In this zone ideas, intuitions, visions, arise spontaneously at first, which mostly have a clearly idealistic character. He either wants to create remedies (for whatever is defective), or thinks as if he could smooth out the wrinkles in the world or even make it anew. The formation of ideas is also dependent on type. Of course he must turn to the actuality of what is feasible, and that means dealing with the reality of existing circumstances and the available means. Observation must play a central role here, and naturally that is done with whatever planets are in this zone, which bring about quite different results. If there are no planets in the previous phase (doubt), then he can even start with a whole flood of ideas (depending on the planets present), although they possibly lack the closeness to reality. Their feasibility is then often in question and disappointments may not be avoided, at least some of the time. These contribute to the necessary store of experience.

3. The Deepening Phase

(Balance point to low point of the mutable house)

In this intermediate phase he becomes caught up in brooding. He thinks over the ideas repeatedly with the available capabilities (according to the planets involved), or tests them out in trials. He can also make enquiries and get opinions of his capacities, or in a sort of contemplative state scour the whole structure of thought for errors, gaps or inconsistencies. Occasionally, however, this phase is marked quite simply by an uncertainty about his own ideas possibly leading to resignation. It is a phase in which excessive self doubt can bring the process to naught. The obstacle can be overcome in that he can pass unconcernedly on to the next phase – and in the event that there are no planets there, can employ the help of competent people who have something to offer in this area.

4. The Will Formation Phase

(Low point of the mutable house to cusp of the cardinal house)

Now it depends if the planning of further action has been gone into with deliberation and care, and that the necessary means, materials and tools have been assembled and made ready. This is a stress zone, it is often misunderstood in our performance-oriented society. He would like to proceed immediately to action (Phase 5). Through impatience and striving to perform, rushed and hasty preparations lead to later mistakes. Placements of Mars and Sun here especially create this tendency. Instead of that, deliberate planning must curb the already-running motor like a brake, so that the strength of the will may be gathered. The fourth phase is an area in which the instinctive, mutually fragmenting drives have to be transformed, to permit that which is consciously desired to happen. All available strengths are to be concentrated exclusively on one goal. Only thus can great success be achieved.

5. The Action Phase (Creative Process)

(Cusp to balance point of the cardinal house)

The potential strengths which have been gathered together now come to the point of release. Here at last is the realisation of all that one has thought about and wanted. **Direct action** is called for and sometimes even adventurousness. The mode of reaction of planets in this zone is quick and basically offensive. The more successful the will-building phase has been, the more smoothly and successfully can any type of creative process follow. He ought, however, to guard against being caught up in a frenzy of activity just because the power to act is freely available in this sector. He should not confuse power with will, otherwise the creative process can degenerate into meaningless activity (♂☉♃♅♇), or become inflated impress behaviour (♄♀☿☽♆).

6. The Reinforcement Phase

(Balance to low point of the cardinal house)

In this intermediate phase the impetus of the cardinal cusp is dying away. Anything new can now still succeed only in the long-term view, and then probably if he can apply the necessary patience. Much more often, and quite naturally, this phase is the completion of whatever was created in Phase 5. It requires foresight and circumspection in dealing with the approaching conclusion of what has been done. If that is not successful matters may go awry along the lines of "Master, the work is finished – may I just fix it?" That is, he is constantly occupied with improvement, cleaning and tidying up.

7. The Consolidation Phase (Stabilisation)

(Low point of the cardinal house to cusp of the fixed house)

In the advance to the next house (in the shadow of a fixed cusp) he often becomes unpleasantly aware that "things just won't do any more". The experience, that uncertainties cannot be sufficiently dispelled through activity, may in particularly extroverted people lead to feelings of apprehension or even **resignation**. Or fears of loss arise and he can take badly to rejection or criticism. He is forced to make the thing solid and economically viable, and may develop the pleasure of **possession** in order to feel more secure. The economic development of what has been created is the right keyword here, because the thing should and must have permanence. That can lead to a process of trying out which can sometimes become hectic and through that can go wrong. Someone with planets here must proceed on the assumption that there is something to be learned in the process of completion, otherwise he will miss out on some of the enjoyment of the following phases.

8. The Utilisation Phase (Realisation)

(Cusp to balance point of the fixed house)

Now is the point in time where all of the final order and optimal use should be found. With increasing readiness and great enthusiasm, but not hectically ("useless energy"), all things are converted into a state of order, all events into reliable routines, and all relationships into agreements. Pronounced thoughts about use guide the functions of the planets here and bring them to maximum efficiency. This creates security, and because of that efficiency is experienced as pleasure. He assumes that he can acquire whatever is needed in order to get control over all life situations.

Because everything in this zone is experienced as objects, human considerations can fall by the wayside. Humans should also be reliable or useful, or function profitably. For those affected, that can produce hardship and can be interpreted as inhumanity.

9. The State of Preservation

(Balance to low point of the fixed house)

In this last zone of the behavioural sequence the whole process comes to rest at its goal. All impulses to movement have died away. For that reason he resorts to the being and having of what he has achieved. Activity is limited to the enjoyment, maintenance and preservation of the creation – and its protection from the environment. The basic position is defensive and conservative. Fears of loss are constant companions, and too often advisers, in daily events. The enjoyment is often restrained by the effort of holding everything together and fending off the environment, and he willingly plays off the power of the possessor against it.

Rules for Interpreting the Sequence of Reflex Behaviour

The Pattern Script (Processor)

Many years of work with these sequences has shown that in the order of the planets laid out in the dynamic quadrants there lies hidden a constantly repeating pattern, indeed a script. As mentioned above, all reflex-controlled sequences of behaviour in daily life take place in this order. Whether it is to do with material, spiritual or intellectual issues, this sequence, this pattern, regulates the individual actions just like a processor with a timing mechanism which sends the planets into action and directs them towards a goal. With this we are dealing with a kind of code that is presumably stored in the brain and can be compared to a computer program. At first one recoils from that thought, believing that it is to do with a compulsion to which one is delivered up. That is actually true to a certain degree. It depends entirely on the state of our consciousness whether we belong to those who blindly follow the pattern of behaviour, or to the free beings who have through self observation (e.g. from the centre of the horoscope) acquired enough knowledge of their reflex-driven modes of functioning to alter something should it be necessary.

Equipment

In reality, this planetary sequence is a tool box which it is advantageous to get to know. We can compare the behavioural pattern with the mode of functioning of a computer in which all programs are stored and available to us through the processor. We can get them to come up if we press the right buttons. Also, if we consciously choose the various programs they appear on the screen on demand and we can use them if we are able.

The same is true of our reflex-driven sequences of behaviour as shown by the dynamic quadrants. If we know and are familiar with them, we experience the individual phases consciously and can cope with them. For example, the possibility exists to slow down or speed up the process, we can control the time factor to suit our goals. We should always be the one who sets the tone, the controlling authority who sits behind the steering wheel. We only have to know it, then we can use these implanted templates of behaviour as a set of tools for the realisation of our goals. However, everything depends on the degree of consciousness. Just as a computer serves us and we do not serve it, we have the freedom to consciously have this timing mechanism at our disposal – but not until we have acquired more knowledge about it. We describe it further in the following rules.

Aspects and Aspect Figures

The natal horoscope should always be placed alongside the diagram of the "sequence of behaviour" and considered in conjunction with it. If we look at certain individual planets in the dynamic quadrants, we should also see where these planets lie in the natal chart. The aspects and aspect figures in the dynamic quadrants are mostly a peripheral issue. If someone has two aspect figures which are separated from each other in the natal horoscope then it means that the person lives in the individual figures at different times. The layout of the dynamic quadrants can be a help if they recognise where the next step is, which planet must now be activated, and in that way they move into the other aspect figure. With this system we can get a better grip on separate aspect figures. Then more order comes into life and we no longer feel so much torn this way and that. That is a great help to consciousness.

Empty Spaces

There can be empty spaces in any area of a behavioural sequence. In the example below they are in the first two zones *Doubt and Criticism* and *Idea Formation*. This woman has trouble reacting properly; she lacks the tools because there are no planets positioned there. Feelings of

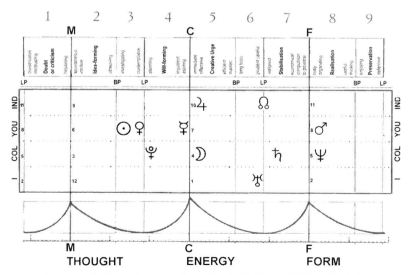

Dynamic Quadrants, female, 1.12.1950, 17:36, Zürich

deficiency, incapability and insecurity may take their place. How does she cope with it? Firstly, it is important to know that there is no shame in having empty areas in the dynamic quadrants – it is quite normal. For this purpose most people seek a partner who can fill out the vacant areas with his or her planets. In that there is a balance, a completion. But first she must understand that and be prepared to accept it as a fact of life. Here the diagram of the dynamic quadrants helps her to recognise the empty spaces and do something positive about it. She is less familiar personally with the subjects which are attributed to the empty areas, they are brought to her by the environment. There are therefore times when she is disengaged and waits for an external impetus.

If, for example, the term *Doubt and Criticism* is foreign, because she has no planets there, then she does not respond to it. Criticism or reproaches cannot set the sequence in motion. Or sometimes she may sit fast without any drive (she is just in an empty phase). Then if someone comes along and makes the reproach "You can't just sit around here like this! You must do something!", she will have feelings of guilt, defend herself or block it out at first. Sometimes such prods are necessary to move someone forwards. A person who has none of the nine zones vacant can generally master all phases of existence.

Empty Creative Zone

We had the case of Markus (below) with an empty space in *Creative Process*. His father had hammered it into him that he could not stand

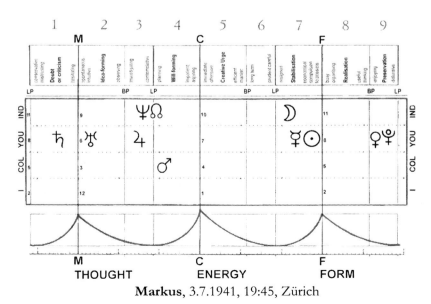

Markus, 3.7.1941, 19:45, Zürich

on his own feet and forced him to help with gardening work. He tried diligently by every means to carry out the work in a satisfactory way, but to no avail. Unforeseen impediments always got in his way and he reaped reproaches, mockery and derision. He was very unfortunate with it. Only when he knew that he had no planets in the area of *Creative Process* could he come to terms with this fact. He has his planets in the first zones, he is a researcher and thinker and really must not work physically at all. When he realised this he was greatly relieved and things went much better for him. That sounds fairly banal, but try it for yourself. Accept your vacant areas and let them be filled by others. It means a lot less expenditure of effort if we can start off from the place where we have talents. This knowledge has already helped many in personnel selection (particularly with team building).

Beginning and End of the Reflex Sequence

Of particular psychological value is to assess those planets which begin and end the sequence. The planet situated at the beginning, the extreme left of the diagram (in the horoscope somewhere after the low point of a fixed house), introduces the cycle. We start with an activity appropriate to its quality. Whether the first planet is in the *Doubt and Criticism, Idea Formation* or *Will Formation* area also plays a part. There is also a great difference if the behavioural sequence starts with Mars, or Saturn or Jupiter or another planet. The planet situated at the end, the extreme right of the diagram (in the horoscope somewhere before the low point of a fixed house), sets a tone in just the same way as the first. According to our observation, the last planet exerts a pulling force on all the planets in the sequence. In a manner of speaking it draws on the first planet and drives the activating energy through the entire row of planets straight on to the end. In that way the end planet is also involved in the beginning of the sequence. In that it has to do with a dynamic motion, it is illuminating that the beginning and end have a relationship with each other. They belong together; the first planet is the sensor that according to its constitution responds to quite specific stimuli, and the last is a constantly driving pulling force, because it knows about the meaning and target of the whole process.

If the **Moon Node stands at the beginning**, it does not signify a power because it comprises a capability, and opportunity to perceive something and react to it. Opportunities must present themselves, however – sometimes one waits on them in vain and must initiate something oneself. For that reason, from experience the next planet (the second from left) must be activated.

With a conjunction we should see which planet is first. As already stated, the sequence begins with the planet after a fixed low point and ends with the planet just before one. It is thus important to establish here exactly whether the individual planets in the conjunction stand before or after the relevant low point – if the conjunction straddles the low point they can have separate functions (beginning or end). Note that all planetary positions are entered in the dynamic quadrants in **house degrees** and not in the degrees of the zodiac.

The computer determines such positions very exactly, so it is advantageous to have the diagram of the planetary sequence calculated and drawn by computer. Of course, a possible handicap can arise from an imprecise birth time. Caution is certainly necessary here. The suspicion of an uncertain birth time can be the motivating factor for a particularly precise self-examination and can if necessary give important clues for a rectification of the birth time.

Circulating Planets

Establishing the exact degree is also important for the interpretation of an individual planet positioned close to the low point of a fixed house. If the distance from such a low point is less than one (house) degree, it can be the cause of an unceasing circulation. So a planet exactly on the low point or within one degree before or after the low point is called a *circulating planet*.

In Example 1, Jupiter is located at the beginning and also at the end. In the diagram it is drawn almost exactly on the first line, but is not drawn in for a second time. However, it stands exactly on the low point of the 5th house and is situated at both the beginning and the end of the dynamic quadrants. It is a *circulating planet*. Jupiter in conjunction with Pluto intensifies the alertness and talent for observation. Nothing escapes the watchful eye. As soon as Jupiter has become aware of something, the sequence starts with this awareness. This person reacts to present stimuli in the flash of an eye and does not question for long whether it brings profit for someone or other. It is to do with the joy of doing and the enjoyment of the moment. Many things are tackled simultaneously, processes run constantly which bring with them an intensification of sensory impressions. The presence of consciousness undertakes all processes uninterruptedly without pausing for rest, because through that there can also be a dissipation of the impulse. With Jupiter there is an overall view, an amalgamation of the goal into a meaningful whole. Beginning and end have grown together, as it were, from which a seamless transition emerges. In this way mostly organic and creative goals are realised which should be for the welfare and pleasure of other people. Pluto

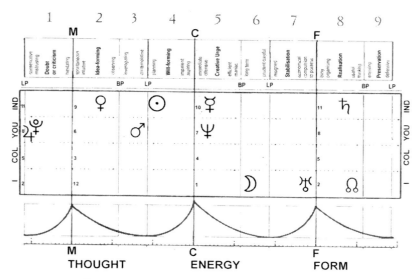

Example 1: Male, 29.11.1930, 12:55, Zürich

in conjunction with Jupiter determines its motivation. It feels called
to give the optimum and realise goals of the highest spiritual value.
Pluto serves evolutionary events and thus the capabilities of Jupiter
are placed at the service of a greater cause.

As is apparent from this example, planets acting as *circulating planets*
are particularly strong in their own characteristics. Some people with a
circulating planet use up their energy without a so-called useful reason;
they burn the candle at both ends if it involves an activity which
enthuses them. That leads to loss of energy and can in the long run
lead through excessive demands to stress symptoms. It is necessary
that this automatic tendency of the *circulating planet* is made conscious
so that this does not happen. Indeed, at the fixed low points the person
can pause deliberately, because that corresponds to their nature.

The role, mode of functioning and characteristic which the
individual planets have in this sequence of behaviour is not too
difficult to make out, especially if one has a *circulating planet* oneself.
For example, one can readily accept that Mars at the beginning is
precipitate in its activity (workaholic), Saturn slows the active flow
of energy, Venus looks for the most comfortable way, Sun is self-
conscious, Uranus is ready to take risks, Mercury is communicative
and enterprising, etc.

Planets at Beginning and End of Behavioural Sequence

In the table on the following page we describe briefly the planets with which the sequence begins and ends. In it we cannot give special consideration to the zone where the beginning takes place. The table sets out keywords which should serve to stimulate the student's thought processes. One should at least understand the first and last planet in an interpretation.

Sequence of Planets = Sequence of Behaviour

As already described, the dynamic quadrant is in its succession of planets a reflex sequence, a process which summons the planets to action one after the other. In this sequence we understand ourselves better, it makes for us something tangible and conscious of what we actually do reflexively. Put in another way, the dynamic quadrant diagram represents a strategy plan according to which the things in our life should run, from the biggest to the smallest. If we want to know how we react and act in individual situations, we can recognise the consequences in the sequence.

In our dynamic quadrant diagram we show, as already described, the positions of the planets. The terms in bold type are the main headings, the others are subsidiary zones in the dynamic quadrants. These subordinate formulations are additional gradual sequential processes. In the mutable zone (M) for example is found *Idea Formation* and that applies to the entire area from the cusp to the low point. Initially one is spontaneous there, intuitive, then observing and enquiring and finally contemplative. The sequence of the terms is chosen consciously, they clarify a sequence of events. They are stages through which a planet goes. The main heading is valid for the stage of the process in general, but the subsidiary headings should also not be forgotten. The planets therefore behave according to the descriptions. There is an amazingly effective mechanism in these sequences. Every process from the smallest to the greatest runs through all the stages from beginning to end. Individual stages which are not necessary for the process in question occasionally act as disturbance factors in the sequence of events, because they nevertheless compulsively want to switch on.

	Beginning Incentive and preparedness	**End** Evaluation and deployment
☉	Dissatisfied with self, goal-oriented, self-willed	Self-satisfaction, ready for new ways to prove oneself
☽	Contact possibility, curiosity, imaginative	Beautiful memories, hope for further experiences
♄	Uncertainty, insecurity, test-reflex, hesitating	Well-being, pride in possession, order, care, protection
☿	Sensitive to words, comparing critically	Pride in knowledge, negotiation and transmission
♀	Sensitive to disturbance, aesthetic, selective	Enjoyment of harmony, intoxicated with beauty, imperturbable
♂	Stimulus to act and to movement, impatient, active	Feelings of strength, pride in achievement, new preparedness
♃	Sensitive to truth, alert senses, judging	Satisfaction of senses, pride in beneficence, reaping and enjoying
♅	Sensitive to imperfection, researching, discovering	Pleasure in finished product, progress, testing of system, improvements
♆	Crisis of need, unloving, helping, healing	Love of letting go, ruminating, meditating, dreaming
♇	Sense of mission, requiring perfection	Peak experience, feeling of power, destroying in order to change
☊	Sense of opportunity, expectant	Retrospective looking at the path, letting go and being open

Key Words for Beginning and End of the Behavioural Sequence

Description of the Sequence of Behaviour

In Example 2 the behavioural sequence starts with Neptune and ends with Mars. Neptune is in the area of *Doubt and Criticism*. How does Neptune react? Mistrustfully, conservative or hesitating? It cannot react conservatively, because that posture is somewhat static and being static is alien to the nature of Neptune. Neptune is flexible and not so easily grasped. It is constantly in flux, awakens inner visions that are sometimes diffuse and sometimes act as intuition. In the area of *Doubt and Criticism* it is sensitive to criticism, it takes as true everything that disturbs or appears false. Often it is not sure what is really going on. It is unsettled or disturbed if it does not know exactly what is happening, it becomes curious and tries to find out, and at that thought is ignited. But unlovingness, disregard for human dignity and a sense of crisis are also aroused. Where Neptune is experienced as a spiritual planet, the process begins with a model of love. Many need a "Great Love", with the certainty that someone needs them, that they can do everything for another person or a cause out of love. To be able to help, to intervene where needed, is an important theme at the start. Some begin with a meditation, they see images or hear voices and know intuitively what they must do, they feel led and guided.

In our example the Moon Node comes next in the area of *Idea Formation*, and then Jupiter. The Moon Node has a special function in the sequence. Planets on either side of it have a significance for spiritual development. They should be taken seriously and specially cultivated. In this case Neptune and Jupiter respond spontaneously

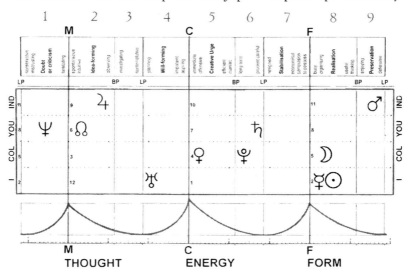

Example 2: Female, 10.5.1924, 03:15, Bamberg

and intuitively to an opportunity (♌). Neptune brings empathy or vision and Jupiter forms the picture which can be apprehended by the senses. The process runs on into the area of *Will Formation* to Uranus. Now a system is worked out and actively improved until it functions correctly. Uranus provides the impulse to find the right technique. It forces a methodical working free of faults – and that strengthens the trust in oneself.

Next comes Venus in the area of *Creative Process*. Venus is only satisfied when her surroundings are orderly, anything defective must certainly come into that. She works to create balance until everything comes into an organic order. Pluto and Saturn are in this zone, and through them long-term goals are pursued, which are approached carefully. Pluto as the ideal of vocation will reach for the highest goals. If it has once had the true visions these endure for the whole of life, they are always effective over the long term as motivational forces. Saturn does not permit these motivations to be shaken, he is their protector and if someone has doubts about it they will be put right. Saturn in this position is a special examiner. Before the leap over the empty *Consolidation Phase* is ventured, everything must be secured and in order. There are situated Mercury, Moon and Sun. An accumulation of ego planets in the *Utilisation* zone plans ahead and organises, the goal must be reached absolutely. Here the whole personality becomes involved, the ego experiences a strengthening on the feeling and rational levels. In our example the Moon comes before the Sun. The two are in conjunction in the dynamic quadrants, which almost always means an immediate gain, a successful work. As soon as one comes to change things around one gets feedback from the environment, and the Moon needs that.

Mars as the Last Planet

Mars is an active planet that because of its nature has some trouble in the *Preservation* zone. As a motor it converts energies into action; it doesn't preserve them but spends them freely. The energy translation succeeds only if there are goals to attain and tasks to be undertaken. If there are, it runs blindly at them, wanting to make an end of the job as quickly as possible. At the opposite end from Neptune at the beginning, it represents a real contrast. It does not wait long and becomes impatient if Neptune spends too long dreaming. It appears to be always short of time. Then it pulls with dynamic force and speed on the whole sequence of the process. Because of that, this person needs a lot of strength, it goes to extremes and just doesn't listen until the task has been dealt with. Ultimately a flagging of energy intervenes regularly (a necessary recuperation), in which it then requires confirmation: "Tell me that I have done well".

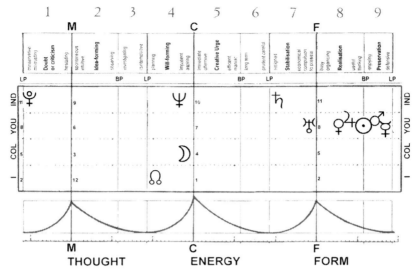

Example 3: Male, 9.8.1955, 17:17, Zürich

In Example 3 the sequence begins with the *circulating planet* Pluto, and ends with Mercury and Pluto. After Pluto, there follow empty spaces in the area of *Idea Formation*, so a jump has to be made to reach *Will Formation*. To reach Saturn and Uranus in the *Consolidation* zone an further jump has to be made over *Creative Process*. This signifies an effort, because this area is prominent in our performance-oriented society. Finally the process ends with a stellium of planets in the areas of *Utilisation* and *Preservation*.

The sequence begins with Pluto, placing the theme of perfection at the beginning. It officiates as the great perfectionist examiner and must link this test with the model of Love (Neptune) right across the empty area, because the Moon Node stands in between and connects the two. This person reacts with Pluto in the area of *Doubt and Criticism* to everything which stands in the way of the vision of a perfect human being. He feels himself called to discover whatever it is that puts this model in question. It is immediately apparent to him what is wrong on the motivational level. He criticises reflexively and tears something up right at the start. That sparks him off, and the sequence is under way. Firstly he encounters the Moon Node and that offers him possibilities to act and react and take an initial step.

The **Moon Node** always signals that the two planets which frame it (here Pluto and Neptune) are enormously important for development. As already said in the previous example, we should take these planets seriously, understand their significance and cultivate their spiritual qualities. Here it involves two spiritual planets which require the highest attention. They represent essential transpersonal powers of the highest quality that are not easy to understand. Neptune, which comes next, follows the image of Love, it can heal the wounds which were caused at the beginning [of the sequence]. Here it is important to pause for a moment and do something out of love. The Moon follows directly after that, the childlike, subjective, feeling ego. It suffers from the incapability of realising the highest ideals and tries to balance that through a surrogate or with something playful. The *Creative* area is empty; here partners have to be sought who will give further help. This knowledge can lead to a development of tolerance with regard to his environment because he has to exhibit this in an empty area. If he tries in this vacant zone to be proud and not ready to accept help, he drops out of the running and lands in a crisis.

Then first in the area of *Consolidation* comes Saturn, and this is in a subsidiary zone in which one can easily give up. Hard facts bring into consciousness the gulf between ideals and reality, and that can cripple enthusiasm. Here it can even lead to short-term depressive feelings. However, Uranus is effective at the end of the consolidation zone and enables a renewed attempt. With a methodical, precise search for mistakes, and the original means, the realisation of the vision can be worked out anew.

After that comes the stellium of planets in the area of *Utilisation and Preservation*: Venus/Jupiter, Sun/Mars and finally Mercury. With Venus and Jupiter the undertaking comes into a final phase of aesthetic polishing, which can be a phase of real enjoyment. Suddenly optimism dispels the mood of Saturn again.

With the cautiously appreciative Sun in this segment there comes consideration and counter-consideration, what is of service to his own self and what is worth preserving. The selection, the removal of whatever cannot be used, plays a big role here. Whatever remains after this sequence has mostly been substantiated in a fermentation process and can also withstand possible criticism. These are results that can be shown and for which one expects proper recognition. Mercury at the end of the sequence can easily pass on one's own realisations and mediate them to others.

Then Pluto immediately goes off into a new cycle, which wants to continue without pause, with criticism of the existing and still higher demands for perfection.

Partnership Comparison

The dynamic quadrants can also be brought into the consideration of partnerships, as an additional dimension alongside more usual methods. Using it, it is sometimes astonishing which essential conclusions can be drawn for the functioning of a partnership.

In comparing the two sequences of behaviour we use the same diagrams as with the individual sequence. We simply draw the planets of one partner in a different colour in the diagram of the other partner's sequence. In that way we can recognise at a glance which empty areas are filled out by either side, and in which areas there are overlaps. As we have seen in the previous examples of individual people, the practice shows a very individual distribution of the planets.

Single subordinate zones or even the main phases may remain vacant. That shows that this personality has difficulty with the particular phase, or that he or she omits it altogether. Because the person feels the deficiency, albeit unconsciously, they look for help. Normally they attract a partner who is well equipped in this area. There apparently exists in people, as shown by experience, a natural selection mechanism by means of which the right choice is encountered. This phenomenon plays a key role in the choice of partner, which is certainly determined unconsciously to a large extent. **Completion through the "You"** plays a central role here.

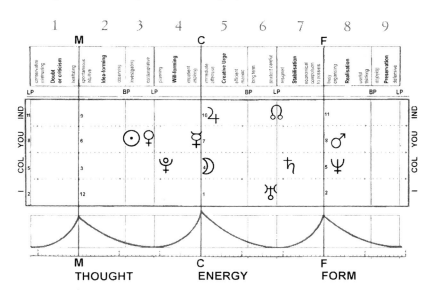

Example A: Female, 1.12.1950 17:36, Zürich

The partnership in our example has existed for around twelve years. Both have the first area of *Doubt and Criticism* untenanted. The area of *Idea Formation* in the man's diagram is occupied by three planets (Uranus, Moon and Mars), that is the completion from the man's side. On the other hand his *Will Formation* and *Creative Process* are empty, as is his *Preservation* zone, in which the woman also has no planets. However, she has planets in *Will Formation* and *Creative Process*. She can thus intervene supplementarily and create equilibrium. If one has the completing planets in *Creative Process* oneself, one can sometimes have the feeling that the other person is "hanging about" and doing absolutely nothing productive. Naturally, that can lead to disagreements. However, in this case she soon noticed that he became active if she took the initiative. From the point of view of the behavioural sequence, he is more theoretical, she is more practical.

His sequence begins with Uranus, hers with the Sun. He mostly has the right ideas, he is stimulated by originality, he wants to be something special. She has to confirm that, a positive personal reaction to his wealth of ideas from her Sun and Venus ought to make him more secure. If the sequence begins with an ego planet, as with the woman in our example, the ego is always the starting point. Thus one begins to become active if one gets a positive response, otherwise not. If they try to react to each other with criticism, reproaches or doubts, that yields no results because that area is empty for both of them.

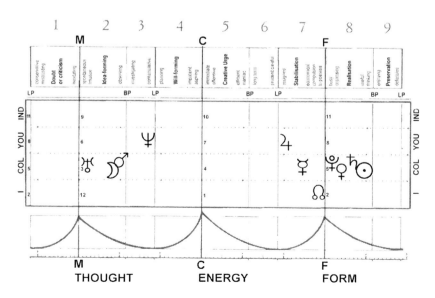

Example B: Male, 12.8.1947, 21:58, Zürich

In the *Will Formation* area, which is empty for the man, the woman has Pluto and Mercury. Of course, Pluto does not always treat the partner gently because it has a high ideal image. Here the man can offer nothing in the empty area, so a lowering of demands on the woman's part might be necessary. The man's *Creative Process* area is also empty. The woman again has an ego planet here, the Moon, as well as Jupiter. She must look for harmony, a feeling of well-being and beauty. He enjoys these, but cannot contribute much to them. That can create problems, especially when feelings of dissatisfaction arise. Uranus stands at the end [of the woman's *Creative Process* area], and the Moon Node between it and Saturn in the consolidation zone. He has something to offer in this area too, Jupiter and Mercury. The security which the woman's Saturn needs is supplied by Jupiter. Both should profit industriously, organisationally and beneficially from this partnership. In the area of *Realisation* there can be problems, because his stellium is situated there, as is her Mars and Neptune (a case of overlap). He gains a lot from this relationship, while the woman with Mars and Neptune at the end of the process gives up too easily what she has struggled for. Neptune also has the job of dispelling illusions and then it is no longer so important if one stands there empty-handed, for it is satisfied if love and humanity remain as the end result.

This comparison shows the possibilities, but also the limitations of a partnership. According to our observations, it is a natural tendency for people to seek or be drawn to others with whom they can follow a common path of development. With this knowledge one can work very well with a partnership comparison. One can also bring in other methods of synastry, such as "click" horoscopes for example (30).

Team Selection

Knowledge of reflex-controlled sequences of behaviour can of course be an essential aid when assembling the right people into a team. In many ways the dynamic quadrants have already been a help in the selection and care of personnel. How often do two colleagues end up at loggerheads because, through having the same zone strongly tenanted, they mutually dispute each other's position.

Completion of Empty Zones by Colleagues

In order to assemble a team effectively it is important to pay attention to the empty areas. As already said, it is difficult to fill them oneself which is why one unconsciously looks for someone else who will do that. With empty areas one tends to reflexively balance them with the capabilities of others. Whoever has an empty zone ought to accept that he has a "gap", an area in which he needs the complementarity and help of others. Many people need first to be ready for that and to acknowledge their own lack of capability. That is an important learning process, especially in partnerships and teamwork.

Nine Phases of the Exercise of an Occupation

The previously described nine phases can be extended to employment questions.

1. The Doubt and Criticism Phase: Here the desire for change and improvement is triggered. He endeavours to recognise existing faults and to even these out through precise information and further training.

2. The Idea Formation Phase: New ways are sought and the setting-up of the project is begun. He considers which projects are promising and works towards their organisation.

3. The Deepening Phase: This requires a first interim appraisal. Realities are worked out through proper market research.

4. The Will Formation Phase: Here he deals with the organisation and its deployment. Forward planning and successful publicity must ensure success.

5. The Action Phase: The creative process begins with the putting into practice of ideas, production is started, performance is measured for quality and yield.

6. The Reinforcement Phase: Now improvement is sought, quality is honed and the optimum achieved. He makes the second interim appraisal.

7. **The Consolidation Phase:** Successful utilisation of whatever is available, public relations, marketing, advertising.

8. **The Utilisation Phase:** He reaches the goal and aims to stabilise the market through administration, organisation and sales.

9. **Enjoyment and Preservation:** The success of the preceding efforts is summarised. The financial result is evaluated.

The Ego Planets in Teamwork

An important innovation in astrological concepts is the attribution of the three-fold personality to the ego planets Sun, Moon and Saturn. We would like to clarify that briefly. Saturn symbolises the ego on the physical level; it is the bodily consciousness with its biological laws. The Moon symbolises the feeling ego that facilitates contacts and relationships as a reflective principle. The Sun, the autonomous ego, functions on the thinking or mental level as a self-conscious entity. The structure of the personality is written about in detail in *Astrological Psychosynthesis* (11).

In teamwork particular attention needs to be paid to the ego planets. The "I" in a work context is always out to be in as good a position as possible and to experience success. For that reason the ego zones must be well defined and in tune with one another. With the dynamic quadrants, we can recognise how this can be done in the employment context. The occupation is not apparent, but the areas where the person has strengths are. We describe briefly below what we must look out for if colleagues have ego planets in the same area. All other interpretative factors must be worked out by an experienced specialist [in astrological psychology].

Sun at the Beginning

Because the beginning of the sequence sets the whole process in motion, the egos clash if they start with the same planet. If the sequence of both parties starts with the Sun then they should not carry out the same duties together. The Sun is the autonomous ego, here he wants to deal with issues independently to let himself and others know that he is capable. With the Sun he needs the feeling of uniqueness according to the motto "Only I can do that, I am the most suitable." He claims his place, his seat, his position. He is also ready to involve his whole personality in the matter, the engagement is honest and strong. He wants to set the tone and determine what happens. Two Suns in the same zone rival each other, act in competition to each other. He is therefore engaged in thwarting the interference of the other and taking the opposite position. Problems of authority will certainly arise from that.

Saturn at the Beginning

If two colleagues begin with Saturn they also hinder each other in the execution of their work. Each has his own well-rehearsed way of working from which he does not want to depart. With Saturn he is not adaptable, he sticks with what he knows, what is tried and proven. In many ways the two Saturns are afraid of each other, there is allocation of blame, suspicion and measures to demarcate boundaries. Saturn is by its nature critical and mistrustful, so in this area it pays particular attention that nothing dangerous happens, that rules and regulations are adhered to. The striving for security can be so important that ultimately nothing creative can result. They play it safe and do only what is most necessary, and are in general most suitable for routine or administrative work. If the sequence of both colleagues starts with Saturn, it would be advisable to create a fixed demarcation of the work area, where no overlaps of authority are possible.

Moon at the Beginning

Here it depends to a large extent on the zone in which the Moon is found. In the *Doubt and Criticism* area it is very sensitive, reacts very personally to all stimuli and is quickly offended if criticised, feeling unwanted. In the *Idea Formation* area it mostly has a number of ideas which it cannot realise itself so that someone has to motivate it to fulfil them. Two Moons confirm each other in their expectations, they are unstable, bend this way and that and want to have fun together, but working and following a plan isn't the Moon's thing. Two Moons reinforce each other in their changeability, then they become dependent on one another and ally themselves against the performance-oriented employees. Often they give up in precise work, leave things undone and cannot set priorities. However, they look for a human climate in the work place and often do not know where they should start with the work. They lack structure, work spontaneously according to inclination and mood and do not like meeting deadlines.

The Moon as the feeling ego at the beginning is probably most suited to artistic occupations where improvisation is called for. The Moon likes to act spontaneously off the cuff. However, work and issues which bring contact with people meet their needs and give them great pleasure. Such work has a social character for them, and in that their work performance is good.

Chapter 3

Stress Planets

What are Stress Planets?

As described in the previous chapter, we interpret horoscopes using the dynamic house system. According to the **static house system** used in classical astrology, for example, the ninth house extends from the cusp of house nine to the cusp of house ten. In the **dynamic house system,** the effect of the tenth house can already be felt after the low point of the ninth house. Two house themes overlap here, which is why this area is ambivalent; a planet here has to cope with two house themes. This dual demand is a great source of stress and can often be overwhelming, due to the effect of two different forces. In any house, the area from the low point to the cusp is the stress area (or shadow area), illustrated below. We call any planets in this area Stress Planets.

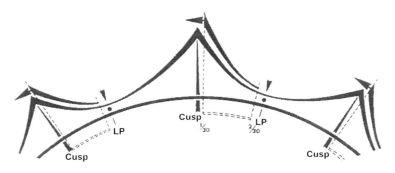

Stress Area between Low Point and Cusp

Stress planets are therefore all planets that are situated before a house cusp (i.e. between low point and cusp), the stress situation arising out of the overlapping of two different house qualities. A planet in this position must simultaneously fulfil the demands of two house themes. That is not always easy, which is why these planets in particular contain compensatory mechanisms on unconscious levels. These remain unconscious until we understand their significance and are then able to transform them. The horoscope enables us to identify and understand them.

Technical Explanation

In our School, a differentiated interpretation of the planets is made using the house intensity curve (page 13). This divides each house into three areas, in the proportion of the Golden Mean. This proportion is used in two directions: calculated in the anticlockwise direction starting from the cusp (i.e. backwards), we find the Balance (or Invert) Point (BP); in the cosmic direction of rotation from the cusp we find the Low Point (LP). By marking these two points we obtain three areas in each house, which correspond to the three cross qualities. From house cusp to BP is the cardinal area, from BP to LP is the fixed area and from LP to the following cusp is the mutable area. Knowing the area of the house in which a planet lies allows us to make an accurate interpretation.

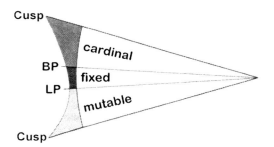

The Three House Areas

As mentioned above, in the dynamic house system the house already starts at the low point of the preceding house. On the intensity curve (page 13), before every house cusp we can see a steeply rising curve that represents the stress area. This starts – depending on the size of the house – approximately two house degrees away from the low point and ends one or two house degrees before the following house cusp (c.f. illustration on page 43). As already mentioned, a planet in this area is forced to combine often totally opposing house themes in different ways.

Behaviour

Many years of experience in the psychological interpretation of horoscopes have taught us that planets before a house cusp have a tendency to compensate. They are under constant stress because they are trying with all their might to reach the next house cusp (aspiration), although they still have to master the task of the house which they lie at the end of (duty). Such planets are burdened with a dual responsibility; they must "serve two masters". On the one hand they want to go forwards, on the other hand they must still (usually against their will) fulfil existing duties. This produces an excessive strain coming from both external and internal sources. The person is confronted with extremely polarised demands, which are difficult if not completely impossible to reconcile. It has been demonstrated in many cases that people use the energies of a planet before a house cusp differently than would naturally otherwise be the case. This makes it more difficult to concentrate on one characteristic, which is why stress situations are so common. This is expressed psychologically in the form of over-compensations, which must be considered as behavioural defects and stress mechanisms. The most distinctive effects of this kind in our "achievement oriented society" occur with planets in the stress areas of the cardinal axes (area at the end of the mutable houses after the low point). We can use this knowledge to research the stress planets and learn to combine them correctly, corresponding to the planetary quality and the sign in which the planets and axes of a cross are situated, in order to analyse the behavioural defect and eventually to correct it.

Compensations

What are compensations? In the psychological dictionary, it says that: *"compensation (lat.) means balancing, for example heart disease, in Adler's Individual Psychology the compensation for inferiorities or feelings of inferiority by (actual or perceived) increased achievement; a psychic defence mechanism. Overcompensations are common, i.e. excessive compensations in the form of the abnormal craving for recognition, arrogance and pride."*

There are therefore different kinds of compensation. We know that the compensation for the withdrawal of love in childhood can be overeating. The unconscious wants to use food to compensate for the loss. Others go to church for the same reason, praying daily for salvation from their own wickedness; others make a career as a film star in order to be loved. Pathological side-effects such as kleptomania, anorexia nervosa, depression, etc. may also arise from overcompensation.

One of the best known compensations – particularly with planets at the end of mutable houses – is a sporting career: skiing, swimming, motor cycling, driving fast cars, etc. Another possible compensation would be setting up a company as a substitute for injured feelings of self-esteem. If, for example, a person has the Sun (which symbolises the father) in a stress area, he desires professional success to show the father what he can do. His personal drive needs the father image in the background; and there is a constant unconscious expectation of the father's unqualified admiration of his achievements. So, if planets have a compensative effect, it is almost always an exaggeration, if not an inversion, of their true character.

Gauquelin Effect

Michel Gauquelin was a French scientist who carried out statistical research, described in his book *Cosmic Clocks* (10). He discovered for scientists a correlation with Saturn positioned either near the AC or around the MC, and for elite sportspeople a correlation with Mars before the AC in the stress area or before the MC, and a lower number before the DC or IC. This led him to discover the principle termed the "Gauquelin Effect" in modern astrology, which corresponds to our stress planets. In the horoscope opposite, we see Mars before the AC in the stress area. This person tried his utmost to find sporting success. He was obsessed with the pole vault and trained for years for the Olympics. Shortly before his goal he injured his hand, which spelled the end of his sporting career.

Mars in the Stress Area

According to Gauquelin's research, elite sportspeople most frequently have Mars before the AC. This stimulates and augments the ego powers. Mars before a cardinal cusp, especially before the AC, makes people want to finish first at all costs. We know that the planets represent a specialised psychic potency, a specific ability that can be precisely described. Mars for example is naturally a motor force, which can be implemented on different levels as required. On all levels, Mars represents performance and achievement. We know that it triggers the adrenaline rush and makes the necessary energy available. On the physical level it is the masculine sexual power, on the next-highest level, in the emotional area, it symbolises the ability to fight, to assert and defend oneself. On the solar, or mental, level it can evoke courage, including the moral courage that enables a person to stake their own life for an ideal or for other people. Here Mars becomes a saviour, a fighter for justice and makes possible transpersonal actions and deeds

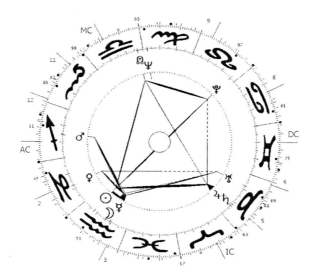

Male 28.1.1941, 05:03 Konstanz

("Robin Hood Syndrome"). This is where the hero, the saviour, the crusader can be found. Mars is always characterised by a release of energy, which becomes excessive in the stress area.

Therefore, if Mars is situated before a house cusp, it may be experienced compensatively. Before the cardinal axes, this energy may cause an increase in potency in men, masculine behaviour in women and enhanced performance in the case of elite sportspeople. It is easy to imagine how a top athlete galvanises all their energy to finish first. Even if he has to train ten hours a day, it doesn't matter, he wants to win at all costs. That is a compensation of Mars energy, which basically serves to glorify the ego (AC = ego point).

The Athlete

Psychological Effect

From a psychological point of view, stress planets are allergic points in the horoscope. They indicate hypersensitivity. If they are in some way questioned, criticised or challenged by the environment, they react with a reflex protective and defensive attitude. This is usually due to hidden psychological injuries. In the case of repressed complexes and problems, like child abuse, feelings of guilt, problems with parents, separations due to accident and death or existential fears that have not been consciously processed, they may also cause psychological compulsion neuroses which require careful therapeutic treatment.

Compensative mechanisms and mental compulsions are an invitation to spiritually inclined people to work on themselves. According to psychological findings, they are forces that one is subject to, which function like reflexes and are external influences on our behaviour. For aware individuals who want to evolve and be free, this is a good enough reason to confront them in order to eventually be able to be freed from them. This usually involves uncovering an illusion, which promises a sense of achievement for the "little self" by means of compensation. Here it is important to be honest enough to admit that one is chasing an illusion. It helps to discover that this is not a stable source of ego fulfilment, but only provides occasional satisfaction.

However, the ego still attaches itself with all its might to the stress planets. As already mentioned, these are sensitive and painful places in a person's character, for some people they feel like bleeding wounds. They really hurt when touched, and attempts are made to avoid or gloss over the pain. Most people react totally defensively, much more intensively than in the case of traumas. If one cannot come to terms with traumatic childhood experiences, one experiences the same fate again and again until one learns to understand what is going on. However in the case of the stress planets, this usually involves misdirected ego powers that are protected by compensative mechanisms. The defensive attitude is therefore very strong. The "little self" defends itself desperately when its survival is at stake. It is really all about the existence of the pseudo ego forms, which are fighting for survival here. They are often only mentally unresolved parts of the self (partial personalities), which are manifested behind the cloak of the "true ego" – that must be seen for what they really are.

But who is willing to admit that he is a victim of self-deception? Someone who is exposed as such refuses to believe it; he has already invested so much energy in it. However, further development is impossible unless the meaning of the stress planets is recognised. They require spiritual truth from us and want to liberate us from deception, from the Maya, from errors of judgement. The horoscope shows us where these compensations are hidden (even from ourselves).

It is a self-deception if one must constantly look for new excuses in order to convince or appease oneself and other people. Breaking down compensative mechanisms is difficult; it requires intuitive feeling, a lot of experience and also humour. Recognising and laughing at one's own stupidity is the cathartic and resolving part of the stress planets' activity. A therapist can work for years on compensatory mechanisms and still not get very far. But with the correct mental attitude, we can try to free ourselves from their constraints by transforming them and setting ourselves higher goals.

Caricatures of the Ego

It already helps a lot if we recognise that what we are really dealing with is a caricature, an "imitation of the self" and not the true self. Stress planets usually surround themselves with masks, forms and fixed behaviour patterns. They always react obsessively with the same masks, although we know very well that they are fake; but it keeps on happening. They are behavioural structures that function automatically, like reflexes. It takes a long time before one can show them for what they are, transform them and thereby liberate the ego from them, for the ego tries to use these behavioural defects to sustain itself, often in a self-destructive way. The top sports person who trains eight hours per day and maybe one day wins a trophy is too one-sided and never gets out what he puts in. Although we may laugh at this today, tomorrow the same thing will happen again. According to our experience, it is easier to transform traumata and therein recognise one's uniqueness, than to free oneself from the compulsive-compensatory behaviour of the stress planets.

Energy Exploitation

Another way of looking at it is that the stress planets obtain the energy for their excessive performances from other planets via aspect patterns; i.e. they exploit their energy. That is also the reason why they are given the highest number of points in the dynamic calculations process. Just as a top sportsperson trains eight hours a day, a stress planet can be so dominant that only this planet is experienced at the expense of all the others. With time, this one-sidedness becomes meaningless; it can even eventually lead to an "atrophy" of much of the personality. The other planetary abilities lose too much power due to this behavioural defect and balanced development is impossible (child prodigy syndrome). That is why change is imperative. The realisation of how much energy these planets consume may encourage a person to decide to transform them.

However, before a transformation is possible, they must a) wholeheartedly recognise and accept this one-sidedness, b) want to return the energy to the exploited planets and c) do this by trying to enjoy the experience of the neglected planets. This calms (satisfies, saturates) the previously compulsive frenzy and produces a new sensation of balance and wholeness. Transformation also requires a profound change of motivation, which precedes a dramatic stage in the overcoming of the ego. There is a transformation of the "little self" into the "higher self", whereby they try to implement these energies for the good of humanity instead of using them to "polish" their own ego.

Compensation, Sublimation, Transformation

Three-Stage Process

Analogy Table of Threes/Trinities

Planet	Saturn	Moon	Sun
Cross	Fixed	Mutable	Cardinal
Motivation	Security	Love	Will
Time sequence	Past	Present	Future
Ego pole	Physical ego	Feeling ego	Thinking ego
Aspect figure	Quadrilateral	Triangle	Linear figure
Colour	Blue	Green	Red
Stress planets	Compensation	Sublimation	Transformation

The three-dimensional interpretation model relates to all elements of the horoscope and of life. To sum it up here briefly: physical existence is on the first level, feeling/emotional existence on the second and autonomous creative thought on the third. These three levels correspond to Saturn, the Moon and the Sun. In astrology we must be able to think in terms of analogies, and be able to discover the analogies on different levels. For the sake of clarity, a few astrological analogies of the threes/trinity are shown in the above table.

A Three Stage Process

It is a proven psychological fact that all developmental processes have three stages or more. The first three basic stages are concerned with the organic division into body, feelings and mind with the astrological analogy: Saturn, Moon, Sun. On the first level one is exposed to Saturnine forces, is blind and ignorant, is asleep. On the second level the forces divide, the emotions start to split into good and bad, we suffer and are confronted with pairs of opposites. On the third level, the intelligence is formed, the powers of judgement and discrimination. The autonomous solar consciousness that has learnt from experience is now in a position to exercise freedom of choice. This three-stage process is a concept of dynamic development and plays an important role in all transformation processes and in our astrology.

The first, Saturnine stage is concerned with compensation, the second with sublimation, which corresponds to feelings, and the third stage deals with transformation, where we want to function autonomously like the Sun. **Compensation** requires a change in attitude, sublimation involves refinement, and transformation a 180 degree motivation change.

According to the dictionary, **sublimation** means "refinement", i.e. energies should therefore be applied in a refined form. In esoteric psychology, spiritual work means among other things a refining of the drives, an ability to handle spiritual energies and a conscious dealing with structures. In astrological psychology too, some spiritual development can be achieved by the sublimation or transformation of the stress planets. How do we deal consciously with these planets and how can they be refined? That happens via a crisis mechanism, which has three stages according to the laws of transformation.

A **transformation** and change of consciousness serves to liberate us from unconscious, static and Saturnine levels. It always starts with a crisis that awakens us, in which a compensation, a rejection, a fear reaches a peak. Once this peak is passed, a breakthrough, a kind of birth into a new dimension of consciousness takes place. Often the balancing, healing process starts with the acceptance of the inevitable. The very instant in which we abandon the resistance or ambition of the "little self" (ego), the change happens. Suddenly we realise the deeper meaning of the whole developmental event and can identify ourselves with it.

Spiritual planets in particular in the stress area before an axis are an indication of constant readiness to change. As higher principles, they represent a superego that can take one over and confer fanaticism. Everything is arranged to correspond to this general principle, which often exaggerates one's powers and can cause nervous breakdowns. In any case, these people swing back and forth between hypersensitive, often neurotic ego-demands and a messianic sense of purpose, and "helper syndrome", self-sacrifice to the point of exhaustion or similar. In the following example, Neptune lies before the 6th house cusp. Although these people are inspired to serve transpersonal principles, the ego depends on such ideal images and acquires an idealised halo. Such a position creates many illusions concerning one's own ego,

Female, 10.5.24, 3.15

importance and self-esteem. Usually one compensates for feelings of inferiority with some eccentricity that is intended to bring one importance and significance. However, since the spiritual planets in particular are subject to constant transformation, the ego is gradually pared off, until it disappears. Only then can the spiritual energies be implemented impersonally for the benefit of others. After this process of "purification", the spiritual stress planets become useful tools for the soul.

Change of Motivation

As we have already stated, in the third stage the stress planets are concerned with a change of motivation, in which selfish motivations are transformed into altruism. This means that the energies of these planets should not be used exclusively for the ego, but should be made available to the inner self, the soul (symbolically the circle in the centre of the horoscope). They can then be used equally dynamically and successfully for the good of others, for the motivation of the soul is to serve and to help. How can this be done?

If, for example, the desire for power is purified by defeats, rejections and powerlessness, sublimation and transformation involves finding an impersonal solution and using the energies to help as many people as possible. That requires a transformation of personal agendas into transpersonal goals, for example in science and research, spiritual aspiration (prayer), social commitment, serving, helping, healing, tolerance, understanding, love, goals that serve the developmental laws, the divine plan, etc.

The Soul

It is an astonishing discovery that at the moment when these energy-laden planets are used to help others, the soul is made effective by these stress planets, and all the implemented energies flow back equally strongly as inner happiness. People may become healers, for example. The stress planets can be used to give to others, instead of exploiting them, to bless them – that is a real transformation. All stress planets can and should be used wholeheartedly for the benefit of the environment.

Energy Consumption

As stress planets always lie at the brink of a breakdown, "home straight collapses" can often occur and one can easily get out of breath. She always pushes herself to the limit and has the feeling that she can never rest. If she allows herself to be conditioned by the expectations and requirements of the environment in the use of these energies, she must be there for others on a permanent basis. Great strength of spirit is required to be resilient, not break down, feel sorry for herself or revert to earlier behaviour. The transformation of compensated stress planets can only be processed and sublimated by introspection and great honesty. One way to do this is by horoscope meditation on the stress planets, which has a purifying effect on the subconscious.

Transformation Meditation on Stress Planets

1st Stage: Relaxation

Sit comfortably in a chair and close your eyes. Breath calmly in and out through your nose – you will become more and more peaceful, relax all your muscles and let go. Be aware of your forehead and relax all your muscles there – your forehead becomes smooth and your face looks friendly. Your tongue lies loosely in your lower jaw. Breathe calmly and evenly through your nose. As you breathe in, think "I am breathing" and smell the scent of a rose.

2nd Stage: Centre Circle

Focus consciousness in your head and let it sink very slowly into the centre of your head, through your jaw, your neck, into your upper chest, where you point to when you say "I". Here in the centre point of your being you see a white-gold Sun shining; allow yourself to sink quite slowly and be enveloped in inner light, where you feel centred and protected. Symbolically, you are now in the circle in the centre of your horoscope.

3rd Stage: Horoscope Meditation

Visualise your horoscope around you. First look at the crosshairs and stand in the centre. Then look left and see the AC with its sign, then look right and see the DC with its sign, below you will see the IC with its sign and above the MC with its sign. In the crosshairs you feel strong and secure. Then you see all the different colours of the aspect structures shining. You can see the planets, the signs and the houses.

4th Stage: Meditation on the Stress Planets

Now look for the stress planets, planets that stand in the shadow of an axis. Examine them closely and reflect on their characteristics and influence. You realise that they absorb and use a lot of energy from the other planets. How do you compensate? Do you want to use these planets to be better than other people? Are you ambitious in the way that the house cusps require? The soul suffers when energy is lost to the outside, because this only benefits the ego. Try to stop this loss of energy and to transform it, by stopping the outward flow of energy and examining the problems it causes. Then guide the energy inwards.

5th Stage: Purification of the Stress Planets

Bring one stress planet very slowly into the centre, into the centre circle, into the white-golden Sun of your innermost being. There in the light of the soul, it is purified of false motives and transformed. Vow to use it to cultivate an impersonal attitude, to change your motivation. You no longer want to compensate your energy and misuse it for your own ends, but allow others to use it and learn to serve with it. Then push the planet slowly back to its place in the horoscope. Bring each stress planet into the centre circle one by one. In this sacred act, they are purified and given the strength to serve.

6th Stage: Final Stage of Meditation

Come slowly out of the meditation, breathe deeply in and out, circle your head, shoulders, hands and feet and open your eyes.

It is a good idea to repeat this meditation several times, particularly if several stress planets are present, as experience shows us that a single sitting is not enough to deal adequately with all of them. It can be very effective to repeat them at longer intervals also after overcoming personal crises for renewed self-control.

The Stress Planets in the Three Crosses

The Three Crosses

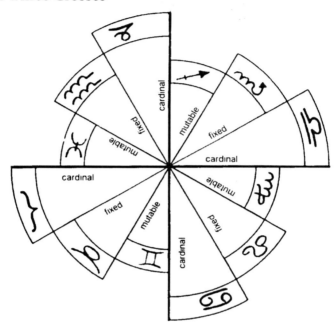

Knowledge of the three basic principles of the three astrological crosses enables a better understanding of the transformation process. They play an important role in horoscope interpretation. A few planetary positions are described below, with their compensative behaviour patterns before the cardinal, fixed and mutable axes. These are guidelines, not definitive statements.

We do not intend to compile a comprehensive list of keywords for stress planets listing every possible variation. Good or bad human behaviour is so complex that it cannot really be set in stone. Sometimes, reactions can be reversed and sudden U-turns may occur. It is therefore in the nature of stress planets to behave contrarily or misguidedly.

For example, compensation before the second cusp can indicate both anorexia and bulimia. Also ego demands often switch completely, changing from megalomania to feelings of inferiority. So it is hard to be sure that one has found the correct interpretation when one wants to make a statement about it. It is best to ask the person concerned what is his experience of the stress planet.

We want to stick to interpreting the three cross principles, as this gives us a system by which we can orientate ourselves. The crosses refer to inner motivations, which permeate everything and create order. But in spite of that, every person has their story, their own compensations. The table below shows the fundamental changes that take place in the three crosses.

Changes in the Three Crosses

1. **Cardinal Cross**   *Power and powerlessness*
   Aries, Cancer, Libra, Capricorn
   AC, IC, DC, MC

   **Changes through setbacks, defeats,
   Waterloo experiences**

2. **Fixed Cross**   *Possession and loss*
   Taurus, Leo, Scorpio, Aquarius
   2nd house, 5th house, 8th house, 11th house

   **Changes through alienation, loss,
   abandonment, insecurities**

3. **Mutable Cross**   *Love and conditions*
   Gemini, Virgo, Sagittarius, Pisces
   3rd house, 6th house, 9th house, 12th house

   **Changes through restrictions,
   imposition of duties, bonds, loss of freedom**

Stress Planets in the Cardinal Cross

(before the AC, IC, DC, MC/ before the 1st, 4th, 7th and 10th house cusps)

Change through Defeat

With planets before a cardinal cusp, the ego is always strongly emphasised. The cardinal energy wants the self to be expressed as a unique experience at all costs. It is the cardinal impulse and will energy that inflates the ego and asserts claims of uniqueness. If one of the three ego planets, Sun, Moon and Saturn, is involved, other people are viewed as rivals, enemies, pushovers or

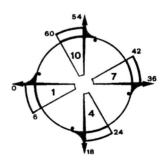

idiots. Manic-depressive states can be produced by stress planets in this cross as pathological expressions of the overabundance, in which phases of depression are followed by phases of euphoria. Below we give a few brief examples for the four cardinal cusps showing how the ego powers are intensified.

Ego Powers before the AC, IC, DC, MC

Before the AC, the ego must always prevail; it does all it can to outdo others as it cannot stand defeat. Before the IC, the ego must have its own family, where it can feel protected. All its efforts are geared to belonging to the family; outsiders or intruders are rebuffed. Before the DC, one is very selective in choice of partner, wants to have the best, most beautiful partner; others are dismissed and rivals are outsmarted. Before the MC, the focus is on individual competence. One does everything to be the best; competitors should expect a fight. The ego planets are placed at the highest level at all costs.

Crisis Mechanism

As already mentioned, every stress planet harbours a crisis mechanism. In the cardinal cross, it is failure and rejection. The change occurs once a "critical mass" has been achieved, when in a "Waterloo" experience the person falls from the heights attained. The inner tension must be so great that they surpass the boundaries of old behaviour patterns, which is the only way that the transformation to a higher level can take place. We could even say that without a profound crisis there would be no transformation, no change in awareness.

Ego Planets

Stress planets are in principle concerned with the ego powers, which is why the three ego planets Sun, Moon and Saturn are particularly potent in the stress area. If one of them is situated before a cardinal axis, then this planet shows Napoleonic tendencies. The motivations of this cross are power and will. A good example is provided by Napoleon, who was defeated at Waterloo. "If you have attained power, you must experience your Waterloo", as we say in transpersonal psychology. From a spiritual point of view, the cardinal type, who sets out always to win and get everything he wants, needs to experience rejection, defeat, powerlessness in order to continue to grow as a person. Someone who wins all the time, a top sportsperson who always finishes first, or a powerful person who enjoys unlimited freedom would have such a strong and hardened ego that they would lose their humanity. The desire to be special is often mitigated by physical suffering, and in this state of helplessness other people are needed again. Also the so-called "type A personality" belongs to the cardinal cross. It is a well-known fact that many successful people only learn to love their families again and to accept their limitations after having a heart attack.

A few examples of stress planets are provided below. In principle, an astrological psychology student should be able to work out the compensation, sublimation and transformation of the stress planets for himself using the above explanations.

Saturn before the MC

One of the results of Gauquelin's research showed a correlation between scientists and positioning of Saturn before the MC. They can only accept that which can be weighed and measured. Saturn at the top of the horoscope means that matter, form and what can be perfected are prioritised. Materialists think in this Saturnine way; their egos are only interested in matter, in what is tangible and demonstrable, and they believe that the world can only be as it is, it cannot be different.

In the case of a transformed Saturn before the MC, we often find people who are able to overcome catastrophic situations with incredible strength and competence. They are masters of form and matter and can use these skills to do a lot of good for others. They usually possess a special ability and are skilled in a certain field. With great concentration, they focus all their strengths on one goal, which they hope will bring them authority, power or status.

Other Planets

It need not necessarily always be stressed ego planets that confer great strength on the ego; all other planets before a cardinal cusp also exaggerate the ego. In any case, the cardinal cusp confers the desire to be special, to win at all costs.

Mercury makes him want to be the only person who knows everything and can talk about anything. He likes to brag about how much he knows, and to prevail over those who know less. A transformed Mercury has a way with words, and communicates his knowledge with great skill.

Venus confers the desire to be the most beautiful and to have as comfortable a life as possible. She strives for harmony, comfort and convenience. The refined, sublimated Venus on the other hand becomes a champion of beauty and the arts; she can mediate and build bridges between warring parties and spread harmony.

Uranus and the other **spiritual planets** are ideal role models, which can be very demanding in the stress area, especially when the ego identifies with them. Personal strength and influence are overestimated. Many people believe that they personally are catalysts for progress in the world. The desire to prioritise spiritual ideas can sometimes take on a grotesque form. Too much is taken on, opportunities are wasted, and ideas are misguided. However, these transformations are particularly strong and eventually the inner nature can serve these stress planets and use them as tools for healing purposes.

Jupiter in the Stress Area AC, IC, DC, MC

Jupiter before the AC

Someone with Jupiter before the AC also has a compensation. This does not involve wanting to be a top sportsperson, but to be the "life and soul of the party" – they want to be the best and the most popular person. They desperately want their friends to like them and to be happy to see them. They want to be the best, the most brilliant ego, who only has the best motives. So that nobody has any doubt about this, they emphasise it constantly. Often this tendency degenerates into a kind of narcissism, which makes them react hypersensitively to the slightest trace of ego rejection. Many annoy those around them with their beliefs of self perfection and achieve exactly the opposite. They lose popularity because their self praise gets on other people's nerves. Their exaggerated self confidence is a front; their ego core is often weaker than it seems. As it is very important to them to live in their own ideal world, there is the danger of imagining their own world where everything is in order. When difficulties are encountered, they prevaricate and look for the easiest way out. Many just avoid problems and live in an ideal world. Others have grand visions and inspirations, but they lack the perseverance to see things through or to change things.

It is not so easy to transform Jupiter. A trine aspect (which has an affinity with the characteristics of Jupiter) can also make a person lazy, arrogant, self-absorbed and unwilling to acknowledge their own mistakes. Many think they are special, their self-image is seen as perfect and godlike, and they look down on other people with contempt. Some follow the latest crazes, keep up with the newest trends and know where to be seen so that they can show off their ego.

A **transformed Jupiter** before the AC returns a sense of proportion to the ego demands; the self-image is reconciled with reality. The unbalanced and inflated ego is refined and deflated by rejections and defeats. People gain wisdom and radiate goodwill and confidence. They care about others and many are important thinkers on social, religious or educational matters. These people are jovial and fair-minded, spreading optimism and joy, which they also evoke everywhere they go, thereby having a positive effect on others.

Jupiter before the IC

In the collective space before the 4th house cusp, it is easy for Jupiter to guarantee itself a comfortable life at home, at the fireside and in the protective bosom of its family. It is very important for him to feel content within his own four walls. It is usually hard for him to leave the family nest. Usually his background is affluent. He has had everything he needs, culture, education and the love of his family. Such fortunate circumstances can restrict his spiritual growth and he may be accused of being spoilt. For many people the compensation lies in outdoor activities, in the experience of nature, sport, riding, swimming, often an excessive love of animals, and children that they cannot give up. The compensation also features gardens and rural landscapes where they can look around freely. Some people travel from country to country in search of their spiritual home.

Others invest a lot of energy in constructing a dream home and become prisoners in their gilded cage. What they really want is the freedom to go where they want and such an elaborate construction only ties them down. It is hard for them to give up these home comforts in order to set off into the big wide world. That is also the crisis mechanism of Jupiter before the IC. On the one hand it wants to have a comfortable home life, on the other it would like to enjoy unrestricted freedom. It usually experiences the crisis through oversaturation, in which it recognises that material things are a meaningless burden. At a certain point, they tie him down instead of making him happy. Many people do a complete U-turn, depending on the sign in which Jupiter and the IC are situated. They leave everything behind them, give up everything, leave home and family and go out into the big wide world and create their own, new reality.

The transformed Jupiter before the IC is free and can serve the collective. The love of nature and the family enable him to commit to making life fun and enjoyable for others. He creates a happy environment and helps to protect and better understand life and nature. He is filled with confidence and optimism, and can pass on courage and faith in life. The transformed Jupiter also strives to live its life according to a clear ethical and philosophical concept. If crises occur, he can overcome them quite easily due to his basic trust and quickly focus on new goals, thus providing a meaningful new start to himself and other people.

Jupiter before the DC

Where devotion to the You is concerned, Jupiter provides outstanding access to the You. These people are very sociable and it is hard to avoid their influence. They adapt spontaneously to the You, their counterpart, and give others the feeling that they are there for them and thereby gain their trust. In the stress area, this auspicious charisma can also be deceptive, it promises more than it can deliver. In the compensation, Jupiter is excessively optimistic about everything, he over or underestimates himself and others. If pushed into a corner, he may even become aggressive. Beliefs and values that are important to the You are disparaged, disrespected, ridiculed and belittled. He has a hundred excuses with which to justify his behaviour. He often loses credibility due to his unfounded optimism and dubious excuses.

Depending on the sign, Jupiter in the stress area is also full of dynamic, conquering energy with which it takes from the partner (the You) what it wants or believes it has a right to possess. It sets out to find partners who have something to give, from whom it can benefit. Some encroach on other people's resources quite deliberately, and appropriate their things. Conversely, they easily fall for someone who promises them the earth and are always bitterly disappointed. When one relationship fails, they are immediately hopeful that the next one will be better. If someone with this Jupiter position never marries, it is because they are afraid of being tied down and unwilling to give up their freedom.

The crisis of **the transformed Jupiter** before the seventh house cusp is rejection, when it loses credibility with other people and is ignored. The moment of truth arrives when the old excuses no longer work and its lies are exposed. Now the person must show what they are really made of and be completely fair and honest with themselves and with others. They are isolated and no longer understand what is going on. They were actually well-meaning and never meant any harm, their motives were noble and good. They cannot see why other people, the You, the partner, do not understand this. In the transformation crisis, the ego is no longer treated fairly. Now it is all about the You. The focus is no longer on the ego and its well-being, but on other people. This Jupiter position can often be a virtue for people in an advisory or helping role, as it gives confidence and hope and adapts itself lovingly to others with understanding and goodness.

Jupiter before the MC

When Jupiter and all three ego planets are before the MC, the theme is individuation and extreme self-stylisation. Great importance is attached to personal goals and he is convinced that he is the best. There is an aspiration to greatness that must be acknowledged by the environment. This can be his downfall, for how can such high Jupiter aspirations be fulfilled? At the MC he must show his true colours, his abilities are constantly put to the test. If he has been too lucky, usually his character has not developed sufficiently for him to be able to stand his ground. Even Jupiter cannot provide protection from the dreaded fall from grace.

Power is the real test in the cardinal experience. With Jupiter before the MC, this is often expressed as indifference, arrogance and pride. Someone with this Jupiter position must learn humility by being forced onto their knees by rejection or redundancy. The compensation can often be an excessive fear of not being able to cope with the challenges and of personal weaknesses being exposed. This provokes a crisis in which he makes mistakes and uses dishonest means to defend himself. Previous attempts to gain popularity by manipulating others then no longer work. It is hard to yield to the inevitable.

In the example chart, Jupiter lies before the MC in Virgo. This Jupiter is usually connected with a certain naivety and a refusal to accept defeat. He is incredulous and stunned when faced with rejection or dismissal. He wants to maintain his high demand, insists on his worth and finds it hard to settle for less. The ego clings to the compensative notion of its own importance. This compensation usually 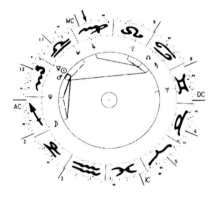 involves restricted ego development in childhood, and the fear of this weakness being discovered and exposed. He builds an imaginary wall around himself as a form of protection in order to make the self feel more secure, but he is sometimes suddenly torn out from behind it.

The transformed Jupiter before the MC, which has renounced its ego demands, is now only there for other people, just like the ego planets. An authority derived from inner strength gives these people dignity and character. They usually have a very positive influence on others. They have a mature and genuine authority and judge wisely and fairly, helping those who have lost their way back onto their feet again. The transformed Jupiter before the MC can handle its acquired abilities and power skilfully. It marks the individuality with an unwavering belief in goodness. It has an unbounded sense of justice and piety. It deals with whatever fate can throw at it good-naturedly and calmly. A particular feature of this Jupiter position is its insight; a deeper meaning is sought in everything which is then quickly incorporated into the new world view.

Stress Planets in the Fixed Cross

(before the 2ⁿᵈ, 5ᵗʰ, 8ᵗʰ and 11ᵗʰ houses)

Change through Loss

Planets before a fixed house cusp always have a strong urge for security, they want to hold on to what they have and defend their possessions against perceived opponents. There is exaggerated behaviour here too, and a propensity to "break a butterfly on a wheel". As befits the motivation of the fixed cross, one seeks security at any price and is always on the defensive. When a planet is situated in this position, the transformation is triggered by loss. In the fixed houses, defensive mechanisms are particularly strong, one defends personal possessions, job, status, influence. Everything is done to retain what one has created and make sure that nothing happens to it.

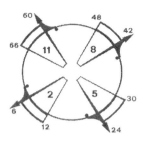

It is in the nature of the fixed principle to suffer from the fear of loss. This is why planets before a house cusp are always afraid that something may go wrong or that something will be taken away from them. In this cross, there is a tendency to paranoia, which causes specific compensations with the corresponding planets. One protects oneself to an excessive degree from all sides, imagines that there is a burglar hiding in every corner, closes oneself in so as to block out external influences. One holds on tightly to what one has so that it does not get lost. But this is exactly what often happens to the fixed cross, for one attracts that which one is most afraid of like a magnet. For the fixed principle, loss is the means of change.

Suggestions for Interpretation

The following descriptions of the ego planets are in a certain sense interchangeable, e.g. some statements about the Moon are also relevant for the Sun or other planets. They do not claim to be exhaustive. Students should learn to work them out for themselves. Sign qualities are also important in interpretation and should be taken into account. It is unfortunately not possible to cover these here, but if you look at your own horoscope, you will immediately see in which signs the stress planets are situated. Further tips for integrating sign and house can be found in Chapter 4.

2nd House

Ego Planets before the Second House Cusp

The second house is known to be concerned with possessiveness, and is where personal resources, acquired means and skills are primarily intended to aid self-preservation and to increase self-esteem. With ego planets before the second house cusp, subtle security measures are carefully built up to defend personal possessions, talents and potential. Personal resources are closely guarded, protected and immediately replaced if lost. Everything of value, sentimental or otherwise, is cherished and nurtured, treasured, hidden and kept secret.

With the Sun before the second house cusp, he strives for (material or spiritual) possessions and would like to accumulate as big a reserve as possible, in order to be equipped for all emergencies. He looks for a job for a lifetime and builds a burglar-proof house. He is constantly trying to eliminate risk from life and makes every effort to remove possible threats, entrenching himself behind walls and becoming a prisoner of these self-constructed protective walls.

The transformed Sun before the second house cusp can acquire sufficient resources and abilities to be able to cope with any task. It has a particular special charisma, vitality and strength and is not easily thrown off course. This enables it to automatically attract the best, ward off negative things and collect everything that is good for itself and others. Because they have enough of everything, and know how to obtain the bare necessities, they are also able to share with others, without worrying that something will be taken from them.

With Saturn before the second house cusp, the striving for security can reach absurd levels, he does not dare to do anything, "hides his light under a bushel" and therefore finds it very difficult to assert himself. He has an excessive fear of loss and takes no risks at all. If he does lose something, his world collapses. He finds it hard to cope with losses, to the extent that he often very stubbornly opposes necessary changes. The protective mechanisms are well-established and efficient and are able to resist change for a long time.

The transformed Saturn here acquires a particular maturity and is able to handle matter. It uses what it has responsibly and productively. With special financial skills he manages what is available and increases it carefully, without running any risks. He can even manage with very little, is thrifty and can go without if necessary.

With the Moon before the second house cusp, he is very demanding with regard to security, loyalty and continuity, especially in relationships. He waits anxiously behind the fence for his beloved to come home. Many do not venture out into the big wide world, i.e. they only open the door to people they know well, when they are sure that they will be treated well and not get hurt. Emotional bargaining is a common compensation here. For example, he says: "if you love me I will always be there for you!" That means that he can be corrupted and speculates about restitution or revenge. If he is promised some kind of advantage, an increase in energy, resources or money, he opens himself up. But this is dangerous and inevitably causes disappointment, loss and separation on the emotional level. He then plots revenge and imagines how he could get revenge for this unfaithfulness. He clings perversely to bad experiences, complains to the world and is not prepared to give, but instead hides behind moral terms or other conditions. The transformation can only come about through true love.

The transformed Moon has savoured many things; it is satisfied and actually does not want anything else for itself. The transformation of the Moon occurs through the change from an immature, infantile state to that of adulthood, i.e. where he takes responsibility for his feelings and no longer expects others to fulfil his wishes. The economic principle of the second house means that the transformed Moon must maintain a balance between giving and taking. Purified by separations and loss, it gladly passes on what it has obtained to others. Eventually he renounces the satisfaction of all desires and is happiest when others feel comfortable and safe.

5ᵗʰ House

Ego Planets before the Fifth House Cusp

The fifth house is dedicated to self-awareness through intimate and very personal relationships. Many people's self confidence is based on the intensity of their relationships, while for some it is also based on their quantity. Love and eroticism, self expression, risk taking are characteristics of this house. Some people become adventurers and gamblers, take too many risks and go for broke. The transformation of the fifth house involves love; it requires letting loved ones go and giving up the conditions she sets on love so that she may learn to love unconditionally.

When the Sun is stressed before the fifth house cusp, personal influence on the environment is important. She sees how far she can go to impress others, is ingenious when it comes to finding ways of asserting her ego. This naturally also depends on the sign in which the Sun is located. In any case, it is about finding an area of expertise and defending her sphere of influence. Personal territory is marked out and no trespassers may enter. Anyone who dares to do this will be thrown out and fought as an enemy. Here the compensation involves her own expertise, her adventurous self-awareness and ego-assertion. Anyone who doubts her ability or competence is considered an enemy and even attacked. Some people may experience the collapse of their own business and go bankrupt, not just because they have made bad business decisions, but also because they cannot accept criticism and cannot admit their own mistakes.

.**The transformed Sun** before the fifth house cusp knows what it and others are entitled to. It can grant other people the same rights that it demands for itself. It lives in harmony with its fellow men and can admit mistakes without losing face. The purified Sun radiates love from the heart onto all living beings equally; it includes everything. Their charisma can cheer up many people, restoring their courage and confidence and freeing them from hopelessness. These people can even use the Sun's energy as a healing force.

With Saturn in the stress area before the fifth house, she is convinced that she can do everything herself and is a master of all trades. Outside help is refused. She is proud of her ability to take risks and hold her ground. But here she must of course serve two masters and suffer the resulting misjudgments and loss of effectiveness. She cannot stand it if others are better than herself and self-control is based on competence. Saturn often makes her treat others strictly and give them little freedom. If she restricts herself, why should other people expect to be free? Other people's mistakes are strongly criticized and harshly judged. She demands the same perfection and effort from them as she does from herself.

The transformed Saturn works daily on improving itself, to which end it is willing to accept difficulties and limitations. Once Saturn renounces personal ego satisfaction, it takes on a maternal function. It is able to master large and difficult tasks and problems with great inner strength and relative ease. It can now protect other people, teach them how to use matter skilfully, stop them making mistakes, solve their problems and help them to overcome illnesses.

With the Moon before the fifth house cusp, the stress effect usually concerns personal, close relationships. She builds a fence around her "own kingdom" and defends her territory by using emotions such as anger, rage, aggression. She protects oneself on all sides against intruders. Self-esteem is dependent on those she loves, which usually makes her possessive and jealous of potential rivals. She intimidates them with threats (display behaviour) and chases them away from her territory.

Loved ones, even her own children, are allowed little latitude. If they make a bid for freedom and attempt to break away, she does everything in her power to stop them. If she is abandoned, her whole world falls apart. Here she must learn that she cannot and should not try to own other people. They must be given their freedom, otherwise they will get up and leave.

The **transformed Moon** before the fifth house cusp has reached maturity through the sorrow of love and gained strength through overcoming emotional pain. She can stop thinking about satisfying her own wishes when she is needed and always places emotions in the service of love. There is often a total about-turn, she wants nothing more for herself and childlike expectations are transformed into creative visions.

8th House

Ego Planets before the Eighth House Cusp

Here the compensations are complex; on the one hand he is dependent on partnerships (seventh house) and does all he can to preserve them; on the other hand, he would like to take his place in society (eighth house). Although he wants to obtain security, he swings between two or more interest groups. A lot of effort is put into building up and securing external status, and the philosophy is that "attack is the best form of defence." Many people get caught up with finding enemies, chasing fears, seeing dangers where there are none and do not actually recognise their true rivals. In times of danger or crisis, they alienate themselves by constructing defence mechanisms, which release self-destructive forces and direct the flow of energy against the self. In the eighth house, he is condemned to go through the motive-purifying process of death and rebirth again and again. The themes of these houses are transformation and change: in the seventh house through the partner, in the eighth house through the enemy image of one's own creation. Paranoid tendencies and associated compensations are almost always present.

Here too, the **transformation** is all about changing motivation. Hate must be converted into love, revenge into forgiveness and possessiveness into renunciation. The experience of polarity is particularly important, which is why the switching from one extreme to the other strengthens the illusory nature of this position and makes it harder to resolve.

With the Sun before the eighth house cusp, he wants to protect himself on all sides and is always afraid of being unnoticed. He tries with all his might to keep his position, to be helpful to others and give them something in order to get something in return. Speculation about others' means and calculated security motives are common compensations. Attempted corruption and the awakening of feelings of guilt are also a speciality of this Sun position. Many simply take what they need from others and advance their own rights with unreflecting matter-of-courseness; they don't question themselves at all. If they are attacked, they fire on all cylinders. They are dangerous enemies and their philosophy is: "an eye for an eye, a tooth for a tooth." In extreme cases, they can be very vindictive, automatically destroying everything that stands in their way.

The transformed Sun before the eighth house cusp is purified by many death and rebirth processes. Here in the fixed area they are quantitative, which is why the change of motivation takes place due to a constant thwarting or non-fulfilment of selfish desires. No job, no matter how well paid, and no authority to exert power can satisfy them any longer. A transformed Sun can demand nothing more for itself. They renounce anything that could jeopardise their spiritual development. Some wear a symbolic "penitent's robe", place themselves at the service of the community and forego all personal advantage. They have found a balance between giving and taking.

With Saturn before the eighth house cusp, compensative mechanisms serve to defend against possible dangers and prevent them. Saturn strives for security and seeks a stable job for life. People with Saturn in this position are masters at constructing bogeymen, at scheming and denouncing others when necessary. They would sell their grandmother if they had to. Some live in the constant fear of being mugged or robbed. They are tormented by the idea of losing their job, being hated or envied, of their partner leaving them or some other dreadful thing happening to them. They are terribly afraid of loss. They suspect that many events could have evil consequences, maybe even the destruction of the status quo, the end of an era, in which all their achievements would be swept away. In time of danger, there may also be a tendency to paranoia, which can take over the whole personality.

The transformed Saturn teaches us to handle this fear of life. All Saturn transformations are very powerful. Before the eighth cusp they lead to limit experiences that resemble death throes, and involve giving up the attachment to matter. The theme of death is important, and the knowledge that the soul continues to exist after death takes away the fear of dying and renders the striving for material security meaningless. Other people can help to demonstrate the immortality of the soul.

When the Moon is in the stress area of the eighth house, he experiences great emotional volatility. The emotional insecurities are significant and are compensated for by ingratiating himself with others. He behaves as though he were ready to make all kinds of sacrifices, often confuses sex and money and shifts the responsibility for his own failures onto others. In the house of the death and rebirth process, the Moon is torn this way and that. On the one hand, it longs for love, for a stable bond that it would like to be unconditional, yet on the other hand, its behaviour complicates and destroys the relationship. If it does manage to have a relationship, it still remains unsatisfied. The transformation here is fundamental. He must renounce all internal and external security measures and be prepared to change. The belief in material security is be abandoned due to the realisation that life is eternal movement. Nothing can stand still, nothing can be held on to, there is no absolute security but just a constant readiness for change, for transformation. As a result, he is called upon to fulfil greater tasks for the community and will be able to serve society.

The transformed Moon before the eighth cusp has overcome and healed many spiritual wounds. It knows the illusions of the astral world and has already looked behind the curtain. Such a Moon has matured through suffering and understands the human psyche with its weaknesses and hopes. It is familiar with the chasing of apparent securities, the longing for protection but also acquisition by unfair means. It has itself been through the abyss and tries to free other people from the tentacles of deception. It possesses a very special ability to help people who have been rejected by society and to set them back on the right track.

11th House

Ego Planets before the Eleventh House Cusp

The eleventh house means freely chosen relationships, perhaps friends who embody the ideal image of man, who one can look up to and be guided by. The influence of the 10th house makes her try to acquire power and recognition, career and prominence through friendships. In the stress area, she demands security and guarantees from her circle of friends. Loyalty becomes a problem, she is nearly always afraid of being cheated by so-called friends. This can even lead to the development of a misanthropic philosophy, even to cynicism as a means of boosting the ego. It is a fixed air house and therefore mainly affects the reasoning and imagination.

The transformation of the eleventh house happens through losses and disappointments in friendships. All false ideas must give way to reality and an ethic should be developed that gives all people the same right to individuality. The highs and lows disappear and all men become brothers. Tolerance and support for high ideals are good qualities of the eleventh house.

With the Sun she constructs thought forms, ideal models and principles by which she orientates herself and which affirm her own importance. She joins powerful groups, which give her security; or she founds an institution, society, trust, church or sect herself. She clings to influential people who increase her self-esteem. With the Sun in the stress area, she easily believes that she is something special or even chosen. Anyone who doubts this is attacked bitterly and declared an enemy. Often, a father problem is the cause of this defensive behaviour, which is compensated either by her own authoritative behaviour or by the fact that she cannot tolerate authority figures and attacks and criticises them. Conversely, others may periodically seek the guidance of a guru, as a kind of a father substitute.

A transformed Sun can here become a model for what a person should be. She develops the most positive qualities and does not allow herself any weaknesses. For this Sun, bad habits and human cravings must be sublimated and make way for the enobling of the spirit. The transformation requires the implementation of high ideals that are free from personal bias and are guided by the laws of evolution.

With Saturn in the stress area, we often find ideas for improving the world and fanaticism in people who are capable of ruthlessly defending their own ideas. She thinks a lot about the world and feels called upon to point out social evils and to accuse other people. These notions can become fixed ideas to which she clings staunchly, even if they prove to be misguided. If these ideas are directed against bogeymen, she also resorts to defensive actions. She fights against people who think differently to herself, accuses them of infamy and belittles them to boost her own ego. There is a tendency to act rather like the inquisition. She seeks out like-minded people with whom she can feel strong and safe and can put her ideas into practice, and seals the bond with vows of solidarity. Terrorism and sectarianism are varieties of this phenomenon. She fights those who are different, which leads to racism, fundamentalism and other radical movements.

The transformed Saturn before the eleventh house has managed to control the ego's fears and defence mechanisms. It is incorruptible and mentally impressionable, opens its inner spiritual powers and – like Moses – communicates universal, unshakeable laws to enable human development. It takes responsibility for whole groups and movements, its mind is sharpened and steeled and the "eternal wisdom" is proclaimed uncompromisingly. Such people are dependable, wise and fair.

With the Moon in the stress area before the eleventh house, she tries to become friendly with high-ranking people. She is always running after them and badgers them until she has gained their attention. As soon as she makes any friends or relationships that correspond to her inner ideas, she never wants to let them go. She projects her ideal model onto the loved one and is disappointed if they do not live up to it. Broken friendships badly injure her self-esteem. She does all she can to please others, to retain their friendship. She gives them an advance, flatters them, gives them the feeling that she supports them and is ready to stick with them through thick and thin. But when it comes down to it, she disappears behind the safety of selfish, anxious motivations. She looks for arguments to defend herself and her behaviour.

The transformed Moon embodies the love of every living thing. The unity of awareness, the universal principle of interconnectedness is completely accepted and lived as the truth. Her own wishes and feelings can easily disappear behind ethical concepts, refinement and propriety. In many cases, it is as though the Moon is living in a glasshouse, and feels trapped inside a gilded cage. It is very noble and cultivated, but it passes real life by.

Other Planets before the 11th House

Although for people with planets before the eleventh house cusp, loyalty is a huge priority, one can usually not rely on them. They attach far more importance to their own security, their own field of relationships than to helping friends in need. The preservation of their own reputation, status, prestige and good name are much more important to them than a once-sworn allegiance. If cornered, they run from truth. They are very skilled at finding arguments to defend themselves and then make the world or the circumstances responsible for their failure. If relationships are no longer useful to them or no longer correspond to their personal ideas, then friends become enemies. "Today they cry "hosanna" to him, tomorrow they cry "crucify him"."

Friendship and ethics are the touchstones of these people. They must decide what is more important for them: their own status in society or friendship and humanity. If they decide against friends, then they will in turn be abandoned. In all fixed stress areas, the karmic law of cause and effect works particularly strongly. Here the unrelenting truth is: "as you sow, so you shall reap."

The transformation happens before the eleventh cusp usually through the loss of human relationships, through isolation. In the eleventh house, she cuts herself off and sits alone in her ivory tower, distancing herself more and more from human warmth. The inner about-turn occurs symbolically after a penitential pilgrimage and in many cases leads to a "Way to Canossa". She must come down from her ivory tower and come back down to earth in order to become one with the people again.

Stress Planets in the Mutable Cross

(before the 3ʳᵈ, 6ᵗʰ, 9ᵗʰ and 12ᵗʰ House Cusps)

Change through Limitation

We now consider a few of the compensative mechanisms of planets before the mutable house cusps. It is impossible to deal with all the possibilities here though, as every person's compensations are unique, so the possibilities are endless.

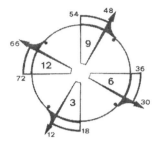

The easiest thing to do is look at the basic motivation of the mutable cross, which is simply for love or relationships. Everything to do with human relationships is important. One does all one can in order to be loved and accepted by others. There is self-denial or resort to addictions, while longing for freedom. There is always the need for something to love, be it people, children, animals, flowers, objects, travel, music or ideas. If someone has problems in personal relationships, and is unfulfilled, they tend to have hysterical outbreaks. Hysteroid symptoms belong to this cross and occur due to a lack of love and attention.

With stress planets before mutable houses, human relationships are constantly sought. One is very active and always searching for something. Without love and relatedness to others, life appears meaningless. One never wants to be alone, but has a strong sense of individual freedom and independence. Many show signs of inner conflict, an ambivalence which makes them appear inconsistent.

In the stress area of houses three, six, nine and twelve, as well as a strong need for love, contact and understanding there is also the desire for independence and freedom. Possible constraints are immediately eliminated and one avoids commitments like loyalty, duty, appointment calendars or schedules. From the outside, such claims to freedom usually seem unnecessary, but these people usually take them seriously.

A truly free spirit must function holistically on all levels. Every experience of individuality involves more freedom. But if someone has a compensatory demand for freedom, and travels the globe spouting ideas of independence, it is not just pretence. Many become welfare cases if nobody takes care of them, refusing to take responsibility for themselves. The worst thing for the mutable principle is to be tied down, and the mere idea of this makes these people panic. The compensation here is to run away when faced with responsibility and the need for commitment. It mainly involves the fear of commitment, and much insight and inner suffering is required for the person concerned to commit properly.

Stress planets before mutable houses frequently lead to caricatures of human nature due to the incompatibility between the fixed and mutable houses. Such people need love and appreciation at any price. Their compulsive need for contact brings them into impasses involving absurd or tricky situations. For example, many are incapable of tolerating unkindness; they run from it and react to it with inner tension or self-pity. Despite this, they always come across people who hurt them and misuse them for their own ends. They give love in order to be loved, make sacrifices so that they will be comforted or admired. But under no circumstances do they want to settle down or be tied down or controlled. They hate using love as a bargaining tool, but somehow always end up being manipulated.

3rd House

Before the Third House Cusp

Here he adapts, wants to fit in, not to stand out, and avoids confrontations. This is often considered to be cowardice. He cannot take a stand and defend his own opinion because he usually has none. If someone is stronger, he hardly dares to intervene – on the contrary, he gives in and tells people what they want to hear. Usually he tries to grab affection and kindness by virtue of conformity and presents.

Other compensations are talkativeness, he wants to make himself interesting and show off what he knows. He always wants to know more and be better informed than others. Confidences are passed on without hesitation, because this enhances his position and gains people's favour and the acceptance of the majority. Here it is often also about the quantity of relationships. He does something because most people do it. He is a slave of groupthink, bows to fashion, trends and stereotypes and propagates them for all he's worth. If many people believe something, he thinks the same in order to conform. He is very easily influenced and believes many things because the teacher, priest or a TV presenter has said it. This compensation can also become part of the family tradition where he uncritically does things because that is what has always been done.

The Conformist
by Wilhelm Busch

The transformation before the third house cusp requires complete absorption in communal tasks. He must serve a group or a collective, pass on his knowledge and give the people the best of himself. The communication and passing on of the internal and external wealth of experience should provide joy and be unconditional.

6ᵗʰ House

Before the Sixth House Cusp

Stress planets easily develop a helper syndrome here as a compensation for the need to be loved. All her efforts are intended to gain popularity and love and she even demeans herself to remain in other people's good books. She prefers to yield than to provoke others' anger. She is afraid of being misunderstood or of the help she offers not being accepted. All too often she does things that she should not have done, or makes promises she cannot keep.

Others are eagerly occupied with making amends for mistakes and righting unintentional wrongs. They apologise in advance for possible failures or incompetence. There is great insecurity and the constant failures, humiliations, insults or suffering caused by the loss of love can also have a psychosomatic effect.

The transformation and refinement of the sixth house involves taking on duties gladly, serving without looking for reward. Really selfless love and dedication to duty requires her to give spontaneously and without ulterior motive exactly what is needed. This behaviour will allow her to fit into the work stream of the collective and experience herself as a small cog in a great machine and not take herself so seriously.

9ᵗʰ House

Before the Ninth House Cusp

This type often resembles "Johnny head in the air", who sticks up his nose and promptly falls into the water. People who go around like this usually think they are right and the rest of the world is wrong. Before the ninth house, mutable "stress people" are totally convinced of their philosophy and their aspiration. They simply cannot conceive that their opinions may be wrong. They construct a philosophy that excuses all their weaknesses. In the compensation, having a mind of his own makes him lose credibility and arouses mistrust. However, that is precisely what these people cannot tolerate, for they want to be trusted at all costs. Their reality simply does not allow them to make such demands, as they are actually always dependent on someone or some idea, although they do not admit it.

They can be terrified of commitment, like the bridegroom who gets cold feet and disappears just before the wedding. The voluntary renunciation of unlimited freedom requires a transformation. Basically, in the mutable cross he wants to serve the community. That means that the ego must be prepared to accept boundaries and responsibilities in order to love one person completely and renounce other possibilities.

The transformation before the ninth cusp happens through recognition and acceptance of transpersonal life goals. He has usually acquired considerable knowledge from which other people can benefit. He has a calling to be a teacher. His acquired knowledge must be good and wise otherwise it will not be accepted. Some people take on an educational role that involves character improvement either with children or adults.

The Teacher
by Wilhelm Busch

12ᵗʰ House

Before the Twelfth House Cusp

Before the house of the "still, quiet room", compensative tendencies are not immediately apparent and tend to be private affairs. She does not like others to access her intimate sphere; secret desires are protected and not revealed lightly. Some people switch between self-sacrificial tasks and random actions. They want to do everything of their own accord; their dedication and help must be spontaneous and must never be forced.

She often gives up on herself and takes a back seat, prefers to pretend not to be there and give in rather than have to face others' demands. All the same, she is deeply hurt if her dedication is not met with recognition, love and attention. In their heart of hearts, these people feel that their noble motives are unrecognised and misunderstood. Love is a noble principle for them, in fact they do everything out of love and intend this to be the case. However, there is usually some kind of self-deception involved. Much of what they do is intended to make others care for them and make themselves look good. To be able to admit this, crisis and suffering are necessary.

The transformation before the twelfth house cusp is usually connected with the loss of love or trust. The desire for affection is frequently met by dislike, the striving for harmony with confrontation and disagreement, good deeds with abuse and exploitation. The increased need for love and unity can even be reciprocated with hatred and argument. Often the only reaction left is to escape into a fantasy world, into music, alcohol or drugs. These people must free themselves from the stream of chaotic feelings before undergoing a death and rebirth process that is even deeper than the one that takes place in the eighth house. In the transformation crisis they can find their way back to the original source from which they first emerged. From there they create a new spiritual power to carry on living and in this way go on to help and serve people in need.

The Age Point through the Stress Areas

In age progression, the areas before each house cusp also have a stress effect. The effect starts theoretically at the low point and increases the nearer one gets to the cusp. The period lasts two years and three and a half months.

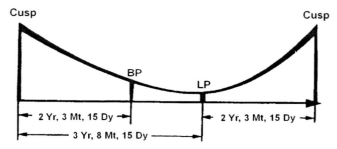

Duration of the Age Point through a House

The actual process of the personal experience can vary though, depending on which planets and signs are situated in this area in the individual horoscope.

As already mentioned, the stress effect is analogous to a mountain climber, who crossed the valley floor at the low point and is now climbing up a mountain whose peak he must reach at all costs. The nearer he gets to the summit, the more energy he has already used up. Yet he must somehow gain enough strength to complete the last stage. He often feels as though he is not getting anywhere at all and would just like to sit down and rest. This is how it feels when the age point is approaching a house cusp.

Age Point Transiting Stress Planets

The age point activates any stress planet in its path. Using the technique of age progression, we can calculate when it reaches the planet's position. In the process we must take into account whether or not there is a sign boundary before or after the planet, because according to the rules of interpretation of age progression, the effect of the planet can already be felt at the start of the sign and can stop again when it leaves. If the next house cusp lies in another sign, between them lies a so-called "ditch", which makes the climb to the next cusp more difficult. We should also know the time orb of the primary aspect (conjunction or opposition) the AP transits. With a 'normal' house size, the effect can be felt from approximately 1° before to up to 1° after the planet's position. It would be a good idea to take another look at *LifeClock* (14) to refresh your memory about the different planetary transits and orbs of the aspects. In any case, most people have an acute experience of compensatory behaviour during the phase of the AP transit.

The Four Main Axes

The stress effect is experienced most strongly before the four main axes, where we are subject to special developmental forces. The cardinal points of the zodiac (AC, IC, DC, MC) are switch points in life, periods of reorientation and rebirth. They trigger vital developmental processes, which start a little while before the low point transit. During this time, we experience increasing internal

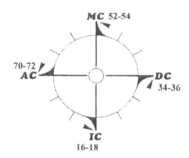

Age Point in the Stress Area of the Main Axes

and external tension. This is usually related to increased performance demands and the concomitant stress. The cardinal house cusps here are like particularly high mountains that rise up steeply before us and which we must climb. The last part of the journey is the hardest for the mountain climber. He pushes himself to the limit and uses his last drop of strength to reach the peak. The same thing happens before every main axis. If we find ourselves in a position of weakness between the ages of 16-18, 34-36, 52-54 and 70-72, this can occasionally be due to a "finishing straight collapse" just before the end of the phase. However, this only happens if we convince ourselves that we do not have enough energy to cope with these increased requirements.

Birth Pushes

At each cardinal point we are subject to a kind of "birth push" that we cannot resist. At the AC, we are born into this world; at the IC comes the birth into the You space, at the DC the birth into the consciousness space and at the MC the highest form of individuality is born. There is a lot of stress at these main axes, which may sometimes even resemble birth pangs. The cardinal impulse force drives us symbolically speaking "out of the womb". We cannot escape these forces; in every rebirth process old skins must be cast off, a process in which our collaboration is required.

Consultation and Critical Reflection

Although the stress planets' compensation mechanisms are interesting from the point of view of behavioural psychology, we should not allow ourselves to be too impressed. When we consider the horoscope from the point of view of spiritual development, it is important to focus on transformation processes, which bring about changes of awareness from one level to the one above or to the interior world.

However, before a transformation is possible, we must make clear that the one-sided implementation of stress planets jeopardises development in the long term. We must be prepared to confront, experience and nurture the characteristics of the neglected planets. This stabilises the compulsive compensation and creates a new feeling of balance. Harmonious development can only be assured by living a full life on all levels; only wholeness can lead to personal fulfilment.

The above interpretations of the stress planets mainly serve to detect spiritual developmental crises and the associated transformation processes in the horoscope and in the consultation. If properly defined and consciously processed, they can also be meaningfully incorporated into the whole. In consultations we should therefore not limit ourselves to or insist upon only one of these statements, but must always draw on the aspect pattern as a whole. An astrological consultation is a many-layered, complicated process, which is most effective when an alignment with the soul takes place, which allows the client to access his own intrinsic spiritual potential.

It is actually only possible to reflect critically on the compensation mechanism with the help of one's own inner source (the inner circle in the horoscope). If we manage to get the deepest life motivation flowing by examining and describing the aspect pattern, the spiritual energy of the core being will automatically correct any misguided behaviour. In other words: derived from the holistic pattern of the horoscope, only the whole aspect pattern can free the inner life motivation and activate the core being. This sets the regulatory forces in motion so that healing is achieved. Ultimately we are responsible for finding our own liberation.

Chapter 4

The Influence of Heredity and Environment

The House Horoscope

The house horoscope is relatively new to astrology. It was developed by Bruno Huber together with his son Michael following many years of psychological research and represents an important behavioural psychology tool in modern practical horoscope interpretation. It is a specific Huber School technique, which calculates the birth chart using identically-sized houses and interprets the resulting aspects as behaviour patterns. In the 1920s, astrologers were already referring to the so-called "mundane aspects", by which they meant the calculation of the aspects of planets at house cusps using the house degree system. This was exclusively used for event calculations. This was the first step towards our house horoscope in which the whole house system is systematically divided into 30 degree sections.

The house chart differs technically from the basic chart in that all houses are 30 degrees wide, unlike the signs, which are either larger or smaller than 30 degrees. The proportional position of the sign boundaries and planet positions in their respective house positions are retained, although some or all of the aspects created will be new (see overleaf for detail of calculations).

The interpretation of the house horoscope is in principle carried out using the same rules as for the radix horoscope. There are no new definitions of the planetary positions in the signs and

---

Calculation of House Horoscope Positions

The calculation must be made for six houses.

1. First, the size of these houses is determined in zodiac degrees: a house of someone born in the temperate zones can measure between 15 and 60 degrees.

2. These sizes are divided by 30, e.g. 42°/30 = **1°24'**. That is the size of a **house degree of a particular house.**

3. The distance of a sign boundary or planet from the corresponding house cusp is established and then divided by the house degree, e.g. 17°20'/1°24' = **12°22'51"**. That is the **position** of the object in **degrees of this house.**

4. This operation must be done for six sign boundaries and for all planets (and otherwise interesting points like Moon Nodes, etc).

5. Finally the new aspects are looked for and marked.

---

houses, so that what is important is the difference between the aspect pattern structures. In astrological psychology, aspect figures and their overall structure (aspect pattern) are interpreted first, as they tell us about the basic life motivation. While the aspect pattern of the radix horoscope reveals the inherited attitude to life and innate behaviour, that of the house horoscope shows the motivations of the educating environment and the behaviour learnt there. Comparison of these two aspect structures enables us to see both the support and the restrictions received from the environment. The aspect pattern of the basic horoscope shows the person's profoundly-felt life motivation, while that of the house horoscope reveals to what extent their motivation is altered by the environment in terms of what they should or must do with their life. So many human problems arise from the discrepancy between the inner will and external duty, and this is precisely what the house horoscope reveals to us.

Discovery of the House Horoscope

By Michael-Alexander Huber

Because the AC, MC and the houses are heavily dependent on the exact time of birth, they indicate our uniqueness. Four minutes correspond to one degree. This explains how, even in the case of twins, different house positions, and by extension different destinies, are possible.

However, very few astrologers have been bothered by the fact that the radix horoscope is not an angle accurate depiction of the heavens at the moment of birth, but is distorted, reduced so that the earth is at the centre (our cosmic reference). I could find no plausible explanation in any book as to why the house system in most radix horoscopes is not square, and why in both the Koch and Placidus systems the houses even have different sizes!

In the terrestrial reality, at the place of birth, the perpendicular, the gravity (IC-MC) is always at right-angles to the horizon (AC-DC). The illustration below, drawn by Bruno Huber in 1970, shows this clearly, and helps to explain how the horoscope puts people in a cosmic context, as the houses are calculated back to the centre of the earth. Seen from the centre of the earth, the zodiac is a regular circle in which the planets are also measured.

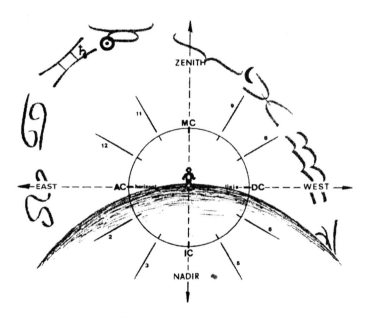

The House System

However, in reality one sees the circle in perspective, as in the illustration. I could not get this out of my head and it gave me much food for thought: why do astrologers draw up horoscopes that do not correspond to reality? Are we cosmic children from outer space? Or does the cosmic reference of the radix horoscope indicate only spiritual people? It was necessary to take the trouble to adapt the fixed, traditional zodiac to the right-angled house system of our reality in order to be able to draw up a proper horoscope.

The reason that such ideas occurred to me was that I had always felt misunderstood. Even when professional astrologers interpreted my horoscope, they did not mention many of what I knew to be important character qualities. This problem of being incorrectly judged was a frequent occurrence. I was usually underestimated by teachers or fellow pupils; they thought I was too sensitive and not able to handle much. I was even told that I ought to pull myself together or I would never achieve anything. In reality, I could put up with a lot and had a strong will. Some people were even afraid of me, because they had once had a glimpse of how strong I could be.

After a discussion with my father one cold January night in 1974, I tried to draw up my house horoscope for him. I calculated the planetary positions from the centre of the earth back to the earth's surface, although I had no knowledge of the basics of Koch calculations. I must therefore have gone about this in a simple, almost naïve way. I remembered the rule of three from school! The very first calculation example produced my house horoscope, which was to go on to become a standard horoscope offering.

I tried for half the night to discover an accurate, logarithmic or continuous calculation, but then returned to the first, simplest solution. If a house is 50 degrees wide and it should be 30 degrees wide, then the distances between the planets are reduced. If a house is

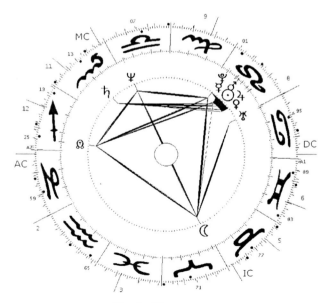

Basic Horoscope
Michael-A. Huber, 9.8.1955, 17:17, Zürich

only 20 degrees wide, it should be stretched and the distances between the planets increased. In other words, the angle between the planets changes as a result of the recalculation so that new aspects are created which must be redrawn.

The result was totally overwhelming. Apart from one opposition, my house horoscope had no more tension aspects! In the radix I have five squares, and here everything was harmonious and blue. This is effectively how I was judged by outsiders, who were almost completely unaware of my inner tensions. During my psychology studies, I was more interested in human behaviour and my research led me to the conclusion that the house horoscope depicted precisely what C.G. Jung had described as "persona", i.e. the effects that a person has on the environment, their appearance or how they are understood by their fellow men.

The following observations allow these experiences to be objectified: only about a quarter of people felt they were misjudged by others, while some were not misunderstood at all. Interestingly, these people's house horoscopes were practically identical to their radix horoscopes, while the house horoscopes of those who were misunderstood were very different. I belonged to the latter group and I wondered if it was really worth calculating house horoscopes if it would only benefit one in four people by helping them to deal with

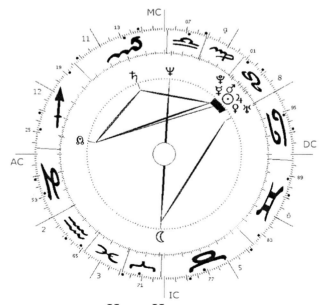

House Horoscope
Michael-A. Huber, 9.8.1955, 17:17, Zürich

their environment and giving them an aha-experience. For this reason and also because at the time I was more interested in pursuing other activities and research, I put the house horoscope on the back burner for a couple of years.

In the summer of 1975, I had the opportunity to present my new discovery to an advanced astrology group. They set about "calculating" all their friends with a mixture of curiosity, scepticism and enthusiasm. In one year, over one thousand house horoscopes were drawn up by hand and researched.

The start of the 1980s saw the introduction of computer horoscopes and the first software programmers, whom I knew, incorporated the house horoscope into their programs. It was now easy for everyone to draw up their own house horoscope. The first Astrology World Congress in 1981 in Zürich triggered the greatest astrology boom of this century and suddenly a great many people became aware of the possibilities of the house horoscope. Demand grew significantly as a result and it was incorporated into the syllabus of the API (Astrological Psychology Institute).

Application of the House Horoscope

Today, the house horoscope is also used in psychological consultation as an additional diagnostic tool and provides valuable guidance for a holistic understanding of the person. It is a unique method both for use in therapy and in terms of the work itself, i.e. measurement of the direct effect on the environment and discovery of acquired or learned behavioural patterns. Sometimes the house horoscope is totally different from the basic horoscope, illustrating the divergence between the person's interior and exterior lives. In cases like these, it usually takes the person concerned a long time to realise who they really are, and for a long time they allow others to live for them, as it were. While the basic horoscope shows what the person perceives to be reality, the house horoscope can be considered to be something completely different, even, if it is noticeably different from the basic horoscope, as something alien. Any discrepancy between the inner and outer worlds is obvious.

Extensive research has shown that in this discrepancy is the cause of behavioural disturbances, illness and developmental crises. The realisation that, often without noticing, we live completely in the house horoscope, i.e. we react automatically as a result of acquired behaviour can be a shock to the consciousness and trigger a process of liberation. Technically speaking, the house horoscope is not really a "new" horoscope, but only a mathematical recalculation giving another perspective to the existing radix horoscope. In the house horoscope we consider the person from the outside (the houses indeed represent our "antennae" for environmental situations), while the radix horoscope is concerned with the interior world. The innate qualities that we are born with are indicated by the positions of the planets in the zodiac. As we use the 30° zodiac signs as a measuring circuit in the radix horoscope, logically in the house horoscope the house system is used as a reference and measuring system. The individual houses are each 30° wide, and the location of the planets and zodiac are squeezed together or pulled apart as appropriate.

Aspect and Aspect Pattern Colouring

The way the aspect colours change is significant in the evaluation of the house horoscope. If we consider the difference between the two horoscopes, we can see immediately when for example a red square has changed into a blue trine. We also examine the planetary positions and note an aspect's colour in the basic horoscope and whether it is the same colour in the house horoscope. In the process, we often find that entire aspect figures change. To correctly evaluate to what extent this change is due to the environment, these differences should be defined very carefully. The table below reminds you of the colours used for aspects in the Huber School, established according to psychological criteria [see *Aspect Pattern Astrology* (12)].

Aspect Colours			
Red	square opposition	= performance and tension	= energy
Blue	sextile trine	= enjoyment/pleasure and relaxation	= substance
Green	semi-sextile quincunx	= sensitivity and and thought	= consciousness
Orange	conjunction	= soft or hard depending on planet	= latent power

The colour tells us a lot about the nature of the consciousness. When we interpret an aspect pattern in the basic and house horoscopes, we start by asking ourselves how many colours are present, which are dominant and which are lacking. We then interpret the colour combinations, as they tell us about the contents of the consciousness as well as about specific attitudes.

Three-coloured aspect patterns give a more or less harmonious picture and indicate inner balance. They do not necessarily express externally harmonious behaviour though, but rather an inner knowledge that everything is subject to laws of development. With red-blue-green aspect patterns, there is a three-dimensional, constantly developing consciousness. We call the three-coloured aspect figures learning or growth figures. People with such aspect patterns strive for holistic understanding; they are not satisfied with seeing only one or two sides of a story, they want to examine as many sides as possible. This quality of consciousness allows them to see more and more subtleties and nuances and to detect deep connections in the developmental process.

Red-Blue aspect patterns show great swings between the need to achieve and the need for pleasure, between activity and passivity depending on mood. One day up, the next day down is how their minds work. This oscillation makes it hard to see a middle way. The "green", the relativising principle, is missing. These people see things in terms of black or white, there are only two possibilities or two sides. The world is either right or wrong. It is too simplistic to divide human motivations only into good and bad, and they often make mistakes, when their harsh judgements can grate on the environment.

Red-Green aspect patterns represent a so-called irritation aspect, as blue is missing. Relaxation, peace and enjoyment are unfamiliar to these people, and such behaviour is alien to them, even the root of all evil for many; for the purpose of temporary relaxation, they tend as it were to "replace" the blue themselves, in the form of compensations. Green (sensitivity) is exaggerated by red (energy, strength), often leading to overstimulation, which gives them the feeling that they are being exploited. However, they often do the same thing to other people without realising it.

Blue-Green aspect patterns, like red-green aspects, are rare. Here there is a certain one-sidedness or lack of stability in the consciousness because red is missing, leading to low energy levels and lethargy. There are great empathetic qualities and a willingness to adapt to the needs of others because they have no great desire to assert themselves. However, they can also be victims of circumstances because they are not good at defending themselves. There is a clear orientation towards harmony and pleasure. They are usually to be found in helping and serving (also artistic) professions, where sensitivity, patience, devotion and loving care are required. From experience, we know that they can care for terminally ill patients with patience and devotion and be content with small successes.

Explanation

This introduction to reading aspect patterns should be enough to show you that the comparison of aspect figures reveals our developmental goals in this life. We understand which changes are necessary and what we can learn from them. If we assume that life is one great evolutionary process, the simplistic division of events or strokes of fate into bad and good is no longer satisfactory. This comparison enables us to see the deeper meaning contained within every event and to identify with it.

Example Horoscope

With this in mind, we would like to take a closer look at the horoscope examples on the following pages 88, 89. In the house horoscope you can see how the signs are sometimes stretched and sometimes squashed, although the proportions of the planetary distances and sign borders within each house remain the same. However, new aspects appear: Moon, Saturn, Venus and Mars all lie at approximately the same distance before their respective house cusp (ca. 2 or 3 house degrees) and are therefore aspected to one another – although they are situated at quite different sign degrees (Moon 2° Aquarius, Saturn 10° Pisces, Venus 9° Virgo, Mars 22° Libra). In house degrees, the balance point lies at 11°27'36" and the low point at 18°32'24", calculated from the house cusp. Previous experience has shown us that in the house horoscope, the aspects to the age point have the most intense effect at the house cusps and low points. These are found in the basic horoscope at the same degrees, so we can talk about a "double effect".

In the example horoscopes, it is immediately obvious that the aspect pattern in the house horoscope has changed with respect to the basic horoscope. It has become much "smaller". This indicates that the child has been misunderstood by its environment, and its development has not been supported, it has been "diminished". Uranus is detached (unaspected) and is no longer connected as it is in the basic horoscope. That indicates that the child was given no spiritual perspectives and connections. They were probably never discussed. In the basic horoscope, Jupiter has two blue aspects, a trine and a sextile, while in the house horoscope it receives a red achievement triangle. In the ninth house, Jupiter's need for a comprehensive, harmonious life philosophy was severely reduced by the father (square Sun). Evidence shows that Jupiter's change from blue to red is linked to a childhood experience that was experienced as a breach of trust and served

Example 1 Radix Horoscope
Woman, 16.07.1935, 20:45

to diminish the child's confidence in life. A change in the opposite direction (from red to blue) would indicate an increase in *joie de vivre*.

The Moon, the childlike self, is trine Mars in the house horoscope and forms a quincunx aspect with Venus/Neptune. Saturn likewise receives a connection to it that was not there in the basic horoscope, but loses its trine to Jupiter. The latter indicates a loss of life confidence. What happened was that during the Saturn transit in the fifth year of life a traumatic experience took place that made a lasting impression and conditioned later romantic behaviour. It was the first sexual dalliances with the boy next door. The mother arrived on the scene and shouted at her and her father hit her for the first time. She could not understand why her parents made such a fuss. From her child's perspective she had done nothing wrong, but the psychological impact was devastating. Misunderstanding, fear of punishment, feelings of guilt, mistrust of the opposite sex and sexual inhibitions kept her tied to her mother's apron strings until the age of 42.

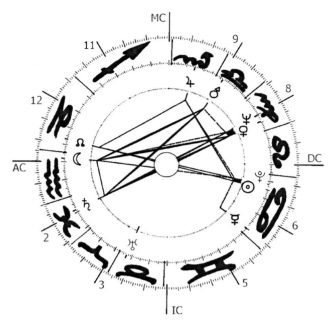

Example 1 House Horoscope
Woman, 16.07.1935, 20:45

The radix horoscope alone gives us no idea of how deeply affected she was by this experience, nor how long-lasting its effects were. Only the house horoscope reveals the cause of such a deep wound in the child's psyche. The radix horoscope shows nothing of the intense aspect between the Moon and Saturn in the house horoscope. There we can see immediately why the age point's effect has been so strong. The Moon and Saturn are aspected to each other (semi-sextile), as are both libido planets Mars and Venus, also in a semi-sextile. In the house horoscope, together with Neptune they form a "Stage Figure" [see *Aspect Pattern Astrology* (12)]. We also notice that Mars in the radix horoscope forms an Achievement Triangle with the Sun/Pluto conjunction and with the Moon Node, while in the house horoscope with Jupiter in the ninth house, Mars has been replaced by Jupiter. This indicates that what marked her so strongly was a false truth, a misdemeanour connected to a guilt complex, from which she was only able to free herself at the age of 42. At this point, her radix age point lay opposite Saturn and on the eighth cusp, thereby also aspecting the sextile aspect of Neptune/Venus to Jupiter, enabling her to see things as they really were.

The Personality Planets

Saturn, Moon and Sun

An important addition to astrological theory is the attribution of the threefold personality to the planets Sun, Moon and Saturn. This is inspired by Roberto Assagioli's psychosynthesis and by Alice A. Bailey's esoteric psychology. Anyone who is familiar with their body of esoteric and psychological work knows that they are always concerned with the synchronisation and integration of the three-fold personality. We have incorporated this useful concept into astrology and have found the following results: Saturn, the Moon and the Sun were the planets that showed the clearest ego characteristics. After years of empirical experience, we developed the astrological concept of the three-fold personality that everyone can recognise in themselves. Saturn symbolises the ego on the physical level – physical awareness controlled by the laws of biology. The Moon symbolises the feeling self, which as the reflecting principle connects us with the world and its phenomena. Lastly, the Sun is the autonomous self, which functions on the thinking or mental level as a self-aware ego unit. You can read in more detail about the three-fold personality in *Astrological Psychosynthesis*, 'Integration of the Personality' (11).

It is obvious that comparison of the position of these ego planets in the radix and house horoscopes is very revealing in terms of the development and synchronisation of the threefold personality. First we determine whether Saturn, Moon and Sun are included in the aspect pattern in the basic horoscope. Do aspects exist between them, do they form an extra figure or are they alone? As the pattern of consciousness, the aspect pattern is one of the most important means of ego motivation and expression. As mentioned above, the aspect pattern in the house horoscope can be different from that in the radix horoscope; aspects to ego planets also frequently change.

Individual Aspects

The individual aspects should also be taken into account when comparing the ego planets in the two horoscopes. After comparing the aspect pattern as a whole, we examine the aspects that contain an ego planet and count up how many red, blue or green aspects it has in the radix horoscope and how many it loses or gains in the house horoscope. From this we can learn about new features of the development of the personality, repression by the environment and possible solutions for existing ego problems. Divisions into good and bad are too simplistic here. According to the law of evolution, in every lifetime we become more whole (integrated), i.e. the necessary balancing processes are carried out. If the development of the ego is restricted by the environment (house horoscope), the next step is to consult the moon node horoscope, where we find the deeper reasons in the whole developmental process.

The Moon Node Horoscope

Here can see how problems are caused, because the moon node horoscope reflects the past (18). The explanation of a misdemeanour can often only be found in the moon node horoscope, as it contains the experiences and achievements of a whole incarnation chain, including what we have already learnt and what we still have to learn in order to become whole, and also what we have done wrong. Perhaps an explanation for an inflated ego (MC or AC position of the ego planets) can be found there too, which may be brought down to size in this lifetime by external repression. Conversely, an ego weighed down by suffering needs a healthy foundation or "blue aspects" to build up its strength.

In the development of the personality, from experience we know that red aspects in the basic horoscope indicate deeply rooted ego problems in the past. If these become blue in the house horoscope, a transformation has occurred. Healthy ego development requires a sense of achievement or a positive environment. If the ego is excessively burdened and repressed by negative experiences from the past, it now receives more favourable conditions in which it can become strong and healthy again. This is the law of compensation that underlies evolution, and which brings equilibration. We often find that tense, red aspects in the radix become blue trines or sextiles in the house horoscope and relieve the pain or suffering. This means that the environment, maybe the father or the mother, has done something good, and has given the person more inner security, life confidence and self-assurance. The transformation of tension into pleasure, from red into blue, is an important criterion in the assessment of the developmental process. In the psychological consultation, this knowledge helps to find moderation and to align the client's experience of reality with their capabilities.

Aspect Comparison

It is apparent from the above that the comparison of the aspects gives us an insight into the respective roles of nature and nurture as far as the development of the personality is concerned. This is a good point to revisit the fundamental difference between the radix and house horoscopes. The positions of the planets in the signs in the radix horoscope tell us about the innate, inherited characteristics; it therefore reveals the influence of 'nature' and also any problems concerning the development of the ego in this life. The house horoscope shows the influence of 'nurture' and the imprinting by the environment into which the child is born. It may take the form of the environmental stimulus that spurs us on to further development, or of restrictions and constraints from which we want to free ourselves. The priority is always the development of consciousness. It is up to us whether we want to continue to be at the mercy of the dependencies and demands of the environment or want to liberate ourselves from them. So the house horoscope always shows the effects and influences of the environment in which we grew up, and once we have recognised them, it is up to us whether we accept or reject them, depending on which developmental standpoint we adopt. The sign positions, on the other hand, cannot be changed; these are our genotype and are, as such, deeply rooted, innate behaviour patterns.

The Three Horoscopes

However, the complete personality structure is only revealed when we also include a third horoscope, the moon node horoscope. It deals with the so-called shadow personality, the repressed side of our character. From the esoteric point of view, the aspect pattern in the moon node horoscope contains all life experiences. The conscious self can use them as inner potential for its further growth and development. It also reveals how far we have come along our developmental path. The three horoscopes are ordered as follows: we start with the moon node horoscope, then comes the basic horoscope, and finally the house horoscope represents the stimulus from the environment that spurs us on to further growth. Contrary to what is often believed, the house horoscope does not represent the goal of individual development. This is only a brief guide; for more information see *Moon Node Astrology* (18).

This is an appropriate point to mention the issue of free will, because it involves aligning the innate abilities in the basic horoscope with the learning processes in the house horoscope and with the past in the moon node horoscope. It largely depends on our will-ability, as to how we synthesise these three things. Integration of the personality needs a strong will that is capable of unifying the diverging psychic factors into a functioning whole. Someone who can reconcile the unconscious depths of the shadow personality with the conscious ego elements of daily life and with the goal setting necessary for further development, is truly a mature and sophisticated human being. It is a well-known fact that the will function plays an important role in the development of the ego. Roberto Assagioli's book (4) makes a valuable contribution to this topic.

Unaspected Ego Planets

It may be that an ego planet in the basic horoscope is not included in the aspect pattern, standing by itself in a sign and house without any aspects. In the case of an unaspected Saturn, we speak of a non-existent mother relationship. An unaspected Sun means that it was the father who was inaccessible. An unaspected Moon is called an "orphanage Moon". Usually this person was misunderstood as a child and felt alone. Throughout life he looked for an emotional relationship that would give him confidence and protection, but usually his emotional needs were not met. However, an unaspected ego planet does not necessarily have these consequences – the house horoscope should always be consulted. Often we find that an unaspected planet or isolated aspect is here included in the aspect pattern. This is illustrated by example 2 (charts on next page).

In the basic horoscope, we see an unaspected Saturn in the twelfth house, which suggests a lack of maternal bonding. Actually the mother died during childbirth. In the house horoscope, Saturn has a small green semi-sextile aspect to Jupiter. The environment has been beneficial; an "old story" could be integrated and enhanced, leading to a new attitude towards Saturn. If a small green aspect does not actually solve the inherited mother problem, at least there is the possibility of changing the negative idea of the mother and to change the physical reality for the better. In fact this girl gained a new "mother" when she was two, who was kind and empathetic enough to become a good mother to her. The age point at the time of this happy event stood exactly over Jupiter.

As we see, working with the house horoscope provides a new, enhanced way of looking at the connections of the human psyche. Much that was previously incomprehensible becomes meaningful. Although working with the house horoscope is more demanding in terms of astrological technique, it is relatively easy to learn.

This is especially true if one is mainly interested in the concept of development. We shall limit ourselves to these few theoretical examples, which should encourage you to carry out your own research.

Example 2 Female, 1.4.1963, 05:20, Geneva

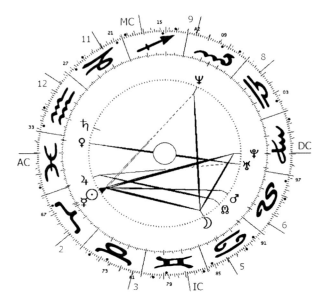

Basic Horoscope

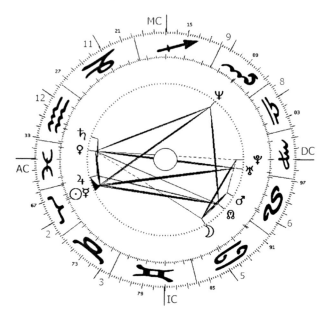

House Horoscope

The Local Horoscope

The local horoscope is a valuable addition to the armoury of modern and future astrologers. The world has become so small that, at some time during our lives, many of us will travel quite far and may change residences often. Now, each place has its own house system, its own environment. In a local horoscope the native's personal planets, sign positions and aspects are transferred to the house system of some place in which he or she once lived, is living now, or is thinking of living.

Perhaps the reader has sometimes wondered why one place is more congenial than another. The reason could be the collective environmental quality of the locality. For each region, astrologically speaking, has its own house system based on a zodiac inscribed on the earth's surface. The figure shows the house system for Zürich. Experience has shown that the global system of coordinates with Greenwich as origin, introduced at the end of the 19th century, actually has a terrestrial zodiac as its basis – even though to all appearances it is a human invention!

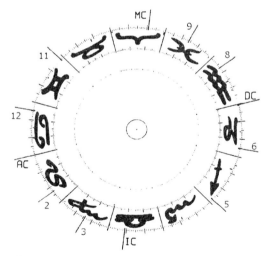

Local Houses for Zürich, Switzerland

Tests made by various modern astrologers on local ascendants and local meridians have demonstrated that the course of events at any given place is influenced by transits of the corresponding degrees of the zodiac. Our own researches have brought further facts to light. Each locality has not only an ascendant and a meridian but a whole house system. And the planets and signs in a person's chart are just as much influenced by this house system as events are!

Planets transferred from a birth chart to a local chart may well be brought to a more favourable house or to a more favourable position in their old house. There are many possible arrangements giving increased vitality or otherwise as the case may be. The local horoscope indicates how the native feels in a collective environment.

Local Horoscope Description

The local horoscope is relatively new in astrology. We have not yet been able to gather a great deal of data on interpretation and on the Age Point. The figure opposite is an example of how the local horoscope can enhance the understanding of the radix. Anyone who wants to do some research for themselves will find this example useful. We have chosen this horoscope because we know the individual well. In describing the local horoscope we shall concentrate on the three ego planets – Sun, Saturn, and Moon. These are decisive for self development and for a sense of well-being in a place.

The Sun is positioned in the birth chart just after the cusp of the 2nd house; in the local horoscope of Zürich, however, it lies in the shadow of the 11th house. And so the symbol of self awareness moves from the lower to the upper half of the horoscope. In Zürich this lady had better opportunities for individuation and self realisation than in her birthplace. The position of the Sun shows that she was challenged by what was going on around her in Zürich to sharpen her identity and to perform a definite function in concert with like-minded people. Solving the various problems that arose was not easy: the Sun stands in the shadow of the cusp and therefore inside a stress zone; what is more, it is in the intercepted sign of Taurus, which has no house cusp of its own. More effort is required from shadow planets; and intercepted signs speak of inappropriate reactions to an environment that is not properly perceived and from which the native gets poor feedback. In the radix, the Sun in the 2nd house shows that the native's material resources had to be fully exploited and that she had to shoulder the responsibility for her finances. She herself had to procure whatever was necessary to bring her plans to fruition.

Saturn moves from the radical 7th house to the local 4th house, that is to say from the upper to the lower half of the horoscope. In the 4th house, Saturn is usually experienced as stress or pressure from the environmental group. The native was always afraid that the neighbours were going to take offence at something or other. She always had to be doing things for the family, for the home, for those around; she felt tied, and responsible for everything that had happened or might happen, and she tried to prepare for all eventualities. Since radical Saturn is in the 7th house, she wanted support from her partner, but

Female, May 10, 1924, 03:15, Bamberg

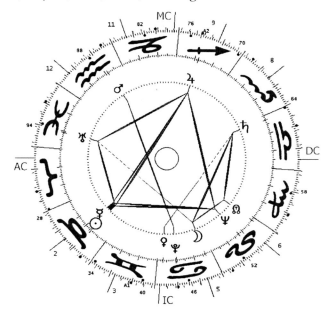

Basic Horoscope (Radix)

Local Horoscope – Zurich

little help was forthcoming from that direction; certainly not as much as previously (square to the Moon).

The Moon moves from the radical 5th house to just before the local horoscope ascendant. Emotional rapport with the place was important to her health. The Cancerian Moon at the AC reacted subjectively to acceptance and also to the slightest rejection; the native was always tense, and uncertain whether or not she was making a good impression. The worry drained her of energy. She quickly senses sympathy or antipathy, and had a hard fight against unjustified fears (shadow planet = tendency to compensate).

The Age Point in the Local Horoscope

It goes without saying that an Age Point travels through the houses of the local horoscope; but here the AP reveals outer stimuli, not the fundamental inner vibrations revealed by the radix. The AP registers the influence of the locality and the local community, and the native's probable reactions to these may be inferred. The method is the same as with the normal Age Point. We look in the local horoscope for the period in which we are interested. The path of the local Age Point starts at birth, but we do not join it until the point in time when the native changed residence. From then on it shows what events and opportunities are likely in the new home – often more clearly and with more accurate timing than the radical AP does. To assess the course of life, we track the local AP as it aspects planets in the local horoscope. The significance of individual aspects can be found in *LifeClock* (14).

In our example, the lady arrived in Zürich for the first time in September 1952. The local Age Point was at 26° Sagittarius, thus exactly at the galactic centre – suggesting that the visit would have something to do with universal values. In October 1952, the native received a proposal of marriage under the sextile to Saturn and quincunx to the Moon. In February 1953, she finally settled in Zürich. The local AP was at 28° Sagittarius trine to the Moon's North Node – so this was an important event for her personal development and spiritual task. The marriage is not indicated by the local AP. However, it was solemnized in March 1953, when the AP was exactly conjunct Neptune in the radix chart.

From February 1954 to October 1955, the local AP was in opposition to Venus and Pluto. This was an intensely critical period as far as decision-making was concerned; and, in August 1956, when the AP was at BP 6, the native left Zürich in order to take up spiritual work full time (opposition Pluto). In September 1962, when the local AP was exactly conjunct Mars, she returned to Zürich. Her absences had lasted from BP6 through BP7, that is to say it practically coincided with the gap between Jupiter and Mars in the local horoscope. In December 1964, at the opposition to Neptune, she started her own service enterprise in the vicinity of Zürich. March, 1968 found her launching a Uranian-type project. At this very time, the local AP entered Pisces, where Uranus was waiting. The preparatory work had already been taken in hand in September 1967, at the opposition to the Moon's North Node. This was the prelude to intense personal and mental activity. There is an interesting connection here with the aspect cycles (see *LifeClock*). At the trine to the Moon Node she came to Zürich. At the opposition she was busy laying the foundations for what was to follow. With the transit of Uranus she set herself up as an independent (9th house) lecturer on esoteric subjects. As her skill improved in this direction, she proceeded to form and lead her own group. Uranus in the radical 12th house shows that even in her old home she liked researching spiritual and hidden things.

During the passage through the 10th house of the local horoscope, success attended all her professional and spiritual endeavours. From 1978 onwards she began to attract attention, her popularity grew and people took her work seriously. In particular, honours came her way and her efforts received increased recognition when the Sun was transited (even though it is in an intercepted sign). Her self-confidence and self-assurance blossomed and she achieved the financial stability for which she had struggled so long – a vindication of the radical Sun's presence on the 2nd cusp.

Discrepancy between Temperament and Environment in Signs and Houses

Another new approach in astrological psychology is the confrontation of signs and houses revealing the interplay between temperament and environment. This facet of psychological interpretation is so important that we have decided, in spite of is complexity, to discuss its bearing on Age Progression. Further information is in (16)

It is a known fact that besides the natural tendencies shown in the radix there are influences that impinge on us from the environment. Therefore, when judging the horoscope, especially the progressed horoscope, we need to discover where disposition and conditioning (signs and houses) are at odds with one another; only so can human problems – not the least our own – be properly assessed. By applying the Age Progression method, we can determine how much the development of our natural inclinations and abilities is helped or hindered by the structure of our environment. This is revealed by the arrangement of the signs and houses, by their relative displacement with regard to one another, and by the planetary positions. As we compare the house system with the zodiac, we see exactly where the inner self is in accord with the concrete life situation, with our milieu, and where it is not. To elaborate a little, consider the following:

1) **The house system** symbolizes both the environment and our adjustment to it. It shows the effect of background and upbringing, the way in which we respond to or have been conditioned by our surroundings.

2) **The zodiac** indicates our natural disposition, our own contribution to life. What is more, hereditary factors can be identified from the positions of the planets in the signs.

3) **The planetary positions** in the signs, together with the aspect structure, also depict our natural disposition; however, it is necessary to observe that the aspect structure expresses a deep-lying life motivation that is not wholly and absolutely explicable in terms of inherited characteristics.

In almost every horoscope, the zodiac is out of alignment with the house system to some degree. This is obvious from the fact that charts have different rising signs, and it is unusual for 0° Aries to be on the AC. The lack of alignment mirrors a friction or tension between the true nature of the individual and the conditioning produced by force of circumstances. It signifies a certain path of development. If, for example, Virgo is on the AC, the zodiac is, so to speak, reversed in the house system. Capricorn, which really belongs to the highest point (10th house) is now at the lowest (4th). See figure.

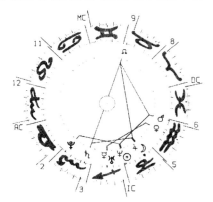

Virgo on the AC changes the position of Capricorn from its natural house (10th) to the 4th.

If the Sun, which is strongest at the MC, stands in the lower half (the so-called collective area) of the horoscope, there is not likely to be a self-confident expression of the true nature, rather a conditioning and inhibition related to the house in which the Sun is posited. Very probably, the native's upbringing will not lead to the free unfolding of a distinct, self-reliant personality.

Differences Between Sign and House
(Temperament and Behaviour)

In working out what is happening in the native's life at any given time, we use the following procedure: first, we find the house the Age Point occupies; second, we find the sign it occupies; third, we see how well the qualities of sign and house agree with one another; and fourth, we note the aspects made by the AP to the planets in the radix. In this chapter we shall consider the third point in detail.

For interpreting the AP, the difference between sign and house (temperament and behaviour) is very interesting and instructive. The house system reveals powerful outside forces that tie us up or push us in certain directions, or maybe aid our development. If we trace the AP through a particular house during a certain period in life, we shall be left in no doubt of the compatibility or incompatibility of sign and house. The sign quality is felt inwardly, causing us to know what we really want. At the same time we experience, through the house, what the world expects and requires of us. The two things can be quite different. The inner will is often contrary to the demands of the environment. The result is unnecessary reverses and apparent failures, as well as difficulties in adjustment with corresponding psychic crises. The latter can be avoided if we learn how to behave; in other words, what and what not to do.

First we need to know that the origin of most problems lies, not in our temperament, but in the conflict between our temperament and real life situations, i.e. between "what I want" and "what the world wants from me." This confrontation between will and obligation begets inner struggles and difficulties, but is also a tremendous powerhouse for development when put in operation by the passage of the AP through the houses.

The Age Point, our focus of consciousness, helps us to distinguish between the demands and opportunities of the environment and our own inner desires and aptitudes. In studying the house theme, we gain an insight into the best way to respond to what is happening around us – whether to go along with it, or to disengage from it because it does not meet our deepest desires. We shall learn something about our freedom when we can take a cold hard look at the clamouring world and then make a judicious, informed decision to give it some, all, or none of what it wants. If we are ignorant of this option, we more or less deliver ourselves up to suffer from "force of circumstances" or from the imposition of others; our dependence on stimuli, baits, opportunities, and commands being due to a lack of the concept of freedom.

So what can the horoscope tell us about the degree of freedom? To answer this, the first step is to discover how far the qualities of the sign and house agree, a point most easily determined by seeing whether or not they belong to the same cross or the same temperament. The second step is to assess the degree of agreement or disagreement, and to find out where we need to improve. As we already know from *LifeClock* (14), the cardinal, fixed and mutable crosses represent our motivations. To outline this concept once more very briefly:

Cross	Keyword	Law	Motivation
Cardinal	Impulse	Power	Conquest
Fixed	Perseverance	Economy	Protection
Mutable	Relationship	Love	Understanding

House/Sign Combinations in the Crosses

We shall now indicate a few of the possible combinations of the crosses. A detailed discussion would exceed the limits of this book. The following figure may help you understand this discussion.

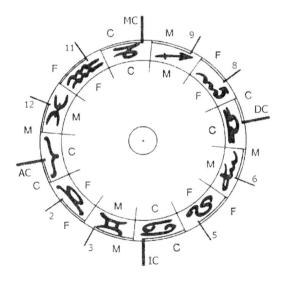

Cardinal (C), Fixed (F), and Mutable (M)
Combinations of House and Sign

Cardinal/Fixed

Fixed houses 2, 5, 8, 11
Cardinal signs: Aries, Cancer, Libra, Capricorn

When a cardinal sign lies in a fixed house, the cardinal and fixed principles form an obvious complementary pair. With this combination, we can be very productive and successful, especially when we make conscious use of the Age Point. If, for example, the cardinal sign Libra is in the 5th house, the typical contact-making, imposing behaviour and self-promotion of Libra can be expressed with charm, adroitness and good taste.

Fixed/Cardinal

Cardinal houses 1, 4, 7, 10
Fixed signs: Taurus, Leo, Scorpio, Aquarius

When the roles are reversed, and a fixed sign is in a cardinal house, the two crosses are well able to complement one another. For instance, individuals with *Leo in the 10th house* can make a good impression. They usually know their own minds, and have no difficulty in striking an individual attitude. The demands of the 10th house are taken in their stride, and no great adjustments are required when the Age Point passes through it.

Mutable/Fixed

Fixed houses 2, 5, 8, 11
Mutable signs: Gemini, Virgo, Sagittarius, Pisces

When a mutable sign is in a fixed house, motives are mixed. The sign favours change and novelty; the house favours stability and the tried and true. The result is internal strife: a conflict between desire and necessity that often becomes painfully obvious when the AP activates it. For instance, if *Sagittarius is in the 2nd house*, the Archer gives a love of liberty and independence from material things which life seems loath to satisfy. In the 2nd, Taurean house, the Sagittarian nature is forced to concentrate on the accumulation of wealth before there is any possibility of living a free life. Often this goal is not achieved until the AP is in the opposing 8th house (ages 42-48).

Fixed/Mutable

Mutable houses 3, 6, 9, 12
Fixed signs: Taurus, Leo, Scorpio, Aquarius

With a fixed sign in a mutable house (e.g. *Scorpio in the 9th house*), desire is at odds with necessity (especially between ages 48 and 54), because the fixed, conservative principle has nothing in common with the fluctuating demands of the environment. This produces an unsettled frame of mind – in the 9th house regarding outlook on life, religious beliefs and inner orientation, and in the other mutable houses regarding their matters. The native has to learn that there is no such thing as ultimate safety, but life is an ongoing adventure.

Cardinal/Mutable

Mutable houses 3, 6, 9, 12
Cardinal signs: Aries, Cancer, Libra, Capricorn

When on the other hand, a cardinal sign occupies a mutable house, the principle of impulse goes well with the changing demands of the house, because there is very little conflict between the two crosses. If *Cancer is in the 6th house*, the efficiency of the native's work will generally depend on feelings of sympathy and antipathy. During the passage of the AP through this house, we should notice that we enjoy pleasant relationships with our colleagues. We work best in harmonious and agreeable surroundings.

Mutable/Cardinal

Cardinal houses 1, 4, 7, 10
Mutable signs: Gemini, Virgo, Sagittarius, Pisces

This combination, too, generally functions without much difficulty. For example, if *Virgo is in the 4th house*, the native could be a woman engaged in the important work of caring for a family. If so, she would make sure she got all the activity and change she wanted by going visiting, moving house frequently, taking trips, or constantly rearranging the rooms.

Chapter 5

The Age Point and the
Four Temperaments

Whereas the crosses represent our essential drives or motivations, the temperaments characterize the types and modes of our behaviour, that is to say they characterize *how* we do things. In short: the three crosses answer the question *why?* and the four temperaments answer the question *how?*

The three qualities of the crosses manifest themselves individually in a regularly recurring series of temperaments. By combining the three crosses with the four temperaments we obtain the twelve signs of the zodiac. To understand the different effects or types of energy of the separate signs (and also of the houses), we can analyse them into their crosses and temperaments and interpret them both as primary principles and as combinations. [See also *LifeClock* (14).]

In many books the four temperaments are also called elements. The latter are the building blocks of all material structures and organic tissues. Each element represents a basic type of energy and consciousness. When the Age Point changes from one sign to another, our temperament alters abruptly – often overnight. As modern physics has shown, energy can be converted into mass; in much the same way, the four elements condense into material and psychic conditions, and crystallize into various characteristics or forms of behaviour. What is more, they have a psychological connection with the four colours, red, green, yellow, blue, assigned to the four temperaments shown in our charts. See the following figure.

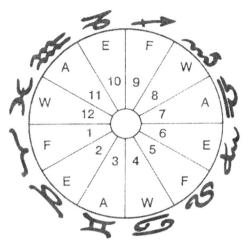

The Sign/House Temperaments
A = Air, E = Earth, W = Water, F = Fire

The four temperaments can be linked to the four states of aggregation of matter:

Colour	The Four States of Aggregation		
Red	Fire	=	Plasma
Green	Earth	=	Solid
Blue	Water	=	Liquid
Yellow	Air	=	Gas

It is life that expresses itself as an organic whole through the four elements, adopts a certain hue or vibration, and changes our inner attitude accordingly. In describing the essential action of the elements, Stephen Arroyo (3) says:

"The birth chart therefore reveals your energy pattern, or cosmic attunement to the four elements. In other words, the chart shows the various vibratory manifestations that comprise the individual's expression in this plane of creation, all of which follow a specific pattern of order which the chart symbolizes. In scientific terms, the chart shows your 'energy field' or what clairvoyants call the 'aura'."

From an esoteric point of view, the elements correspond to the four subtle or fine-structure bodies of the human being. These interpenetrate one another and, taken as a whole, may be likened to a force field that envelops the physical body and supplies it with life-giving energy. All four elements are present in each of us, even though individually we incline to one type more than another.

The element earth is a symbol of the physical body that binds us to real life, to the tangible world. The element fire corresponds to the vital or etheric body. This has a close connection with the physical body and provides the coarser substance of life. The element water is linked to the emotional or astral body, which is animated by subjective ideas, hopes and wishes. The element air is connected with the mental body, in which all thought forms are contained and into which new thoughts are continually pouring from the universal thought plane. The esoteric paradigm is as follows:

Physical body	Earth element
Etheric body	Fire element
Emotional body	Water element
Mental body	Air element

Typology

Psychologically speaking, the four temperaments are the basis of astrological typology. This has been confirmed in modern times by the work of C. G. Jung, who opened up fresh vistas in personal psychology with his four functions. The table shows a useful scheme:

Element	Jungian Type	Planet	Colour
Earth	Sensation	Jupiter	Green
Water	Feeling	Venus	Blue
Air	Thinking	Mercury	Yellow
Fire	Intuition	Mars	Red

There follow brief descriptions of the four types, including planetary analogies that will help readers gain new perspectives and throw a distinguishing light on the characteristics of the temperaments.

Fire or Intuition Type

(Corresponding to the planetary quality of Mars)

Its properties are active, m0asculine, dynamic, decisive, able to seize the initiative, positive, freedom-loving, pugnacious, thrusting, ambitious, pushy, individualistic, full of bright ideas, creative, intuitive, fickle, insensitive, choleric.

Earth or Sensation Type

(Corresponding to the planetary quality of Jupiter)

Its properties are objective, practical, economic, purposeful, profiting by advantage, close to nature, alive to the world of the senses, epicurean, persevering, tenacious, patient, cautious, lazy, phlegmatic.

Air or Thinking Type

(Corresponding to the planetary quality of Mercury)

Its properties are objectifying, theorising, studious, clever, intelligent, collating, impartial, critical, analytical-logical, intellectual, culture-conscious, informative, negotiating, communicative, matter-of-fact, adaptable, relativising, fickle, superficial, sanguine.

Water or Feeling Type

(Corresponding to the planetary quality of Venus)

Its properties are selective, sensitive, subjective, feminine, imaginative, receptive, impressionable, healing, peaceable, harmony-seeking, easy-going, compassionate, devoted, in need of protection, anxious, vulnerable, reserved, temporising, passive, capricious, melancholy.

Typology and the AP

It is easy to apply the above to Age Progression. When the Age Point passes through the houses, intuition and creativity are activated in each of the fire houses (1, 5, 9), realism and powers of realization in each of the earth houses (2, 6, 10), learning ability and thought in each of the air houses (3, 7, 11), and feeling and a need to belong in each of the water houses (4, 8, 12).

Naturally, the same applies to the AP and the signs in a given horoscope. For example, say the AP passes through the *air sign Gemini in the 8th house* (at some time between age 42 and 48 depending on how much of Gemini occupies this house), then during this period the native will be very interested in acquiring new knowledge; it meets his or her inner need (sign = disposition). However, we have to take into consideration that the environment (fixed 8th house, a water house) confronts him or her with rigid conditions. Psychologically, this means that emotional ties, obligations, constraints, or lack of time or money make life difficult. But as the individualistic 9th and 10th houses are being approached at this stage, the native will be able to break free for further development, learning, communication and variety.

I and You Temperaments

A further instructive distinction is that between the "I" and "You" temperaments. This is very significant for psychological interpretation and for the Age Point. The fire and air signs oppose one another in the zodiac and so do the water and earth signs; these represent the confrontations between the I and the You, between the inner and outer worlds. They symbolize the law of polarity of our being, and our striving for completeness. Fire and air can be regarded as masculine-active, water and earth as feminine-passive. Air and water, air and earth, fire and earth, and fire and water do not oppose one another across the zodiac, but stand side by side in a brotherly-sisterly relationship. They are mutually supportive. On the principle "as above, so below," we apply to the houses what has just been said about the signs. The division is the same. On the I side of the horoscope (houses 12 and 1), we see water (Pisces) and Fire (Aries); on the You side (houses 6 and 7), we have earth (Virgo) and air (Libra). From this we derive the following classification:

Fire and Water are I temperaments.
Earth and Air are You temperaments.

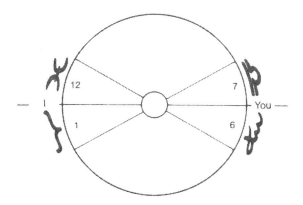

As far as the Age Point is concerned: when our AP is passing through a fire or water house (1, 4, 5, 8, 9, 12), we can cultivate the I, promote our personality and become self-aware. This is a good time for realizing our wants and wishes. When the AP is passing through an earth or air house (2, 3, 6, 7, 10, 11), the time has come to respond to the You and to set aside our I (our own hopes and desires) or at least to subordinate the I to the environment.

House/Sign Combination and the Temperaments

Each combination of house and sign is psychological evidence of the native's problems and development; so let us take a quick look at some examples, confining our attention to a single zodiac sign in each case. The reader will note that our conclusions are drawn from first principles, not from symptoms of concrete events. Generally speaking, it is much easier to work out an interpretation from inner to outer than the other way round. By starting from primary qualities and not from appearances, we avoid contradictions. If we reason from cause to effect, we shall obtain a useful overall picture of the modality, blending and interactions of the astrological elements. Not being lost in a mass of details, we can orientate ourselves correctly and see where the connections are. Only by making a synopsis, by seeing things as a whole, can we see the truth. But before we go into describing the house/sign combinations, the following principles should be considered for interpretation:

1) It is not often that sign and house coincide. Usually there is a certain amount of overlap, in which case it is always the sign on the house cusp that counts.

2) When a sign fills the greater part of a house, but the preceding sign is on the cusp, the qualities of the two signs should be combined.

3) If the sign is intercepted, the sign quality is subordinate to the house theme.

4) Another important factor in making a judgment is whether or not a sign is occupied. Planets represent important psychic forces which must be taken into consideration.

5) In a sign/house combination, we must always bear in mind that signs show what is innate – our disposition – whereas houses show what is expected of us – that is to say, external conditions.

6) Therefore we need to discover whether the qualities of sign and house agree or disagree.

7) In making an interpretation, we should start from the fact that any discrepancy between sign and house indicates developmental tensions that stimulate inner growth. These have an aim, a hidden meaning, that ought to be figured out.

8) The key to this is given by the Dynamic Calculations method [see page 120]. In this context, a note can be made of whether we are dealing with a minus house – in which the case the sign is stronger – or with a plus house – in which case the house is stronger.

Fire Houses 1, 5, 9

Combined with fire, earth, air, and water signs

Fire/Fire:

Aries, Leo, Sagittarius in fire houses 1, 5, 9

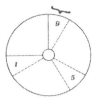

Here is agreement. The inner temperament finds confirmation in the world outside, and does not need to adjust to it. However, different qualities of the crosses will produce a complex motivation. Say the *cardinal fire sign Aries is in the mutable 9th house*, then motivation is the field in which there is a transition from the cardinal will cross to the mutable contact cross. As far as the temperaments are concerned, like temperaments can complement or potentize one another. The fire sign is at home with personality development and with the manifestation of the ego in the world. So the ego reigns supreme in both sign and house. In the 1st house, all experiences revolve around self-assertion; in the 5th, they have to do with strengthening the personal influence; in the 9th, they concern the winning and defence of personal freedom.

Earth/Fire:

Taurus, Virgo, Capricorn in fire houses 1, 5, 9

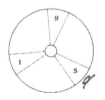

Earth and fire have a knife-edge relationship. If the fire blazes too fiercely it is disruptive and scorches the earth. Earth supplies fire with materials for burning, and this is mutually beneficial provided everything is kept under control. Growth is brought about by warmth and light. With an earth sign in a fire house there is great practicality. The fire house gives willpower, ambition, courage, and a fund of ideas which earth helps to formulate. The person with this combination will move unerringly toward his or her goal and will not easily be diverted from it. Creative talents and activities make their presence known. If, for instance, the *earth sign Taurus is in the 5th house*, the fire house gives love of action, a readiness to take risks, and the courage to experiment. Safety-first Taurus loses much of its hesitation, but supplies the endurance and stability required for the creative forces to do something concrete. With the passage of the AP, this house can realise its potential.

Air/Fire:

Gemini, Libra, Aquarius in fire houses 1, 5, 9

Since air and fire signs are in opposition, it is possible for them to complement one another. The capacity for thought given by the air signs breezes (so to speak) into the intuitive fire houses. But a very strong wind either extinguishes fire or fans it into an inferno. When the airflow is moderate, the fire burns quietly and steadily and throws light and heat on the path. In other words, the natural intellect express itself usefully in the environment; yet, at the same time, intuition supplements verbal knowledge, so thinking becomes more comprehensive and universal, and the expansion of consciousness is a goal. For example, if the *air sign Libra is in the 9th house*, the attitude of the native is normally cultivated and philanthropic, and there is a willingness to allow others their rights. However, this fire house will not accept the Libran need for harmony where the integrity of the life or the inner attitude to others is concerned. Real values have to be upheld.

Water/Fire:

Cancer, Scorpio, Pisces in fire houses 1, 5, 9

As types of energy, water and fire are inimical to one another. Fire shrinks from being doused by the element of feeling (water) and water is agitated by fire's threat to disperse it into steam. Nevertheless, processes like these are creative: consider how the sun's rays suck up water and gather it into clouds, ready for the next shower of rain. And the cycle of transformation is at work not only in nature, but also in the horoscope. For instance, if the *water sign Cancer is in the 1st house*, the native's ego will be expressed very emotionally. He or she tends to have subjective reactions and will take many things too personally. Such individuals usually spend themselves for those they love or for those with whom they are closely connected. They do not make selfish demands unless backed into an emotional corner. Passive water signs take a certain amount of rousing. Water/fire transformation alters the ego, and purges it of emotions (such as an exaggerated fear of the environment) – the sort of thing that hinders ego development.

Earth Houses 2, 6, 10

Combined with earth, air, water, and fire signs

Earth/Earth:

Taurus, Virgo, Cancer in earth houses 2, 6, 10

The earth temperament manifests itself fully here. This individual relies on the five senses, on what can be physically observed. He or she sets a premium on common sense and practicality, does not rely on inspiration or theory but on hard facts, and knows how to make the best of his or her abilities. The 2nd house encourages

one to conserve energy, and to plan for a big return on a small outlay. In the 6th house every effort is made to safeguard one's existence, and in the 10th house much hard work goes into winning professional advancement. The practical earth element gives patience, perseverance, skill, and stubbornness. Those in whom it is strong try to make sure that no one can get the better of them. Often they cling to order and routine and are interested only in material comfort. Yet even here the basic motives are modified, all according to the crosses involved. If *Taurus is in the mutable 6th house*, the obstinacy of the fixed sign becomes rather more flexible and accommodating. Nevertheless, one must not place too many demands on the native: a Taurean does not take kindly to being exploited.

Air/Earth:

Gemini, Libra, Aquarius in earth houses 2, 6, 10

In the earth houses, the air temperament has to adjust to matters of fact, and this gives greater depth. Theoretical and high-flown ideas are compelled to prove themselves in practice; something which is often perceived as due to external pressures or constraints, yet gives good results in the long run. For example, if the *air sign*

Aquarius is in the 2nd house, ideas and spiritual goals must be turned into deeds. The earth house reduces the soaring thoughts of Aquarius to viable proportions, and this the air temperament finds limiting. The earth house policy is slow but sure, but Aquarius wants the future now, if only in imagination. Bringing ideas to birth in the material world is the task; making one's vision useful to others the aim.

Water/Earth:

Cancer, Scorpio, Pisces in earth houses 2, 6, 10

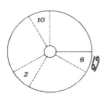

Water and earth are also polarities, and oppose one another in the horoscope. But they are complementary in the sense that facts are understood and absorbed through the emotions. These elements go well together. Earth acts as a container for water and leads it in fixed channels. This gives water signs the confidence, security, and sense of direction they seek. For instance, if the *water sign Cancer is in the 6th house*, feelings for others can be fully released. Maternal functions, such as caring, supervising and nursing, or the desire to be responsible for others, have plenty of scope in the 6th house. If people with this combination find that their concern is not wanted or appreciated, they will creep into their shell and will not come out again without repeated reassurance and expressions of regret from the other party.

Fire/Earth:

Aries, Leo, Sagittarius in earth houses 2, 6, 10

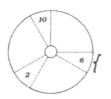

Fire signs in earth houses suggest that inner goals are likely to be achieved. The onrushing fiery energy is moulded into concrete realisation of the correct form. For example, if *Aries is in the 6th house*, the latter puts an environmental brake on the egocentric impulses of the former, and the native must learn to serve the You, i.e., to serve others, before achieving the eagerly desired recognition.

Air Houses 3, 7, 11

Combined with air, water, fire, and earth signs

Air/Air:

Gemini, Libra, Aquarius in air houses 3, 7, 11

When the temperament is repeated its properties are potentized. In this case, the air quality of thinking is stimulated. The native seeks verbal and intellectual exchange, and needs confirmation of his or her opinions, beliefs and doubts. He or she may move in a rarefied atmosphere and lose touch with the direct experience of daily life. Admittedly, this does tend to promote objectivity and discourages fixation on material things, but practical accomplishments are lacking. *Aquarius in the 7th house* can make it easy to get on with people as long as the native keeps them at a distance and deals with them in a general way; but loving care of the current partner is not so much in evidence. In the 3rd house, the views of other individuals or of the group seldom impress, and elicit no more than a brief "I hear you." Someone with Gemini in the 7th house has no respect for the privacy of others and is intrusive. Air signs in the 11th house prompt the native to place too high a value on education, intellect and culture, and go with a refusal to admit that the value of ideas has to be proved before they can be treated as dogma.

Water/Air:

Cancer, Scorpio, Pisces in air houses 3, 7, 11

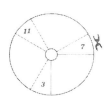

In a person with this combination, feeling and understanding either clash or stir one another up. The water signs have difficulty in meeting the requirements of the air houses. Personal feelings always enter into the native's attitude. The aloof objectivity of the air houses is quite foreign, and even painful, to sensitive water. For example, if the *water sign Pisces is in the 7th house*, the native will invest a lot of his or her emotions in relationships and will be very devoted. But the 7th house calls for a balanced relationship, a genuine partnership which, either by contract or mutual consent, leaves to each their own. Pisces finds this hard to accept, because it craves emotional commitment and reassurance. Pisces wants to love and be loved: it believes in genuine human ties not legal arrangements.

Fire/Air:

Aries, Leo, Sagittarius in air houses 3, 7, 11

Fire and air are poles of a single axis, so the two temperaments have a complementary function. Fire burns by means of the oxygen in the air to produce both light and heat. With their intuitive dynamism, the fire signs can react quickly to the mental challenge of the environment. To bring air house ideas to fruition takes concentrated willpower, and this is just what the fire signs supply. When this combination is discordant, inspiriting energies and creative forces are set free. With *Leo in the 3rd house*, educability depends (from inner necessity) on the quality of the environment. The opinionatedness natural to the fire sign makes for a nonconformity that is often in conflict with orthodox views. If teachers are too dogmatic during the passage of AP through the 3rd house, the fire sign reacts individualistically and the native becomes obstructive or generally shows no interest at all. The central fiery force of Leo must find in the 3rd house's relativizing and equalizing a highmindedness worth accepting. Only then can the lion say a wholehearted Yes, and throw himself heart and soul into the 3rd house, filling it with vitality and living values.

Earth/Air:

Taurus, Virgo, Capricorn in air houses 3, 7, 11

Earth and air can coexist happily. Earth finds it pleasant when wind blows gently over it (although it is disturbed when a storm rages.) The practical intelligence of the earth temperament usually meets the requirements of the air houses. For example, if the *earth sign Virgo is in the 11th house*, Virgo will give approval to the ethical standards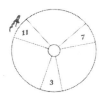
of friends and others. It will also have a desire to keep the world in order, so that life can proceed smoothly and undisturbed. The slightest disruption of vividly imagined hopes and wishes is keenly felt and remembered. With the accumulation of minor disappointments, trust in friends, in the future, and even in life itself can be lost. However, the air house is always ready with new ideals to solace disappointments.

Water Houses 4, 8, 12

Combined with water, fire, earth, and air signs

Water/Water:

Cancer, Scorpio, Pisces in water houses 4, 8, 12

The emotional element flows strongly and steadily here, like a river hurrying to the sea. The natives are largely controlled by emotional impressions. Their evaluation of reality, which is emotionally coloured, is derived from their feelings. Today, they are positive and full of optimism; tomorrow, negative, despondent and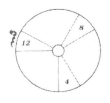
passive. They react emotionally to all sorts of nuances and subtleties. Others often fail to notice these things, but to them they are very important. In the 4th house they are deeply disappointed if others do not share their perceptions; they feel misunderstood, and are liable to take offence at what they imagine is a personal slight. In the 8th house they passionately desire that others reciprocate their

feelings. The 12th house links them with invisible currents from the unconscious or from the universe – often they are kept by protective forces from within themselves, led like small children, guarded and preserved from danger. The element water is closely associated with processes of transformation and purification. This is particularly noticeable when the crosses differ. For example, if the *fixed water sign Scorpio is in the mutable 12th house*, the safety motive dissolves in this uncertain area of universal sharing, breaking down of barriers and transcendence. Inclusiveness comes before safety here. However, those who are unaware of the need for transformation are driven by compulsive ideas and wishes and by irrational fears. The least threat makes them uneasy and defensive.

Fire/Water:

Aries, Leo, Sagittarius in water houses 4, 8, 12

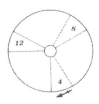

Here again are two hard-to-synthesize elements. In water houses, fire signs will usually raise a lot of steam: the native's goals and wishes conflict with the emotional claims of others. Fire is not accommodating but makes a decidedly egoistic temperament, in which personal interests occupy the foreground. Because of insensitivity, the feelings of others are easily hurt. If, for example, the *fire sign Sagittarius is in the 4th house*, inner freedom, and a clear personal identity will naturally be important; however, the 4th house calls for conformity with the group and serious attention to the duties of family life. Sagittarius instinctively opposes these claims, which are felt to be impositions; so there are problems with the immediate environment. With the passage of AP through the 4th house, quarrels, misunderstandings and conflicts with relatives must often be endured. It is then that the urge to be free, and the longing for the wide unfettered world, leads to early departure from the parental home. Nevertheless, it is through the family friction that the native gradually loses something of his or her "cold individualism" and develops more understanding for others.

Earth/Water:

Taurus, Virgo, Capricorn in water houses 4, 8, 12

A natural appreciation of the basic essentials of life, shown by all earth signs, holds the emotional side in check. The earth element bestows on the water element structure and form. Feelings are given an aim, are directed into certain channels, and can be employed constructively. The flowing water element finds a dependable solidity in the earth sign. If, for example, the *earth sign Capricorn is in the 8th house*, the fluid element can be harnessed for use. In practice, this may mean that a secure, preferably top executive, position is sought that will last until retirement. Of course, as the AP passes through the 8th house, the purifying and purging water element is likely to meet powerful resistance. The native will not give way, holds on to what he or she already has, and refuses to grow further. The Saturnian forces of Capricorn gain the upper hand all too easily, especially when the sign is occupied by planets of the same nature as itself.

Air/Water:
Gemini, Libra, Aquarius in water houses 4, 8, 12

Air signs think and talk a great deal, water signs react to the slightest vibration or stirring of air. This combination is always in motion, and responds immediately to everything that is perceived either internally or externally. The thinking principle of the air signs is kept busy by the water houses, but it is not easy to create anything of lasting worth.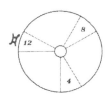
Thoughts are fleeting and have to be caught and made concrete. The best that can happen in this case is for them to soak into the astral body and fertilize the desire nature; then the natives have an inspiring effect on those around them, and are rather like expectant mothers waiting for the birth of their ideas. Now suppose *Gemini is in the 12th house*; this usually purports an ineffectual struggle for academic honours. The natives are soon irritated, and may even feel threatened, when their opinions are ignored or their intellectual ability is doubted. They believe their ideas deserve serious attention. But there is something they need to learn: their wealth of thought will pay dividends only when cleared through the deep emotions.

The Synthesis of Sign and House

As already mentioned, in working out the meaning of temperament and cross, notice must always be taken of the house concerned and also of the phase of life. A synthesis is derivable only from joint activity. The first thing to do when trying to understand the life situation and problems of an individual at a given age is to define explicitly the basic inner attitude of the sign character (of the cross/temperament combination). This will make it possible to use the basic attitude consciously and positively in tackling external tasks. And here it is worth observing that, even when the environment appears to present hopeless difficulties, the sign quality (our natural talents) can help us solve them.

To illustrate what we mean, suppose that Pisces is in the 6th house. Both Pisces and the 6th house belong to the mutable cross; so to this extent they are in agreement. By temperament, however, Pisces is a water sign; but the 6th is an earth house. This water/earth combination has 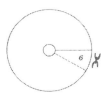 already been described. Watery Pisces is all for sitting down to watch the world go by. The native will do nothing that is not part of his or her job – unless it is to help someone in need. When others approach, they will be kindly received, and an interest will be taken in their problems; but, after they have gone, the native will do nothing further. It is no good expecting from Pisces the love of activity seen in earth house 6. During the passage of the AP through the 6th house, the native is torn between two minds. The 6th house prompts them to get busy, do their duty, work conscientiously, keep good time, attend to everyday affairs, etc.; but with Pisces, none of these promptings will be heeded unless someone else is supervising or begging for help. The activity reflexes are strongest in this and the 7th house, but reactions are still typically Piscean. How the person goes about things depends on the sign quality and on any 6th house planets. To bring the house into harmony with the sign, he has to know and use his temperament. How then does he go about it?

Let us stay with our example. The quality of Pisces can be used correctly if we learn the "magic of wait-and-see." By keeping quietly yet expectantly active, we develop a certain magnetism which draws to us what we need. But it would be a mistake to sit around without enthusiasm treating the world as boring: opportunities would pass by unnoticed. The synthesis of Pisces and the 6th house is achieved by cultivating inner growth, a readiness to react, a receptive, sensitive response to people and situations. Pisces encourages us to perceive nuances and depths, to react to things going on behind the scenes – to what are seen as the fundamental energies behind appearances. This is the reason why, even when the AP is passing through Pisces in other houses, we are quite likely to start taking an interest in occult and esoteric matters.

In synthesizing sign and house, we do not oppose the theme of the house, or simply live in accordance with inner need, but endeavour to unite the two – often very disparate – qualities. The secret lies in bringing our inner needs to bear on external problems in a way that will help us to solve the latter more constructively. This is the right approach. The two themes being highlighted by the AP in house and sign must always first be seen and understood in combination. As already mentioned, it is the obligation to develop as a human being that is apparent in the confrontation of sign and house. We have devised a numerical method which shows the difference between sign and house as plus and minus scores. Since the method plays a part in refining the psychological interpretation of Age Progression, the following section contains a brief description of how it is used.

Discrepancy Between Signs and Houses – Dynamic Calculations

In the Dynamic Calculations method devised by Bruno Huber (17), the discrepancy between disposition and behaviour (sign and house) is assessed numerically. The individual houses or signs are scored with plus or minus qualities. The values are to be found in the chart data of computer programmes based on the Huber method. See the following example.

	Crosses: Motivation				Temperaments: Behaviour			
	Total	Car.	Fix.	Mut.	Fire	Earth	Air	Water
Sign	96	38	44	14	18	23	20	35
House	104	28	52	24	29	39	14	22
Difference	8	-10	8	+10	11	+16	-6	-13

Virgo 6th house

Cancer 4th house

Dynamic Calculations

On the left of the table are the values of the planets in the three crosses, on the right are the values of the planets in the four temperaments. The upper row of figures gives the values of the planets by Sign position, and the middle row gives their values by House position. The third row shows the Difference in value between the sign and house values.

First we consult the table to determine the values of the planetary positions in cardinal, fixed or mutable signs/houses and also in fire, earth, air or water signs/houses; positive and negative values being used to offset the signs and houses against one another. If the house values are bigger than the sign values, the result is positive; if smaller, the result is negative. If the result is positive, the houses and therefore the environment override the disposition; if it is negative, the signs and therefore the disposition dominate the environment. Certain signs, and the houses derived from them, are thrown into prominence when we combine positive and negative quantities in the crosses and temperaments. This happens according to the following rules:

1) Positive is combined only with positive, and negative only with negative.

2) Only the highest numbers are combined; those less than 5 can be ignored.

In the above example we combine -10 in the cardinal cross with -13 in the water temperament. This gives us the cardinal water sign, which is of course Cancer. And Cancer corresponds to the 4th house. Thus the 4th house turns out to be a "minus house." Also, on combining +10 in the mutable cross with +16 in the earth temperament, we get the mutable earth sign Virgo, which corresponds to the 6th house; therefore the 6th house is a "plus house."

Generally speaking, most people are strongly influenced by the plus houses, and have learned to function in that area of life. In the minus houses, the signs (i.e. disposition) are stronger. Our milieu has made hardly any impression at all on us, and may have ignored us. We do not have much idea of what goes on in this area of life, have acquired no know-how, and so are either insecure or else uncluttered and free.

The AP Through Plus and Minus Houses

With the passage of the Age Point through the 6th house, which has a high positive value in our example, 6th house problems will be keenly felt between ages 30 and 36. Possibly we shall live in a state of uncertainty, or find ourselves under continual pressure from the circumstances of life with no apparent means of relief. Experiences of this sort will last as long as we resist the demands of the 6th house. A high positive number always indicates an ability to stand stress; in the case of the 6th house, it is important to learn to fulfil daily duties. We ought to accept them gladly, because the process of recognition and acceptance eventually leads to freedom. The very knowledge that a problem and a special task await us in this house offers a solution, because we can consciously come to grips with them.

In the example the 4th house is a minus house and, when the AP passes through it (age 18 through 24), life will probably become rather uncertain. Perhaps the parental home provides little security and is not a cosy nest. Or perhaps, feeling homeless, we wander around looking for some kindred spirit with whom to form a relationship, though anything permanent seems to be out of the question. Society can be an unknown quantity; often it is a threatening factor – and so is the family. When the AP passes through a minus house, we feel rather insecure and helpless; needing know-how, needing to grasp that we have a freedom we can use. By bringing our natural disposition (as represented by the sign) into play, we can become more self assured.

Interestingly enough, a house with negative numbers offers room to manoeuvre. To combat a feeling of helplessness, we can take ourselves in hand. Since this area of life has not been over-structured, we are relatively free to be ourselves; that is to say, we can live in the spirit of the sign occupying the inherited disposition. But this is possible only if we are capable of using our freedom constructively and if, on the strength of what we see and know, we adopt an individual or independent attitude.

As a rule, during the passage of the AP through houses with negative values, it is fairly easy to express our natural disposition; whereas during its passage through houses with positive values, a whole pack of habitual reactions or over structurings must be removed before we can get in touch with our own true will.

More importantly, the study of sign and house brings a conscious realization of the unity of temperament and environment, of inner and outer worlds. The development of this awareness of complex unity is known as individuation. The person who has achieved wholeness by synthesizing the two worlds is free from the horoscope, and is guided entirely by the self and by the real requirements of life, not by imposed standards. In him or her, nature and human nature agree, and it is possible to risk being individual – to the extent of passing one's own moral judgments and taking full responsibility for what one does or does not do.

Having reached this stage, we face the world positively and assimilate it, because we perceive ourselves as part of the whole. We may perform the same tasks as others, but our attitude is different, and usually they recognise it. When we have achieved this inner wholeness and are at one with the universe, our assured personality structure and our expanded awareness make us a tower of strength to many and we become a helper and servant of humankind.

The person who is at loggerheads with the world or who ignorantly refuses life's duties has abandoned the harmonious process of exchange between inner and outer, between above and below. So it is important to seek our centre and to remain firmly anchored there;

then, in the light of what we know, we can freely decide how to treat the world and its claims.

As long as we repress a part of our being – to which the environment also relates – the horizon is limited and we fail to take advantage of life's possibilities. Our decisions are not well thought out because they do not come from our inner selves; we go by what is customary, or blindly follow the advice of parents or other authority figures who have conditioned us to act according to those standardized forms of behaviour which the world calls good or bad, black or white. By escaping from well entrenched systems, we gain inner freedom, and our ideas of right and wrong become based on conscience and personal knowledge. In other words, our attention is directed more and more to our own centre, we become aware of our selfhood and individuality and so recognize the tasks we are meant to accomplish in the world. All this requires a process of continuous self interrogation and self control, in which the unconscious is not forgotten. Only when we have discovered for ourselves why we ought to do this or that can we assume responsibility for how we live; perhaps doing exactly the same as we did before, but now with a new awareness. There is no further room for the superego, for collective norms, codes, and authorities, or even for the horoscope; the self, as the centre of the personality, becomes the arbiter of behaviour and approaches the world in a positive and creative manner. This self within, symbolized by the cross in the middle of the horoscope, lives in harmony with cosmic laws – in unity that is with the entire plan of creation. He or she whose life is attuned to the Self can do only what serves the Whole. To give an experience of wholeness and to increase human freedom are two of the worthwhile goals of Age Progression.

Chapter 6

The Temperament Age Point

Four Lines of Development

Since the four temperaments are so closely bound up with the way we do things, a further interesting perspective opens up at any age phase if, beside the normal Age Point, we consider an Age Point travelling through the individual temperament houses.

Following prolonged research and many observations of the various ages and their characteristics, the fact has been confirmed that a combination of the two Age Points is needed for deeper insight into psychological connections. What is more, we may safely say that while the normal Age Point registers the outward behaviour noticed by others, the Temperament Age Point reveals our inner development, the maturing processes taking place inside us. The latter is determined by the four temperaments; and it is remarkable that, in practice, the normal Age Point (AP) and the Temperament Age Point (TAP) move synchronously in the horizon houses (the "I" houses 12 and 1, and the "You" houses 6 and 7), move in opposition in the meridian houses representing the confrontation of the group and the individual (axes 4/10 and 3/9), and, finally, move square to one another in the fixed houses (having-being) and are thus in strenuous but activating tension. To make matters clearer, we begin by giving the following table showing the four temperaments and their houses as four different lines of development.

Personality development • Bearing • Self-presentation • Ethics I-extroverted	FIRE 1st quadrant	1	STRUCTURE TYPE: basic form, figure, outer life (image), objectives, self-interest	
		5	ACTION TYPE: conduct, imposing behavior, aggressive contact-making, erotic adventures and their results, exploitation	
		9	THINKING TYPE: outlook on life, sense of justice, consciousness of own worth, philosophy of life, a tendency to be opinionated	
Social development • Authority • Possessions • Performance YOU-introverted	EARTH 2nd quadrant	10	VOCATION: place in the community, self-development, career, aims, authority or presumptiousness	
		2	BASIC EQUIPMENT: talents, energy store, advantages, acquisitiveness, one's means, life substance (vitality, finances)	
		6	STRUGGLE FOR EXISTENCE: aptitudes, way of working, performance, weaknesses, psychosomatic processes	
External relationships • Ties • Morals • Adaptability YOU-extroverted	AIR 3rd quadrant	7	LEGAL UNIONS: interest in commitment, secure social relationships, contractual relationships, sacrifice of the ego	
		11	CONGENIAL ASSOCIATIONS: freely chosen affiliations, friends, ideals of humanity, the moralist	
		3	NATURAL CONTACTS: neighborly and brotherly – externally given, collective thought standards	
Inner orientation SELF –understanding –conquest –existence I-introverted	WATER 4th quadrant	4	DESCENT: tradition, home and hearth, family, group membership	THE SMALL I
		8	DEATH and TRANS-FIGURATION: law of give and take, obligations to the you	THE I IN CRISIS
		12	INTROSPECTION: You-loss, isolation, the non-secular individual	THE BIG I

Four Lines of Development

The Spiral of Development

When dealing with the Temperament Age Point, we should note that it does not travel regularly from one house to the next, and yet every now and then, at the cardinal axes AC, IC, DC, MC, it makes an immediate transition to the next temperament house.

Ego development	Fire houses	1	5	9
Social development	Earth houses	10	2	6
Contact development	Air houses	7	11	3
Emotional development	Water houses	4	8	12

The resulting spiral of development runs through the houses as illustrated in the following diagram.

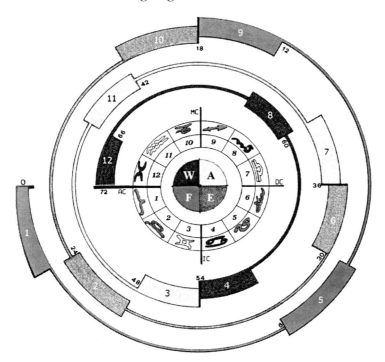

The Spiral of Development

In this spiral line of development, the TAP takes eighteen years to move through the three fire houses, and similar periods of time to move through the three earth houses, the three air houses, and the three water houses. This eighteen-year cycle has already been described for the quadrants in *LifeClock* (14). We shall come back to this later. Incidentally, it is interesting to note that the temperaments were assigned to the quadrants in antiquity. Even the Babylonians saw a correspondence between fire and the 1st quadrant, earth and the 2nd quadrant, air and the 3rd quadrant, and water and the 4th quadrant.

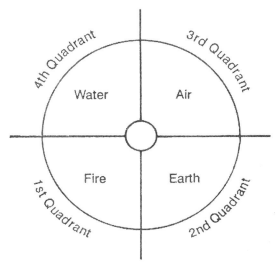

Quadrants and Temperaments

Our study of development starts with the assumption that life can be equated with growth. Each temperament has its line of development, which begins in a cardinal house, jumps to a fixed house, and ends in a mutable house. The three-stage development process is organic and always leads to greater integration. Those who recognize the pattern try to resolve their problems in a way that allows for growth. Whether or not a situation pleases them, they will forge ahead every now and then and be more or less creative. They tend to be perfectionists, and want to improve themselves and the world; even though they know it is unrealistic to expect a state of perfection on this earth. The urge to make things better is the first step on the road to further development and marks the life of someone with originality, for whom there is no standing still, no resting on their laurels, no holding fast, but a continual advance under the laws of cosmic progress.

1. Personality Development

Bearing, Self-presentation, Ethics – Houses 1, 5, 9

As we know, it is from the ascendant that the Age Point sets out at birth to journey through the house system. In the first six years it transits the 1st house. Now this is the first fire house. Therefore, in the first six years of life, the AP and TAP move side by side. At the age of 6, the AP enters the 2nd house, but the TAP jumps to the next fire house, the 5th, and stays there until age 12. Between 12 and 18, the normal AP travels through the 3rd house, an air house, while the TAP travels through the facing 9th house, a fire house. During this stage of life, the two Age Points are in opposition. After the first 18 years the fire cycle is complete. The normal AP now moves into the 4th house, while the TAP crosses directly from the 9th house into the 10th, an earth house. The Age Points remain in opposition. And so, when the native is 18, the normal AP leaves the I-side of the horoscope and enters the YOU-side, and the TAP commences its earth cycle.

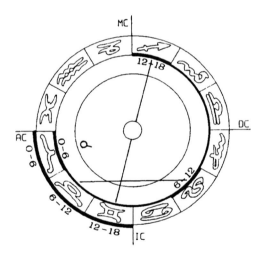

Development in the Fire Temperament.

The Fire Phase

1st quadrant

The fire temperament is an I-temperament. Therefore all the fire houses (1, 5, 9) have to do with ego development. The personality starts to develop in the 1st, or Aries, house. In the 5th, or Leo, house it continues to make progress, and in the 9th, or Sagittarius, house it has fully-formed consciousness. Fire begins with the raw ego and ends with the complete individual. There is a time of crisis in the 5th house during which we graduate to personal autonomy. Any planets in fire houses can be used to promote the development of the native's personality.

If we now bring back into the picture the normal AP, we see that as the latter is moving through the 1st quadrant (ages 0-18) the TAP is encouraging ego development in the three fire signs (1, 5, 9). Either way, the unfolding of self consciousness is the theme.

In the 1st house we build our ego image; in the 5th we are confronted by our own world. We make a deliberate effort to see how far others will let us go, and in encounters with the You we learn a great deal about ourselves. We want to make an impression on others and show them our best side. Failed friendships and love affairs reveal our weaknesses. Then there is the question of how to treat people. The right way is to be fair and honest, and to act responsibly. When we have learned this, our development shoots into the 9th house. Here there arises a balanced perception of how to use authority and individuality. And the journey continues, as consciousness crosses the MC/IC axis into the 10th house.

Ages 0-6
AP and TAP in the 1st house

From ages 0 to 6, the AP and TAP both go through the 1st house, keeping in step with one another. "Here I am" is the main theme of this manifestation phase of the ego. The fire of ego manifestation is stoked by the two Age Points so that the I can be cast in its proper form. In infancy concentration on self is very strong. Many children even display autistic traits. Usually a child does not pay close attention to its surroundings until the Low Point (the fourth year of life). All its energies are absorbed by ego development.

Ages 6-12
AP in the 2nd house, TAP in the 5th house

Between ages 6 and 12, the AP is in the 2nd house and the TAP in the 5th, a fire house. The temperament combination is earth and fire. The 2nd house makes the child intensely aware of, and eager to relate to, the environment. It has to win a place for itself and, at the same time, expects to be acknowledged by others. But there are social pressures on the developing ego. The fire theme of the 5th house also comes into play, and it comes into play like this: the child is determined by all means to make an impression. It measures itself against others and wants to excel, wants to have more than they have, plays all sorts of tricks to get its own way, brags, and shows off its possessions. The child is always testing how far it can go and is constantly pushing at social barriers; and so it experiences a lot about the world and the world's rules, and is continually learning how to get on better with people. At this stage, impressions are formed that govern contacts and behaviour later in life, even in the sexual sphere.

Ages 12-18

AP in the 3rd house, TAP in the 9th house

In this phase of life, the two Age Points move in opposition. A tension exists between the desire to learn (3rd house) and the conviction that one already knows everything worth knowing (9th house). There is a wish to preserve self respect when in the company of adults. At this age, many young people would like to have all their questions answered, but their comprehension is limited. Nevertheless, these are the years in which one learns most, not because one thirsts for knowledge, but also because the entire 3/9 thought-axis strongly stresses learning ability. Many youngsters develop grand ideas about life in this period, build castles in the air, construct an imaginary world that usually bears little resemblance to reality but makes them feel good. They cannot stand criticism or reproach, and hate the compulsory instruction represented by the 3rd house. Often they fail at school for this reason. Some of these young people display a practical wisdom beyond their years, and many are true philosophers. But most of them must suffer not being taken seriously, even though their judgment on many issues is usually sound. Their 3rd house AP keeps them tied to their desks, being lectured by teachers.

2. Social Development

Authority, Possessions, Performance – Houses 10, 2, 6

With the earth cycle, social development starts; this, too, lasts for 18 years. Up to age 24 the TAP passes through the 10th house, which is of course an earth house. See figure overleaf.

As the normal AP moves into the 5th house at 24, the TAP makes a sudden drop into another earth house (2nd) and remains there for six years. At 30, the AP and the TAP both enter the last earth house (6th). At 36, when the AP and TAP arrive at the DC, the phase of social development is over. After this, the air cycle begins with the entry into the 7th house – and the two Age Points continue to run side by side.

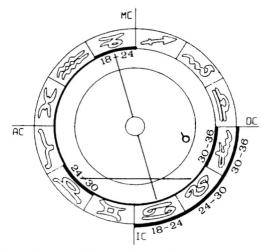

Development in the Earth Temperament.

The Earth Phase

2nd quadrant

While the AP is travelling through the earth quadrant (the 2nd) at ages 18-36, the TAP is travelling through the earth houses. Starting in the 10th house, it continues in the 2nd, and ends in the 6th.

The development of a given temperament always finishes in a mutable house and begins in a cardinal one. Here in the 10th house the interest centres on wielding authority and on becoming proficient in some field. The 2nd house theme is the acquisition of material wealth; and the theme of the 6th house is handing on to others what has been acquired. While developing socially in the earth houses, it is important to prove that one is not an asocial hustler who is simply out for power. True satisfaction arises from benefiting others with the gains gleaned in the 2nd house. This is growth. First comes ambition and planning a career, then the production of wealth, and lastly sharing with the community what one has earned. One must go as an individual to the You in the spirit of helpfulness. This is social progress.

Ages 18-24

AP in the 4th house, TAP in the 10th house

In this phase of life, the two Age Points are again in opposition. Repeatedly, the adolescent feels that he or she is being pulled this way and that by conflicting tendencies. Young people at the IC often behave as if they were already at the MC. They jib at tutelage and authority and try to claim in advance the power of the 10th house. They want self determination before they are really ready to look after themselves. In the 4th house most of them are still dependent on their families. All the same, the seed of the individual human being lies hidden here, trying to sprout vigorously via the 4/10 axis. Many parents do not understand these things and feel hurt; they become authoritarian and are met by stubborn resistance. The tension is part of the process of leaving the parental home – normally something which has happened by Low Point four (at the age of 22).

Ages 24-30
AP in the 5th house, TAP in the 2nd house

Here the fixed houses are square to one another. This usually means an intense, exhausting period of life that holds in store both duality conflicts and learning processes. Hard tests await us in each fixed house, and we ourselves have prepared them in the preceding cardinal house. Our plans and wishes are now ready to be verified and carried out. The fiery expansive egoism of the 5th house presses outward and seeks to conquer the world. However, the TAP in the 2nd house discourages us from being too pushy. In the 5th house the emphasis is placed, among other things, on erotic and sexual experiences. Sexual activities begin to follow a routine. We discover how well we are able to manage our contacts with others.

Ages 30-36
AP and TAP in the 6th house

Now the two Age Points are travelling side by side once more, and in this way reinforce the quality and demands of the earthy 6th house. Social development is forced, and therefore we are kept very busy doing useful work. Besides earning a living, we want to do something meaningful. In the 6th house, the idea is to offer the world what it needs. Success can be ours if we are prepared to help others with their problems. Even when we feel that we are not needed, or even that we are being exploited, it is more important to understand and help others than to cater to self-importance. If we are to make the most of the 6th house, we need to integrate, to make less of ourselves, and to recognize that others have problems too. People at this time of life often change jobs and take up community work: they want to help, to heal, to serve.

3. External Relationships

Ties, Morals, Adaptability - Houses 7, 11, 3

From the 6th house, the TAP crosses over into the cardinal air 7th house. This change to a cardinal house brings resurgent growth, a fresh beginning, new birth. The air temperament deals in externals, so confrontation commences with other human beings, as does a permanent relationship with the environment, with the You.

Until the 42nd year of life both Age Points are travelling through the 7th house. Then the normal AP carries on through the 8th house while the TAP skips to the 11th. Subsequently, right up to age 48, the Age Points are square one another. A square does not inevitably mean conflict; it can signal a fruitful learning period where much occurs and progress is made. One longs to exploit one's talents and to do something useful. The final phase of external relationships brings an adaptation to necessities, seeing the TAP is in the 3rd air house; but, at the same time, increased wisdom and a more mature outlook on life, since the normal AP is in the 9th house.

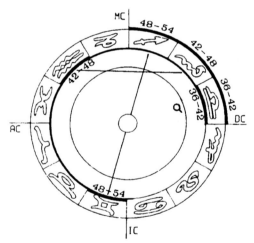

Development in the Air Temperament.

The Air Phase

3rd quadrant

When the normal AP is in the 3rd quadrant (ages 36-54), the TAP is travelling through the air houses (7, 11, 3). The theme of this phase of life is the intelligent understanding and organization of all external contacts. Since this quadrant relates to the air temperament, one could hardly expect otherwise. The development spiral begins in the

Libra cardinal 7th house, continues in the 11th individual friendship house, and ends in the collective 3rd house. (See figure opposite.) This line of development starts out from abstract intelligence, from pure thought-power. Getting to know the You boosts intelligence. Air always implies contacts, and the thinking we do about these is intelligence. At the root of all comprehension lies the contact with object or subject.

The 7th house principle of utilitarian alliances must change if there are ever to be any deep 11th house relationships. At this stage, the realization may dawn that one's motives for getting married were not entirely selfless: personal advantage played a part. We observe the consequences arising from this and start being selective. We look for people possessing spiritual and human worth, not simply material prosperity. Our new contacts must be much more in tune with our inner nature. And so we come to the 11th house and an enhanced and extended knowledge of human beings as such: of their characteristics, their make-up, their ethics. Friendship, in the 11th house, is a solid relationship that is fairly objective. This gain in objectivity brings one to the Gemini 3rd house. The individual feels impelled to transmit his or her universally valid knowledge to the public; perhaps becoming an author, scholar, lecturer or teacher, whose perceptions or learning can then be made widely available.

Ages 36-42

AP and TAP in the 7th house

Again the two Age Points are moving synchronously, and they stimulate the air temperament and thus the reasoning ability. Now there is a good chance of not repeating our mistakes. We can put into practice what has been learned. No longer so much involved in working and serving, we can make rewarding intellectual and cultural openings for ourselves. In the 7th house we embark upon a process of conscious communication with those around us, because we want to know who is who. Fresh light is thrown on the unconscious, instinctive relationships of earlier periods. The environment becomes a mirror in which we see ourselves and others as we really are. By and large, this is also a period of disillusionment. The 7th house is an "echo chamber," and it sends back to us what we give it. Therefore in confronting the You, whether in marriage or in a business partnership, clarity and honesty of thought are needed. By following this rule, we shall learn a great deal not only about others but also about ourselves.

Ages 42-48

AP in the 8th house, TAP in the 11th house

Now the upper fixed houses are activated. The two Age Points are square one another, and this means that the forces of transformation are armed for conflict. The 8th house holds Scorpio's themes of life and death: things thought to be defunct are now revived. We are confronted by past conditions or habits, and fate lends a hand in testing the humanity and ethics of former pet ideas or avocations, and in probing their fitness for future development. If they meet the demands of the 11th house, they will help us on our way; if they do not meet them, they will become destructive or lead to premature change. Resignation is the result. Thus our inner hopes and wishes (activated by the TAP in the 11th house) encounter the established patterns of the 8th house. For best results, we need to adopt a new mental attitude. This is hard to do in the 8th house, because we are still encumbered by (quite legitimate) matters of social status.

Ages 48-54

AP in the 9th house, TAP in the 3rd house

In this phase the two houses are again in opposition. The 9th house is where our knowledge of life crystallizes into a creed. So, added to the teaching imparted to us by the community in the 3rd house, are the personal experience and independent thought of the 9th. Therefore this period is very suitable for plunging bravely into whatever answers to our inner convictions. In this individualistic house, we ought to become more self reliant without losing touch with people. Say we developed an inferiority complex in the 3rd house period because we were not as clever as the other children; this is the time to shake free from it – possibly by summoning up the courage to step forward and advocate something we know to be true. Often we come back to those leading ideas of which we dreamed in the 3rd house; now with a real chance of doing something about them. If we are prepared to fight for these ideas, our life will take on a new and deeper meaning that will lead to further progress.

4. Inner Orientation

Self understanding, Self conquest, Self existence – Houses 4, 8, 12

With the advent of the water cycle, there is a turning from outer life to inner life. Between ages 54 and 60, when the normal AP is traversing the 10th house, the TAP is moving through the 4th house. At 60, the TAP springs into the 8th house, while the normal AP remains in the quadrant by crossing into the 11th house. Usually this phase of life is beset with difficulties, because detachment from outer things does not come easily. Between ages 66 and 72 the two Age Points meet again in the 12th house. See figure below.

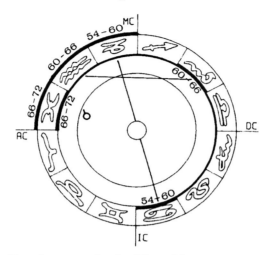

Development in the Water Temperament

The Water Phase

4th quadrant

In the 4th quadrant (ages 54-72), the TAP passes through the water houses (4, 8, 12). This is a time of introversion for the purpose of finding oneself and of cultivating inner values – a goal shared by both the 4th quadrant and the water temperament. At 54, the AP reaches the MC and the TAP reaches the IC. They are now in exact opposition. We are confronted by ourselves and by all that has already been achieved, as well as by what still needs to be done. We change direction: the normal AP re-enters the I-side of the chart and the TAP begins its cycle through the water temperament.

The cardinal 4th house is where the cycle commences. At the outset, we are emotionally embedded in collective life without really giving it much thought. Whether we belong to a sports club, a religious community, a family, or some other group is beside the point; very much to the point is the security provided by an association. What matters is to be with people who think and feel as we do and share the same hopes. The next port of call is the fixed 8th house corresponding to Scorpio. Here we learn that the benefits of safety and security entail obligations. We are required to play our part and to recompense the group or community in some way. There has to be give as well as take. The group's claims are asserted in the name of established custom. It is the group that is found to have rights: the individual has only a limited degree of freedom. Finally comes the 12th house, a water house corresponding to Pisces. Here one seeks a deeper security in the sense of belonging to the cosmos or to nature. Directing one's attention to higher values and goals opens up sources of spiritual strength, brings contentment and a feeling of being back home at last.

Ages 54-60

AP in the 10th house, TAP in the 4th house

In this period of life, on the vertical individual axis, a mature personality structure is formed which is strong and stable. But the TAP embarks on a water-type development, an inner orientation. This is a paradox. Because of it we are often beset by crises that arise quietly and affect us internally; crises that we do not reveal to others because we do not wish to lose face. Even if we enjoy outward success, wealth and honour, we may suffer from inner loneliness. We long for peace and safety, for the cosy nest of the 4th house. Frequently one possesses a certain prestige in the 10th house, and is seen as something of an authority in one's field. It is gratifying to be "somebody," to bask in the recognition of others. On the other hand, we realize our dependence on those who admire us. If they stopped admiring us we should be deprived of the pleasure obtained from their reinforcement of our self-image. Therefore at this time of life there is always a fear of falling from the heights we have scaled. So we must do our best to keep the affection of others, even when we occupy an elevated position. Above has no meaning without below.

Ages 60-66

AP in the 11th house, TAP in the 8th house

The individuation process is resumed in the 11th house. This presumes, of course, that we now have a wiser head on our shoulders. We have reached a stage when people will expect us to exhibit genuine humanity, culture and morality. The 11th is an air house, and its contacts will challenge our mental and spiritual strength and flexibility. Relationships are fewer but more rewarding. The TAP is in the 8th house of social structure at the very time when our social position is firmly established but we are no longer in society's pocket. We effect the quiet detachment that comes from inner reorientation (8th house), and step back without being left out. A philosophical attitude needs to be developed that is in touch with reality and accepts that there must be fresh growth everywhere. The person who enters this mature dimension of consciousness will not be lonely, but it is important for the foundations of spiritual development to be laid well in advance if anything is to be solidly and usefully built on them, and if our creativity is still to flourish. As likely as not we shall make friends with individuals to whom we can give something and who are important to us – especially intellectually important; in other words, we shall look for kindred spirits to share our interests.

Ages 66-72
AP and TAP in the 12th house

Once more the two Age Points coincide. In the 12th house we need to be at one with the universe, or to return to source laden with the fruits of experience. There is a tremendous realization of belonging to a cosmic whole; which may be religious in character but also be based on a materialistic concept of the physical universe. We differ as individuals on this point, but the experience is real enough. It is a process that conducts us to the limits of existence and gives either a genuine taste of reality or else a fear of death, before the end. Those who can make peace with themselves and with the world are ready for a new birth and are equipped for a fresh start in life. At the ascendant there is a renaissance, another beginning, which shuttles us back into the 1st house.

New Beginnings

Ages 72-78
AP and TAP in the 1st house

At the 1st house a new cycle begins. The dynamism of the fire temperament imparts a fresh impulse to the remaining years of life. Pep and verve return, and for many senior citizens this is the first time they have really been themselves. In this 1st house, the I-house, one can find out entirely new things about oneself after being given a new inner direction by contact with the boundless space of the 12th house. If one journeys on with the AP, and this is always possible, one starts the cycle all over again, but in a way that is richer and wiser, with fresh standards, fresh outlook, fresh joy of living. Many now stop worrying about the good and bad in life.

Chapter 7

The Age Point in the Twelve Signs

Having dealt with the significance of the crosses and temperaments, we shall now describe the qualities of each of the zodiac signs as they come into play during the passage of the Age Point. For the sake of simplicity, we shall ignore the modifications introduced by house, temperament, ruler, planets in sign, planetary aspects, and stage of life. So what we now have to say is by no means comprehensive, and should not be treated as such. Readers may like to work out the modifications for themselves. As already mentioned, the signs consist of a combination of temperament and cross. For example, the mutable air sign is Gemini, the cardinal earth sign is Capricorn. Signs are also categorized according to the ascendant. Each ascendant has its own 7th house sign, 11th house sign, and so on. All told there are 12 x 12 = 144 combinations. Within the limits of this book it is impossible to deal with 144 house/sign combinations; nevertheless, we think it will be helpful to the reader to learn the effect of the Age Point in the various zodiac signs and to study the characteristic mental attitudes associated with them.

AP at the "Zero Point"

The zodiac ends in Pisces and begins in Aries. At this juncture the circle is closed; end and beginning, death and rebirth mysteriously meet. There is more on this in the next chapter on the astrological colour circle. As the AP ushers you into Aries, you step across the so-called "zero point" of the zodiac where you will probably feel a strange attraction to transcendental matters. Consciously or unconsciously you will be stirred by something that may seem strange and yet familiar. The experience is one of refined energies from subtle spheres reaching you through this "gap." Many individuals are greatly stirred by this, but others are hardly affected at all; it depends on the degree of openness to spiritual influences. Many are unsettled and do not know what is wrong with them; especially if they are immured in the material world and know nothing of the Self, their true home. Crises involving radical changes may occur in which new life seems to proceed from death. Many feel they have been left defenceless in the grip of some power. Others deliberately await a contact from the spiritual world. They open up in prayer, meditation, or religious retreat to subtle, healing forces, or seek a mystical experience of God. Many who have crossed this threshold with the Age Point speak of a "pull," of a longing to return to the home of the soul. The "pull" frequently brings about an inner reversal, a change of motivation, and with it a decisive turning point in life. At all events, a new cycle begins with the entry into Aries, and one ought to prepare for it properly.

AP in Aries

As the AP enters the fire sign Aries, the dynamic fire element springs into action. The "zero point" experience" is over, and you prepare for a "rebirth." Now you pluck up the courage to do new things, and are full of vitality and the joy of living. This feeling may prompt you to accept yourself cheerfully for what you are with a sort of youthful unconcern. Even when you are frequently disappointed and do not succeed straight away, you can move hopefully on to new aims. You should not ponder too long, because then you will lose not only the courage but also the power to act and may even become depressed, usually from groundless feelings of guilt. In the Aries period, success lies in quick, decisive action. You will be more of a pioneer, advocating progressive ideas and inspiring others. Aries is an I-sign, so you can also benefit yourself. Quite possibly you must summon up the courage to "look after number one" if you have neglected the needs of your ego during the Pisces period or have sacrificed any of your ideals. Self development and a sense of identity are now important; your impulses and deeds will be genuinely your own and will not be prompted by others. You are favourably placed to carry out your projects, even against opposition. In everything you do, you may be expected to be yourself and to stick up for yourself, and to be very dynamic, fearless and spontaneous, refusing to be discouraged, and always making independent decisions.

AP in Taurus

When the AP is passing through the fixed earth sign Taurus, you need to watch your economic situation. Your existence has to be stabilized, with a realistic approach to aims, plans and tasks. You will be more sparing of your energies than you were in the previous period, and are likely to be busy turning to account the ideas and impulses of Aries. Success comes by working steadily and systematically, and by refusing to be sidetracked from your purposes and designs. It would be wise to sustain a regular daily rhythm and to finish whatever you take in hand. Your life should now become more stable, with an increase in material, intellectual or emotional wealth. Whatever you have achieved or obtained can be exploited usefully and economically in life. You should learn to safeguard what is yours, in case your claims are contested. You accumulate, consolidate and utilize, to husband your strength and make controlled use of what you have. For this you need to be undisturbed, with time to attend to every detail step by step. The unfolding of your talents, and the successful deployment of your material assets, occupy the foreground of your attention. You can now put something by for a rainy day.

Venus, too, as ruler of this sign, is probably active, especially if in Taurus. You should be able to enjoy the aesthetic and pleasant side of existence, live life to the full, and get ready to prosper in comfort. Now you can cultivate a well-rounded personality and can grasp what has always been denied you. You can create a solid base of wealth and goodwill, and earn the capital to cushion you for many years.

AP in Gemini

When your AP crosses from Taurus into the air sign Gemini, you immediately feel as if a great burden has been removed, and you take many things more easily. There is a gain in flexibility; you are more open, more inquisitive and more versatile. Anything new intrigues you. During this Gemini period you exhibit greater learning ability and can mend the gaps in your education. You can learn languages, attend courses and lectures, or return to school. This is the time to strive for knowledge and a broader education. You should try to make new friends and acquaintances and should respond positively to the approaches of others. In Gemini you are more accommodating and flexible than you were in Taurus, can adjust more quickly to changed circumstances, and are grateful for variety. Your spontaneity is enlivening and makes you adventurous. You are in your element passing on information and knowledge that you yourself have just found useful. By showing what you know, you may win the recognition that has so far eluded you.

The time is ripe for being open to impressions from the environment and to whatever will improve your mind – this includes things that put you in touch with your surroundings, such as travel, conversation, correspondence and lectures, to name but a few. And your matter-of-fact approach solves emotional problems in human relationships. Truthfulness and objectivity can now be cultivated consciously. Abilities that have lain hidden are ripe for development, and this makes for professional and social success.

AP in Cancer

When the AP enters the emotional sign Cancer, your reactions to your environment are considerably more sensitive than they were in the Gemini period, which promoted intellectual development. You will experience your emotions in a new way. It is no longer easy to hide your feelings; people notice much more quickly what is going on inside you and whether you are happy or not. Now it is opportune to take seriously your longings and desire for love and security, and to learn to show them too. You become more capable of giving and accepting love and tenderness. Often, when the AP passes through Cancer, images emerge from unconscious; childhood memories and parental problems are recollected and call for fresh consideration. Youthful dreams revive, possibly with a chance of being realised at last.

Cancer, the family sign, provides a splendid opportunity for patching up quarrels with relatives, for strengthening the ties of love, for drawing closer to kith and kin, and for becoming more firmly rooted in the community, the family and one's home ground. With the entry into Cancer, you notice a greater emotional involvement with others and recognize how much a part of your environment you are. The cry for security, for a nest where you feel safe and cosy, is more insistent; but you must avoid isolating yourself and withdrawing sulkily into your crab's shell. Your dear ones should be shown how much they mean to you. There is no longer any point in hiding behind formal behaviour, intellectualism or other defence mechanisms. You can openly and honestly tell those you care about that you need them. Most likely you will work to make a "home sweet home," a safe retreat, a protection from harsh reality. If your age is right, you might start a family during this Cancer period.

AP in Leo

Often extra heat is generated by the transition from watery Cancer to fiery Leo. Conformists may become rebels. If, during Cancer's period, you have kowtowed to the opinions of others and have given overmuch credence to them, there is no longer any need to do so. Now you are free to organize your life how you want.

During this period, the structure of your living space is important. It would be good to break away and be your own boss. You can risk doing what you think is right, in accordance with your inner convictions. The opinions of others have lost much of their influence with you because you have found the courage to act on your own initiative. With the AP in Leo, you go by what you yourself think and not by the "done thing." Perhaps some of the emotional relationships formed during the Cancer period will irk, because they impede your progress. This may mean that you are on your own again and have to win through independently. For many of us, the lessons to be learned from the experience are to love ourselves a bit more, to adopt a personal stance in society, and to take the views of others at their true value. If you feel that you are the centre of your circle, you obtain the full benefit of your innermost powers.

You ought to develop as perfect a picture of yourself as possible, a close-to-life ideal, radiating out from you into the environment and setting an example to others. According to the house theme or stage of life, you can take the lead mobilizing the energies of others and activating their talents, so that good work is done under your management. You stand out as an individual but, on the other hand, have to take the responsibility for what you do and allow. With your strong personality and increased awareness, you become a support to many and in this way mature from within into a recognized authority.

AP in Virgo

The change from Leo to Virgo is usually very obvious. It may not be particularly comfortable to fall from a ruling into a serving role. You should now confine yourself to whatever is significant for your professional development. You have to forego the distractions and exaggerated ideas of your own importance that arose during the transit of Leo, and must learn to adjust to hard facts. Problems of existence come to the fore in Virgo. Perhaps you need to concentrate on earning a living, to learn new skills or to go on a retraining course. This will involve you in practicalities, technical details or procedural problems, requiring a sense of order, thoroughness, and the paying of strict attention to the matter in hand. It is wise to deal with things systematically, setting sensible targets and keeping them. The emphasis is no longer on the impression you make on others but on your skills and productivity. A social or humanitarian occupation can help to make the most of the qualities of Virgo. You can care for people, put things first for them, and prevent them from making false moves in the first place. With growing confidence, greater fulfilment is possible, thanks to the discernment, selectivity, and analytical gifts of the Virgin, who knows what is good or bad for her. Visits to health farms, dieting, and medical checkups are timely now. Many at this period in their lives (if the house and age allow) enter altruistic callings. They are high-principled and indefatigable, display a social conscience and are happy just to be needed.

AP in Libra

The attitude to partnership changes with the transition from Virgo to Libra. The dependence, not to say submissiveness, of Virgo gives way to freer relationships. Now you can learn more about the You, and take more of a personal interest in people. If you concern yourself with others, you will not stand alone; but you must give something before you can receive anything back. Others come first; you will adapt yourself to them and strive for an equal partnership. For this, tolerance, a readiness to compromise, understanding, tact and diplomacy are required.

As far as possible, you will avoid conflicts and try to bridge the gap between opposing sides. Where there is an impasse, you will make the first move to break it, and will restore peace by resolving problems fairly. You no longer deal in stark black-and-white, good-and-bad, either-or, but in subtle qualitative differences. Perceptiveness needs cultivation during the passage through Libra, in order to find true wisdom and harmonious relationships. Probably you will crave love and understanding, and may do all in your power to make yourself agreeable. Your efforts will be devoted increasingly to beauty and harmony, to balance and cultural enjoyment. You are inclined to lean on others and to get by on charm. You tend to avoid unpleasant confrontations and court popularity. This helps to improve your self-image, and you show your partner your better side. But great care is required not to waste time on worthless individuals. You must always seek the right measure, the golden mean between the extremes. Then human relationships will be fulfilling; you will find the right partner and there will be a proper balance between the I and the You.

AP in Scorpio

Scorpio is the sign of transformation, of the processes of change, of death and renewal. Experiences should not be sidestepped now, even when they jeopardize the peace and comfort of the Libra period. You should meet life actively and see where your limits lie. In this period you find that many things alter, because progress never stands still. Nothing lasts forever; everything falls to the scythe of time. Perhaps you will suffer loss or, conversely, gain something for nothing. Many experience the misery of loneliness, yet find in it a challenge to scale spiritual heights. Others are forced to learn wisdom by gazing into the abyss of human nature. After the crisis of change, one should be able to bear up against extremes of sorrow and joy, and should be able to build a solid inner dyke against later floods. Whoever responds to a higher motivation will penetrate deeply into the secrets of life during this period, often overcoming obstacles vigorously if not ruthlessly.

In Scorpio, sexuality can become a problem for many; it ought not to be repressed, but lived positively. In each act of creation, each transformation process, there is a clash of forces. This is nothing to be afraid of, but should be treated as an opportunity to transcend one's limitations. For the most part, the path in this period leads through perpetual destruction and reconstruction and requires constantly renewed effort, and the shedding of anxiety, outmoded forms of behaviour, and false certainties. What has formerly proved successful may now prove to be useless. Times have altered, and some readjustment is needed. The conquest of fear of the unknown implies a letting go, an abandonment, often an annihilation of the very things to which you used to look for security. But by giving a positive welcome to irrevocable change you will develop new abilities and prepare for the greater freedom offered by Sagittarius.

AP in Sagittarius

The transition to Sagittarius always comes as a respite. Now you can be more mobile and can rise above the limitations life has imposed. You can shake off your fetters, and wholeheartedly espouse some cause you suddenly see is right. You can adopt a positive and affirmative attitude to life and view it in a pleasanter light, feeling it is there to be enjoyed. Now the emphasis is laid on your own autonomous thinking and independence; and you ought to demonstrate that fact. Where there are conflicts you are in a position to lay down the law and to defend the weaker party. You win sympathy as well as influence by your lively interest in the welfare of your fellow-creatures. It is possible for you to transcend your ordinary self, to cast aside the fears of the Scorpio period in order to take a share in life on a larger scale. What is more, you should now indulge your desire for more living space, and undertake journeys, in order to expand your consciousness. You can and should let people see what you know and pass on your experiences of life. You should have clear-cut goals and should think out new ways of achieving them. But you must also be prepared for the isolation that is natural to each individual consciousness. Even when you yourself long fruitlessly for understanding and love, you should not stop sharing with others your insights and your humanity. If you do this, you will be serving higher ends, your life will be meaningful and you will be of use to the greater Whole.

During the Sagittarius period, many are seized by a vague feeling of unrest, which does not allow them to settle down anywhere. The love of freedom, the wanderlust, the irrepressible desire to ferret around, and the constant temptation to set new goals keep them with their luggage packed and ready to go. The time is now ripe to make major journeys. Others discover a new direction in life and are inspired to seek spiritual goals that benefit not only the individual but a higher good. By being ready for action and having the courage of one's convictions, one can bring within reach plans or projects that have been lying on the drawing board for a long time, or have not been attainable until now.

AP in Capricorn

Capricorn is the sign of individuality in which the mature personality takes shape. By this time you should be clear about your personal and occupational goals. You need to take command of your situation in life or assume some kind of leadership. You are unlikely to be deterred by hindrances or failures but, with unflagging strength, doggedness and willingness to work, slowly but surely make your way in the world. You should accept the risk of individuality; or, in other words, should learn to manage your own affairs. The idea now is not to pay too much attention to the opinions of others but to do what you have learned is right.

Capricorn is the sign of the person who stands head and shoulders above the crowd and gets himself or herself noticed. Therefore in the Capricorn period one cannot commit errors without having to pay for them straight away. You need to set to work carefully and not allow yourself to be pressurized or irritated. It is important always to follow a settled pattern, and to develop self discipline and personal responsibility. Whatever happens you are keen to preserve the quality of your work: not slacking but keeping to the highest standards with perfection in mind. This applies as much to the elaboration of plans as it does to material things.

When you have mastered any area, and have become an authority on it, you are able to insist on concentrating on your aims. People with strong personalities need thick skins; and during the passage of the AP through Capricorn (at any age) they know how to safeguard both themselves and their projects. Their self-belief and sense of mission give them the confidence to tackle the task in hand. They are indomitable, and overcome difficulties with great competence and skill; it is no exaggeration to say that they thrive on difficulties.

AP in Aquarius

In Aquarius, contacts are made with a view to finding true friendship. So-called friends may often have let you down in the past, and now you can give them the cold shoulder without feeling guilty. You have become selective: you recognize your own worth in your association with other men and women. No longer everyone's friend, you learn who will suit you and who will not. Your interest in the happiness of others is not merely intellectual or psychological but represents genuine philanthropy, fairness and warmth. The spirit of fraternity – universal empathy – can come into its own in Aquarius. The value of everything is correctly judged. Passion, sexual desire, delirious love affairs no longer shake you because you feel neither false emotion nor fanaticism, but can cultivate genuine relationships and strive for spiritual ideals. With this detached attitude, you are in a good position to find others who are on the same wavelength as yourself – others with whom you have a mental affinity. Once you have located your real friends or social unit, you will no longer feel like a stranger on the earth, but will be supported by a bond of loving understanding and shared dreams. Community spirit and teamwork are to be encouraged, as long as there is no sacrifice of individuality within the group.

In these conditions, you will gain in human values, make loyal friends, and will no longer be a slave to the desire for possessions, security and personal advantage. If you concentrate on spirituality and idealism, moral improvement, on the ethics of human equality, the period will be one of great happiness and inner strength, and you will mean much to your friends.

AP in Pisces

In Pisces, the last sign of the zodiac, problems often solve themselves. Things that used to look serious lose their significance. However, with the fishes, one swims out into deep waters for a while. Many feel familiar ground give way beneath their feet when they enter this sign.

Their interests may suddenly change. Perhaps they wish to know what lies behind visible appearances. Quite a few dip into religious, occult or esoteric books, start studying the border sciences or astrology, or become aware of subtle influences. Others develop devotion, the spirit of sacrifice and great sensitivity. They feel called to do good and to care for the sick and the poor.

This is the time to show increased concern for others and their needs. You may have to forget your own, often quite minor, complaints in order to relieve major suffering elsewhere. During this period you should willingly concentrate on your duties and throw yourself wholeheartedly into whatever you do, preferably into social or humanitarian service. In a kindly, sympathetic way, you will see people's good points rather than their bad ones.

It is not possible to be very enterprising at this time, your initiatives come and go so quickly. You must learn to wait patiently for a chance to be more active. But now you can meditate, enter the chambers of the soul, and listen to your inner voice. You will experience the world through an emotional sense that conveys subtle experiences to you. Your ego-nature is gradually dissolved: in Pisces the boundaries between the individual and the universe are often obliterated. Due to your deep inner longing for union with the transcendental, you are now prepared to receive guidance, and you summon psychic powers from a source within you by mystical introspection – in order to be ready for a fresh start in the next cycle starting in Aries.

Chapter 8

The Zodiac in Colour

Life From Red Through Violet

The colour spectrum (the rainbow), when laid round the horoscope, gives a picture of personal development very similar to that given by the theory of Age Progression; it also expresses the same life cycle idea. A rainbow spanning the sky may be viewed as a bridge, or heavenly gateway, symbolizing high spiritual advancement. The law of development – of evolution even – lies within it.

The rainbow is an impressive natural phenomenon. Most of us have gazed in wonder at this bright arch springing out of nothingness; and we are also familiar with the bands of concentric colours (red, orange, yellow, green, blue, indigo, violet) produced when a light source shines on a glass prism or on a drop of water. Now, the Age Point is comparable to a light source, and radiates like a sun from the central circle of the astrological chart. As it travels through the chart, it "lights up" the planets, signs and houses in many ways. These changes can be symbolized by colour, and this is why we work with colour in the chart. See figure on next page.

The Colour Spectrum

Various attempts were made by astrologers to assign colours to zodiacal signs and planets, but not in connection with the spectrum until Bruno Huber compared the colour circle with the course of life through the houses. The results are astounding; but, before discussing them, we must explain what we mean by the colour spectrum.

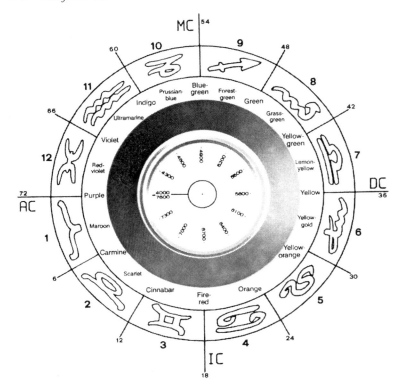

The Colours of the Natural Zodiac

The spectrum, also known as the rainbow phenomenon, is the splitting of a beam of white light into various colours. This happens either through the refraction of light in a prism or through diffraction. White sunlight is actually composed of bright colours – the spectral colours. A distinction is made between the three primary colours, red, yellow and blue, and the three secondary colours, orange, green and violet, plus all the intermediate shades, as well as the invisible infrared and ultraviolet. The latter lie just beyond the red and violet ends of the spectrum respectively.

The spectrum can be explained scientifically and its colours have been carefully number-tagged. The light perceived by the human eye consists of the visible part of the spectrum with wavelengths varying from 4000 (violet) through to 7600 (red) Angstrom units. Since the spectrum is continuous it contains innumerable tints, not just what are popularly known as "the seven colours of the rainbow." People with good vision can distinguish between 2,000 and 10,000 shades of colour.

Astrological Colours

In the figure opposite a circle of colour is represented inside the zodiac and the houses. The spectrum used is an ordinary continuous spectrum. For convenience of reference, we have listed certain wavelengths at regular intervals. The spectrum, which in reality would be straight, has been curved round the zodiac in such a way that it begins and ends at 0° Aries (or the ascendant): The colour circle formed in this way can readily be compared with the path of life. There has been no distortion by stretching some parts of the spectrum and squeezing others; on the contrary, the prismatic spacing of the colours has been faithfully preserved.

To make it conform to current theory, the spectrum has often been pulled out of shape (a crime perpetrated for a long time in the art world); the underlying assumption being that opposite colours in a colour wheel are bound to be "complementaries" giving white or black when mixed. This assumption is not founded in fact, because pure black is virtually non-existent; that is to say, by chopping the spectrum into equal sections, one is never going to obtain the ingredients of pure black. Nearly all mixtures reveal some hue or other, as we see for example in the browns or dark greys.

In our philosophical moments, we have an inveterate tendency to think in terms of black and white. The force of our logic compels us to see polar opposites as stark contrasts. This is a human fixation, and has nothing to do with the natural world where things are not simply black or white. On examining the colour circle, we should let nature correct us and begin to allow our ideas to agree with reality.

The Three Primary Colours

The spectrum contains three primary colours that are recognized by physics. These are pure red, yellow, and indigo (or deep blue). These three primaries are very important: in the spectrum they blend with one another in varying proportions to give an infinity of intermediate shades. As indicated by the small inner arcs in our horoscope colour circle, red extends more than 180° (in fact for ca. 210°) from Aquarius through the beginning of Virgo, yellow extends even further and traverses eight signs from Taurus through Sagittarius (ca. 240°), and blue, which starts in the lemon-yellow region, extends from Scorpio through Pisces (ca. 150°).

It is interesting that yellow occupies the most space. You can see that it is also the lightest colour. It is more dazzling than blue or red. This ties in with the fact that we have a yellow sun – even though we may see it as white. A glance at the chart shows pure yellow at 5800A. The surface temperature of the Sun is 5800°, so it is not a white star but a yellow one.

By the law of analogy, the three primary colours of the spectrum correspond to the three-part division of the horoscope already described in *LifeClock* (14). This being so, we are in a position to evaluate the Age Progression colours qualitatively.

Red = 1st third = Houses 1-4
Colour of manifestation, purposeful, dynamic movement.

Yellow = 2nd third = Houses 5-8
Colour of contact, attitude, urge to make relationships.

Blue = 3rd third = Houses 9-12
Colour of retreat, self-orientation, peace, isolation.

Psychological Effect of Colours

The psychological effect of colours, or colour psychology, is a field that has already gathered a great deal of interesting data. The subjective meaning of colour was appreciated by Goethe (9) many years ago; and he wrote at length against the rather matter-of-fact physics of Newton (27), who was the first to make a detailed scientific investigation of light and colour. Ostwald (28) and Müller (26) can be regarded as modern creators of the colour wheel, which still has an appreciable number of devotees in the art world and may be seen in the complementary colour wheels illustrated by Itten (19) and Grob. Following the Pythagorean tradition, Kaiser linked colour with mathematical and musical studies, while the painter Kandinsky (21) was enabled by his artistic sensitivity to produce one of the most psychologically valuable contributions to colour theory that have so far appeared. Finally, the psychologist Lüscher (24) developed a colour test that seems to be appreciated more by the public than by professionals. It is fairly well known that colours can affect people's moods. For example, green has a calming influence, red rouses one to be active and enterprising, yellow imparts a sense of warmth and a desire to make contacts. Dull and faded colours easily lead to depression and melancholy. Lively colours help to make work a pleasure, but colours that are too glaring break concentration. Findings like these have been utilized to some extent by physicians and teachers, but most of all by industrial psychologists. For instance, a person whose favourite colour is yellow will not look at life in the same way as a person who prefers red or blue. Lovers of red are thrusting and egocentric, and often ruthless (1st third); lovers of yellow are intensely contact-oriented and therefore dependent on their environment (2nd third); lovers of blue are fairly passive, upward looking and spiritually minded. These are fundamentally different attitudes to life, and it might be a good idea to consider the effects of the three primary colours in more detail.

The Three Primary Colours

Red

Red strives to develop and to spread beyond its natural borders. It represents a love of life, the survival instinct common to us all even in childhood. This will is a primary urge, an inherent activity; and psychologically it is embodied in a dynamic restlessness that continually presses forward, although occasionally it amounts to nothing more than movement for movement's sake.

Yellow

Yellow is the chief colour in our solar system, because we have a yellow sun. It is the contact colour and is important to us as social beings. As a contact colour, yellow induces people to approach each other to give or ask favours; under its influence, they agree with one another, grow attached, and form alliances. In other words, relationships of all kinds are the province of yellow. Such relationships can be based on practical considerations, or on personal affinity, as in erotic or platonic friendships. Yellow can signify harmonious companionship with give and take, but also exploitation and endless demands. Yellow is our most important colour as it is the contact colour, and without contact human beings cannot live. "No man is an island," and, after a while, seclusion becomes unpleasant and even unbearable. We are social animals and the urge signified by yellow is remarkably strong in us. The move toward community life, toward union with You, toward synthesis and oneness, is mysteriously connected with our yellow sun.

Blue

Blue is diametrically opposed to red in quality. Whereas red – to some extent – binds us to the earth, blue lifts us from the earth and removes us from mundane existence. We feel something of what space travellers must feel as they watch our planet vanish. As it recedes, so does everything gross and earthbound. We return to the self. Breaking free from the material, we enter another and spiritual dimension. So transcendental blue corresponds to retiringness: we want to be on our own, to be left in peace, to enjoy solitude, to distance ourselves from the world and the things of the world.

It seems that each one of us has "three people" inside him or her. The first simply desires to live (red), the second seeks encounters (yellow), and the third returns to itself (blue). However, we must not forget the secondary colours, which have their own significance in Age Progression.

The Three Secondary Colours

These arise from the three primaries.

Orange = red and yellow.
Penetration, extroverted contact-making, erotic, aggressive.

Green = yellow and blue.
Desire for protection, self-control, reserve.

Violet = blue and red.
Transcendence, dreams, unreality, innocence.

These tints are always a mixture of two primary colours. What is more, all other tints in the spectrum arise through a proportioned mixture of two primaries. If we begin with lemon yellow, for example, we find a high percentage of yellow with only a trace of blue, but enough to make the yellow cool. With the addition of a little more blue, the yellow darkens to light green, lime green, etc. As the blue increases and the yellow decreases, the greenness becomes more pronounced until blue predominates to give blue-green (malachite green). Finally blue takes over and yellow completely disappears. Between the pure colour points lie the half-colour points, where there is a fifty-fifty mixture of the two colours. The orange half-colour point is at the cusp of the 5th house. Somewhere near cusp 9 is the green half-colour point, and just before the AC is the purple half-colour point. The arc from the pure red point (carmine) to the yellow point subtends an angle of 150° (quincunx); from yellow to blue (indigo) we have a trine and from blue back to red we have a square aspect. This means that the measured distances between the pure colour points are not equal. The configuration is a dominant triangle containing three distinct aspects. Psychologically speaking, this is a dynamic structure signifying growth or learning. As we see, nature is not symmetrical; a grand trine would have been symmetrical. Thinkers of the past always sought for symmetry, because for them it represented absolute purity or perfection, but nature is in fact asymmetrical and therefore dynamic.

Turning now to the half-colour points on our circle, we discover that they are spaced symmetrically – they form a grand trine. But here we are dealing with colour mixtures, colours of the second order, and no longer with pure colours. Symmetry does not appear until we come to colours of the second order.

The Colour Circle as a Life Clock

The experimental meaning of the colours follows their distribution by the light spectrum through the house system. As we know, people in the same age group have much in common with regard to attitude towards life, basic interests, and problems; they are coloured the same, so to speak. On examining the colour circle, we observe an interesting correspondence between the qualities of the colours and the course of life through the twelve houses. Our sequence of experiences in terms of colour is very much the same as our sequence of experiences in terms of the movement of the Age Point through the house system.

Because, as the old adage says, the microcosm is like the macrocosm, the pattern of our lives must mimic that of the cosmos and of the spectrum. The zodiac belongs to the reality of the cosmos, the spectrum belongs to the reality of light, and the house system belongs to the reality of our lives. In the colour circle, these three realities are welded into a functional whole. We exist within this circle. We grow, mature and die in it; and our self expression is governed by its colour changes. In the course of life we pass from pure red through more and more yellowy reds, pure yellow, various greens, blue, violet and finally purple.

Beginning and End

In the colour circle, we have put the start of life at Aries in the zodiac and at the ascendant in the house system. On the purple edge of the visible spectrum, life starts with the AC, in dimness, before the dawn. The individual emerges from nothingness, from the invisible realm; and on the other side of the AC he or she comes to the end of the journey. Life and death meet one another here. Now, if we try to make the spectrum "bite its own tail," we find that it does not quite manage it: there is a gap, an area of seeming nonexistence, separating the beginning (red) from the end (violet). At the junction of the spectral red and violet arises the mixed colour purple, a colour that is not spectral. It is not seen when white light is refracted by a glass prism because the spectrum apparently peters out. In reality the blue end of the spectrum is continued by an ultraviolet band, and the red by a band of infrared, although neither band is visible to us. There is something strangely significant about this, because the gap is like a gateway of incarnation through which the soul steps onto its life-path at red.

At the ascendant life begins, and red is at the beginning too. It signifies our will to live, to manifest ourselves, to succeed, to be someone. The power of self-manifestation and self-assertion lies in red, which persists through to the 5th house. In the 1st house, the self-motivated drive is expansive. Red is a highly active colour, especially when mixed with yellow – which makes it even more intense and dynamic.

Yellow, the contact colour, helps us to make contact with the You, also with whatever objects we encounter. Yellow stands at the You-point in the chart. As yellow comes more into the picture, there is a growing desire to press on in the yellow direction so as to find a You. When there is practically no yellow in the red, for example in the 2nd house, we are still more or less asocial, and refuse or hesitate to have anything to do with a You. Only at puberty does the longing for a You slowly make itself felt (3rd house). Probably we start thinking of ways and means of meeting a partner. Success has to wait until we are properly in the yellow phase. Then we enjoy ardent contact with the You – until the colour blue steals in to cool things off a little.

Blue begins in the 8th house, with the need to break free from mundane affairs in order to be ourselves once more. The blue sector gives us knowledge of what we are like when not shackled by the bonds and obligations of the lower houses; it bestows a freedom and independence that are uniquely an upper house experience. Blue characterizes the phase of withdrawal; perhaps that is why Goethe termed it spiritual. Although not entirely so, it does denote a certain aloofness from the duties and cares of everyday living (11th and 12th houses). It signifies retirement from the world and a turning toward the higher life. Blue is the colour of detachment, self-knowledge and individuation in a loftier context. It is inherently restful, and gives us an opportunity to identify with the greater Whole.

Pure blue symbolizes infinity. The night sky verges on pure blue, especially before it is quite dark. If we avoid the horizon when gazing into the night sky, this blue will put us into a mystical frame of mind; in some countries, the twilight hour is also known as the blue hour (*blaue Stunde, l'heure bleu*).

Purple

The reader will readily work out the effects of mixtures of primary colours. However, one or two points are worth mentioning here. One of the most intriguing of the secondaries is the colour opposite yellow, namely purple. This colour is not contained in the visible spectrum, which becomes black at its red and violet ends; in fact the blackness contains infrared and ultraviolet radiation. Purple overlaps the ascendant, which symbolizes the start and close of life. There is an underlying logic in this.

The colour purple consists of a fifty-fifty mixture of red and blue. It is a special colour. Who wears purple? Ecclesiastical dignitaries, kings and emperors – in other words, those who are over everyone or who stand apart from everyone. A king is untouchable, beyond the reach of many things affecting ordinary mortals; so is a cardinal. Because ordinary human standards do not apply to them, they dress in purple.

Purple and violet (corresponding to the 12th house) are associated with nothingness in colour psychology; violet in drawings or paintings has a zero function, showing something nonexistent or so transparent as to be intangible. Purple might be called an unreal colour, it is not in the spectrum. A more understandable effect of purple is illusion. In the drawings of the mentally ill this colour occurs quite frequently, because these people exist in an illusory and non-existent world. Colour psychology regards purple as indicating an unreal state of mind in which the person concerned lives with at least part of his or her being somewhere that is "not of this world," in a fantasy world. When we find a planet at the zero point of the zodiac (0° Aries), the planet has something of this quality; what it represents is not fully incarnated; part remains "on the other side."

Students who wish to go more deeply into the study of colour should see the Bibliography for the most important books on the subject.

Chapter 9

The Moon Nodes

We come now to a new line of research into human destiny – the moon node system. Since this is an advanced and highly important element in interpretation, both for spiritual development and for modern therapeutic practice, we give here a brief description. For more detail see our book *Moon Node Astrology* (18).

The moon revolves round our earth in the same way as the earth revolves round the sun. The two orbits, when superimposed, cut one another at points we can calculate. These points of intersection are the Moon Nodes. The point where the moon crosses the ecliptic to move out of the southern half into the northern half of its orbit is the ascending node. Exactly opposite this is the descending node. The imaginary line joining the two points is known as the line of nodes, and is important for predicting eclipses of the sun and moon. See figure below.

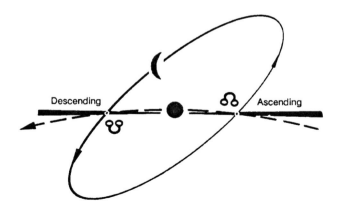

The Moon Nodes.

The Lunar Houses

Just as we divide the sun's apparent path into twelve zodiac signs, so – taking the ascending node as our starting point – we can divide the moon's path into twelve lunar houses. Technically, this is quite simple: commencing at the ascending node, thirty degrees are counted in a clockwise direction. This brings us to the cusp of the 2nd lunar house; another thirty degrees brings us to the cusp of the 3rd lunar house, and so on.

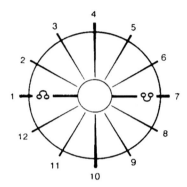

Determining the Lunar Houses

This is the basis for the so-called Moon Node Horoscope. For details on how to draw up the Moon Node Horoscope, see *Moon Node Astrology* (18). This can be drawn up using a computer programme producing Huber-style charts (2).

The Shadow Function of the Moon Node Horoscope

In essence, the moon node horoscope has to do with our desire nature, all the controlled and uncontrolled psychic factors from the past that are stored in the moon node system. Looked at esoterically, it symbolizes our astral body. It is the so-called mirror sphere, where our motivations, wishes and deeds are projected from the past (our karma) into the present.

In terms of depth psychology, the moon node horoscope makes the shadow of our personality visible. We all have an invisible part of our being containing drives, wishes and projections. The latter are not amenable to everyday consciousness, and we tend to suppress them as being unusable in ordinary life or even potentially dangerous. So the shadow is often regarded as negative or "black."

Of course, there are also positive factors which indicate good karma. There are, for example, spiritual longings that may be totally suppressed because they do not fit in with some mental dogma or because they do not happen to be fashionable. But even if we ignore them they are still a part of us. Modern reincarnation therapy is concerned with such factors; by reliving past experiences, these factors are made conscious and reveal causes that can exploit the apparently acausal.

C. G. Jung speaks of the shadow; a rather inaccessible part of the unconscious, which today is explored only in depth psychology. The human conscious and unconscious resemble an iceberg with no more than the tip projecting above the surface of the sea. The visible part is the conscious, the invisible part is the unconscious and in this we find the shadow personality. We are hardly aware of the motivations, secret wishes, or splinters of the ego hiding in this shadow region; often we cannot even envisage, let alone admit them. At most, they appear in our dreams. Nevertheless, they do exert an influence on our lives; but usually we fail to associate them with ourselves, because they manifest as results of our unconscious projections. They appear right out of the blue, in the guise of situations, issues, or people entering our lives from outside. They seem to attract to us with magnetic force the very things we dread and repress. Many an external situation is misleading because, like a mirage, it is only a reflection. We cannot handle it properly while we see it as "out there" and not belonging to us. All too often, the consequences of this shadow function remain beyond our control. They seem to be forced on us or to be things we do automatically. Generally speaking, they have to be experienced negatively before we are able to connect them with ourselves. However, in the moon node chart using modern techniques of interpretation, we can achieve a conscious understanding of our "shadow." (18)

The Moon Node Age Point

The moon node system has a time dimension and Age Progression of its own. We allow the same period of time (72 years) for the Moon Node Age Point to move round the chart, as we do for the radical Age Point. The Moon Node Age Point (MN-AP) sets out from the ascending node and travels clockwise (i.e., in the opposite direction to the normal Age Point) through one house after another, spending six years in each.

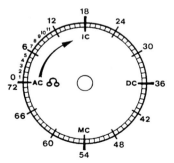

The Age Point of the nodal chart travels clockwise

Since the lunar houses are a uniform thirty degrees, five degrees always equals one year of life. The years corresponding to a given number of degrees can be read directly from the MN Age Point sheet from a Huber-style computer programme. Thus we can immediately see where we are in the lunar house system at the age of 45. (See figure). As the Moon Node Age Point travels along, the previously mentioned qualities of the shadow can enter consciousness in many shapes and forms, and can produce behaviour for which it is difficult to give a reason. Also they can stir up powerful emotions, compensatory actions, and regression to earlier forms of behaviour, in which we keep repeating the same old reactions. With regard to the Moon Node Age Point, it is quite possible to see as karmic components things which, in reality, are nothing more than psychic automatisms. They come from the deepest layers of the unconscious, from the repressed or unlived shadow region of our psyche; when the MN-AP transits a planet, they can look like the workings of fate or karma.

An example may make this clearer. A lady had Venus on the cusp of the 9th radical house. At a certain stage in her life, she lost her entire fortune. She could not understand why and blamed her husband. Further calculation placed Venus on the cusp of the 2nd lunar house, which suggested that in the past, and especially perhaps, in some past life, there was an accumulation of material goods and wealth (Venus on the 2nd cusp) that was balanced in the present life by the loss of everything (Venus on the 8th cusp.)

However, the interpretation is not always so straightforward. Our example is something of an exception in this respect. The reader is urged to write down the fateful events in his or her life. Often the MN-AP has no perceptible effect; but often there is a vague stimulation due to planets activated by the MN-AP.

Comparisons of the Radix AP with the MN-AP

Interesting facts emerge when the two Age Points are compared. With spiritual development, the MN-AP frequently plays a bigger part than does the radical AP. At the end of this section we discuss the horoscope of an important spiritual teacher, Jiddu Krishnamurti, for whom the MN-AP brought essentially spiritual breakthroughs. It is fascinating to observe the joint action of the two Age Points. With the radical AP, we are looking at the rational side of the psyche and at comprehensible processes that either produce events or are evoked by events. On examining the moon node chart, we come face to face with subliminal motives, the real reasons why we did or are doing this or that. Here we are digging down to a deeper layer of motivation capable of explaining a great deal that was formerly inexplicable. Now, if we are sufficiently strong-minded and our powers of intelligent discernment are in good working order, we can start rooting out some of the things responsible for our faulty attitudes.

Encounter of the Two Age Points

There are two points at which, twice in a life-time, the AP of the normal house system (moving anticlockwise) meets the AP of the moon node house system (moving clockwise). See figure below.

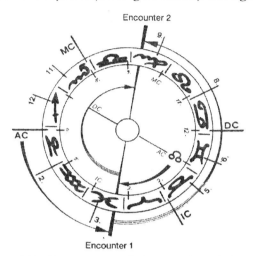

The Encounter of the two Age Points

These encounter points can be pivotal in our experience. Maybe we do not know this at the time, but it usually becomes obvious when we look back. In general, the changes involved take place slowly and sneakily. They can commence two or three years before the encounter but may not be noticed until two to five years afterward. The two encounter points lie on a house axis and are defined by the theme of the house and the axis. When, for example, the "encounter axis" is on the 1/7 plane from the AC to the DC, there will be an I-You problem sometime in the native's life. If the two encounter points are on the 2/8 axis, possessions will pose problems; if they are on the 3/9 axis, the problems will be intellectual.

The first meeting between the Age Points happens between birth and the thirty-sixth year of life; the second between the thirty-sixth and the seventy-second year of life. Exactly thirty-six years separate the two encounters. The timing of the encounters is different for each of us, because it depends on the positions of the nodes in the individual chart. If the encounter points lie on the 3/9 axis, the first meeting will occur in the 3rd house (about age 14), and the second will occur in the opposite house (around age 50). These encounter axes must not be confounded with the line of nodes however. In general, it is true to say that if the life has been rather passive prior to the first encounter and we have been led and moulded by others, then afterward we become more dominant and tend to go on the offensive in life; whereas, if previously we have been more extroverted, afterward we become more quiet, more passive, more defensive. The first encounter of the two Age Points is usually quite striking. If our subsequent development is considerable, the second encounter may almost escape notice. Should the effects of the second encounter be strong and drastic, this shows how little we have learned in the intervening thirty-six years.

There is also a good chance of sharp, incisive events occurring at the encounter points; events such as ruptures and bolts from the blue that alter the very nature of our existence. For instance, sometimes those by whom we have been dominated and restricted simply pack up and go, leaving us free to live our own lives. Many will say, "I have paid off my karma and can do what I really want to do at last."

Everyone is more or less exposed to sudden twists of fate which defy rational explanation yet completely change our lives. More than one astrologer has vainly looked to traditional prognostic techniques for some clue to the mystery; but often the only astrological solution is to be found in an encounter of the two Age Points. Anyone baffled by some experience would do well to consider the possible effect of one or other of the encounter points.

The Horoscope of Jiddu Krishnamurti

A Contribution by Marianne Glunz

Krishnamurti has a very special place among the numerous Indian gurus who have imparted spiritual knowledge to the West in this century. He spoke of an "uncharted land of truth," to be found neither by a special path nor by chelaship, but only through the most unflinching self-observation, as the only thing that can bring freedom from the ego and lead to full union with the truth.

As a youth, Krishnamurti was named by the Theosophical Society in Southern India as the vessel for the expected appearance of the highest master, and was given an appropriately rigorous upbringing. After years of internal struggle and in an unparalleled act of repudiation, he rejected this idea and dissolved "The Order of the Star in the East" founded in his honour. Subsequently, to all who were willing to hear him, he spoke merely as a spiritual philosopher with no disciples and no organization.

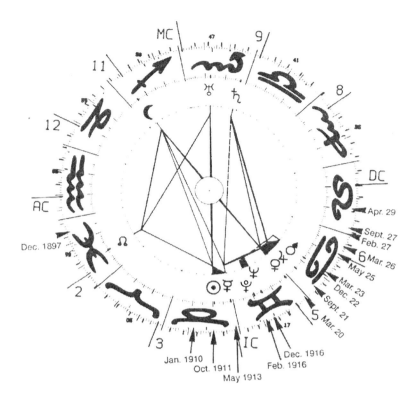

Jiddu Krishnamurti, 12.05.1895, 00:30, Madanapalle, India
Chart includes Age Point Dates.

Krishnamurti's chart is strikingly vertical in its planetary arrangement. The Sun-Uranus opposition is practically perpendicular; and so is the quincunx, the long green "ideas" aspect occupying the thought axis between the two planets of intelligence, Mercury and Saturn. Only slightly tilted, in the 11 th and 9th houses respectively, we have the Moon-Venus opposition and trines of Saturn to Venus and Jupiter. So there are clear indications of a striving toward spirituality and toward becoming conscious as an individual. The centre of gravity of this striving lies in the 9th house, the upper pole of the thought axis, with Uranus at the Low Point and Saturn near the cusp, both in the dying and becoming sign of Scorpio. Thus an inescapable link is forged between the opposition and the quincunx. Original thought (9th house) and the transmission of ideas (3rd house) are the main themes of this life. While Uranus makes an ambivalent configuration with the Sun and the Moon Nodes, Saturn "stokes up" a prolonged conjunction of Venus and Jupiter with a minor influence from Mars.

Venus, on her part, is the pivot of the tense Venus-Moon-Mercury configuration, which makes contact with the ambivalent configuration via a weak conjunction of Mercury and the Sun. Potentially, there is great spiritual power through the conjunction of Neptune and Pluto in Gemini, which, scarcely affected by the other forces of the psyche, leads a life of its own in the soul's depths.

The obvious supporting pillar of Krishnamurti's being is the Sun-Uranus opposition and the Saturn-Mercury quincunx along the thought axis. Uranus carries great weight not only from its position at the top of the chart, but from its rulership of Aquarius, the rising sign. Krishnamurti's revolutionary spirituality, his unrelenting calling-into-question of ideologies and religious dogmas, derives from this opposition and this quincunx: on the one hand there is his early education in Theosophical theory, represented by the 3rd house, and on the other hand there is his 9th house abandonment of the inculcated forms of thought, his abrupt rejection of all assertions on spiritual matters that do not come from innate cognition. He overstepped normal limits not only geographically (he travelled widely), but also in two great changes of life-style: first, through his contact with the Theosophists, he left behind his familiar traditional Hindu milieu, and then he broke free from Theosophical circles to go his own way. By so doing he fulfilled an inner urge, indicated by the Moon Node. As it happens, the latter showed a possible way out of the opposition via the blue aspects: he could rely on considerable private resources given by the closeness of the node to the 2nd cusp. With Pisces on the cusp, these resources were spiritual rather than material, and he was able to share with others the personal knowledge springing from the fullness of his inner being.

The person who initiated Krishnamurti at the beginning of his spiritual journey was Annie Besant, president of the Theosophical Society, who was surrogate mother (he lost his mother when he was young) and spiritual guide rolled into one. Saturn in the 9th house marvellously expresses the two things, and its placement mirrors his relationship with this woman. The love and esteem with which he repaid her (Saturn trine Venus and Jupiter) were undiminished by Krishnamurti's rejection of Theosophy.

In addition to its relevance at this personal level, the Saturn-Jupiter trine was particularly important in his spiritual development. With Saturn in the 9th house in Scorpio, we have pronounced philosophical leanings: a looking for basic truths and a searching inquiry (Saturn) into the meaning of life (Jupiter). Interestingly, the same aspect appears in the charts of Kepler, C. G. Jung, and Heidegger.

At the entrance to Krishnamurti's path stood the image of the spiritual guru: the highest master, whose vessel he was said to be. However, through mental and physical dying and becoming processes (Saturn) Krishnamurti attained a highest knowledge that invalidated, for him, the highest master role. With a Scorpionic hatred of compromise, he then refused all master-and-pupil relationships, all devotees and followers.

The second, upward-striving opposition, between Venus and the Moon along the relationship axis, reveals a certain difficulty in his approach to contacts. Owing to his tactful, sensible behaviour he soon became universally loved, which is not surprising with the Venus-Jupiter conjunction in the 5th house; yet from time to time he suffered from great loneliness and could hardly bear to have anyone near him while his fiercest inner struggles were going on. The 11th house cusp placement of the Moon denied full enjoyment of the social popularity promised by the 5th house. More and more he became a teacher of the present generation: endeavouring to instruct the general public (3rd, 4th and 5th houses) from the insights he had gained (11th house). Among other things, he displayed a great interest in the question of education (Jupiter, 5th house, Cancer) and founded various schools, the first being in his native India.

The stimulating Moon-Sun-Mercury-Venus constellation signifies his teaching ability; he tried with the utmost perseverance (given by the fixed signs Taurus, Aquarius and Scorpio) to familiarize his listeners with his central concern (Mercury conjunct Sun), deliverance from the ego, and to call them to consciousness of the self (green aspects of the stimulating constellation). Krishnamurti's tragedy, which he himself often mentioned with an air of resignation, is that his gift as a teacher bore so little fruit: the blue aspects that would have helped him are missing from the constellation. He was constantly communicating with a public that eagerly sat at his feet waiting for him to do the impossible – namely to hand them his own spiritual knowledge on a plate.

Krishnamurti's Moon stands at the cusp of a fixed house in mutable Sagittarius (in conjunction with the galactic centre 25°24´); a painful position which imposed a massive weight of suffering on him, especially in his younger years. For a temperament alive to a wider, unrestricted outlook (Sagittarius), the Theosophical training and the prodigious hopes placed in him soon became a prison. Krishnamurti finally freed his sense of self (Moon) from the tight confines of his world (Sun in 3rd house), but his letters bear eloquent testimony to the tremendous conflict of loyalties (in the 11th house one is loyal) by which he was torn. He discarded the alien destiny foisted on him earlier through Sun in the 3rd house, and in the process gained a new and personal ideal, that of spiritual friendship (Aquarius on the AC: direction of individual development). He said in a talk at Saanen (1984):

> *But those who genuinely want to understand, who are on the watch, who seek the imperishable, the beginningless and endless, will close ranks with greater determination and become a threat to all that is inessential, to what is unreal, to the phantoms. And they will combine, will be aflame, because they understand. We must create such a community. That is my aim. In true friendship of this kind – which you do not seem to know – each has the will to cooperate. Not at the behest of some authority or in order to be made safe but because they really understand and therefore live in the imperishable. This is greater than all worldly friends, than all sacrifices.'*

The Age Point in Krishnamurti's Horoscope

We will now discuss the Age Point in Krishnamurti's chart. The table on pages 172-173 shows the radix AP. Also pertinent to this discussion is his moon node horoscope (facing page). We have also included his Moon Node AP (page 174). The dates discussed in the text are highlighted in both AP tables with arrows.

Dec. 1897

One of the most important people in Krishnamurti's life was his brother, Nityananda, who accompanied him on his many journeys and was his closest friend and second self until he died of tuberculosis at age 28. When Nitya was born, the AP of Krishnamurti, who was then 3, made a fine trine to Jupiter-Mars, which augured well for a close, harmonious relationship between the brothers.

Jan. 1910

At the end of 1909, at 14½, he met Annie Besant and was initiated by her into the task of being a representative of the highest master. With a sextile to Mars and a semi-sextile to Pluto, the AP builds an information figure, making possible a first step in the direction of spiritual awareness.

Oct. 1911

The year 1911 was very important. Krishnamurti was 16 and his AP transited the Sun. "The Order of the Star in the East" was expressly founded for him in view of the role he had to play. He also travelled to England for the first time with Annie Besant and his brother. One can imagine what a culture shock this was for the young orphan. In this portentous year, the AP activated the ambivalent Sun-Uranus-

Moon Node constellation. What resulted was the sudden uprooting from the homeland (Uranus 9th house) and the imposition of a life task within the context of the "Star" (Sun 3rd house).

May 1913

In 1913, when the AP transited Mercury, making a semi-sextile to Venus and a quincunx to Saturn, Krishnamurti came to know Lady Emily, a motherly woman who gave him the security and love he sorely missed. Unfortunately, they were constantly being separated (the quincunx is a separation aspect), which was a great trial to them.

Feb. - Dec. 1916

The passage of the AP over the Pluto-Neptune conjunction was not marked by any spectacular events. But shortly afterward Nityananda wrote a letter to Annie Besant in which he said:

> *Krishna is incredibly altered. He can look into people's hearts [Neptune!] and is capable of making up his own mind. He stands much more firmly on his*

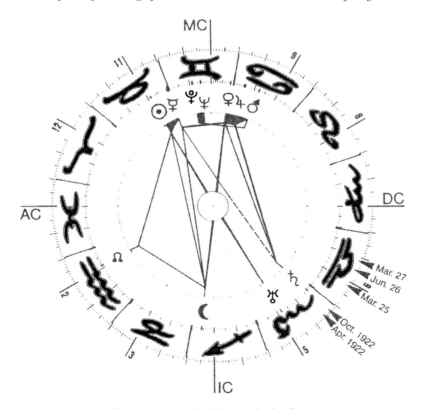

Krishnamurti's Moon Node Chart

1895 / Age 0			1901 / Age 6			1907 / Age 12		
28 Feb	⚺	☋	12 May	S	2	12 May	S	3
9 May	□	☉	6 Jul	□	G	5 Jun	⚹	♀
11 May	S	1	2 Aug	□	☾	6 Jul	⚺	☿
						23 Sep		☋

1896 / Age 1			1902 / Age 7			1908 / Age 13		
7 Feb	⚹	G	16 Feb	□	♀	29 Mar	☍	♄
5 Mar	⚹	☾	17 Mar	⚹	☿	25 Sep	⚹	♃
24 Sep	△	♀	27 May		☋			
23 Oct	□	☿	14 Nov	⚻	♄			

1897 / Age 2			1903 / Age 8			1909 / Age 14		
5 Jan	⚼		27 Apr	□	♃	26 Aug	I	3
28 Jun	△	♄	27 Aug	I	2	25 Oct	⚺	♇
25 Aug	I	1						
➡ 13 Dec	△	♃						

1898 / Age 3			1904 / Age 9			1910 / Age 15		
15 Dec	□	♇	20 Apr	⚹	♇	➡ 6 Jan	⚹	♂
			26 Jun	□	♂	21 Jul	⚺	☿
			21 Dec	⚹	☿			

1899 / Age 4			1905 / Age 10			1911 / Age 16		
25 Jan	L	1	25 Jan	L	2	26 Jan	L	3
21 Feb	△	♂	17 Jul	⚻	♅	7 Mar	☍	♅
22 Aug	□	☿	26 Nov	⚺	☋	31 Jul	⚹	☋
						➡ 6 Oct	♂	☉

1900 / Age 5			1906 / Age 11			1912 / Age 17		
23 Mar	△	♅	27 Jan	⚺	☉	26 Jul	⚻	G
6 Aug	♂	☋	21 Oct	△	G	24 Aug	⚻	☾
7 Oct	⚹	☉	16 Nov	△	☾			⇨

Radix AP Table for Krishnamurti.
S = Sign; G = Galactic Center;
I = Invert/Balance Point; L = Low Point.

1913 / Age 18	1920 / Age 25	1926 / Age 31
30 Mar ♍ ♀	➧ 19 Mar ♂ ♀	➧ 10 Feb ♐ G
➧ 1 May ♂ ☿	24 Apr ♍ ☿	13 Mar ♐ ☾
12 May S 4	25 Jul ♋	27 Oct ♍ ♀
2 Aug ♓		29 Nov ✶ ☿
1914 / Age 19	**1921 / Age 26**	**1927 / Age 32**
16 Mar ♐ ♄	28 Feb △ ♄	➧ 19 Feb ♌
20 Oct ♍ ♃	26 Aug I 5	27 Aug I 6
	➧ 26 Sep ♂ ♃	➧ 4 Sep □ ♄
1915 / Age 20	**1922 / Age 27**	**1928 / Age 33**
27 Aug I 4	➧ 30 Dec ♍ ♇	10 Mar ♍ ♃
1916 / Age 21	**1923 / Age 28**	**1929 / Age 34**
➧ 9 Feb ♂ ♇	➧ 25 Jan L 5	25 Jan L 6
7 May ♍ ♂	25 Mar ♂ ♂	➧ 27 Apr ✶ ♇
➧ 29 Dec ♂ ♅	8 Nov ♍ ♅	13 Jul ♍ ♂
1917 / Age 22	**1924 / Age 29**	**1930 / Age 35**
25 Jan L 4	1 Aug △ ♅	2 Feb ✶ ♅
2 Oct ♐ ♅		30 Sep □ ♁
1918 / Age 23	**1925 / Age 30**	**1931 / Age 36**
27 Mar □ ☊	17 Jan △ ☊	1 Mar ♐ ☊
16 Jun ♍ ☉	6 Apr ✶ ☉	10 May □ ☉
	➧ 12 May S 6	12 May S 7
1919 / Age 24		
12 May S 5		
4 Jun ☍ G		
9 Jul ☍ ☾		

Radix AP Table for Krishnamurti. (continued)

1913 / Age 18	1919 / Age 24	1925 / Age 30
3 Mar ♐ ☉	4 Mar ☍ ☉	➡ 3 Mar ♐ ☉
12 May S 4	12 May S 5	12 May S 6
12 May □ ☊	12 May △ ☊	12 May ♐ ☊
9 Oct ⚹ ♅	9 Oct ♂ ♅	9 Oct ⚹ ♅
1914 / Age 19	**1920 / Age 25**	**1926 / Age 31**
2 Jun ☍ ♆	1 Jun ♐ ♆	➡ 2 Jun △ ♆
21 Dec ♐ ♂	20 Dec △ ♂	21 Dec □ ♂
1915 / Age 20	**1921 / Age 26**	**1927 / Age 32**
6 Mar ☍ ♇	6 Mar ♐ ♇	➡ 6 Mar △ ♇
27 Aug | 4	26 Aug | 5	27 Aug | 6
1916 / Age 21	**1922 / Age 27**	**1928 / Age 33**
17 Apr ♐ ♃	➡17 Apr △ ♃	16 Apr □ ♃
19 Oct ⚹ ♄	➡20 Oct ♂ ♄	19 Oct ⚹ ♄
1917 / Age 22	**1923 / Age 28**	**1929 / Age 34**
25 Jan L 4	25 Jan L 5	25 Jan L 6
1 May ♐	1 May ♏	1 May ♎
21 Jul ☍ ☿	22 Jul ♐ ☿	21 Jul △ ☿
23 Aug ♐ ♀	23 Aug △ ♀	23 Aug □ ♀
1918 / Age 23	**1924 / Age 29**	**1930 / Age 35**
5 Apr ⚹ ☽	4 Apr ✳ ☽	4 Apr □ ☽

Table 5. MN Age Point Table for Krishnamurti

own feet than he did before, and although he is not aggressive and never will be, many folk are irritated by what they call his sudden obstinacy. (31)

This suggests that Krishnamurti had undergone a profound inner change. Obviously he had acquired a spiritual (Neptune) authority (Pluto) of his own. The evidence appears in that from this time forward he ceased to give blind assent to the proposals of the Theosophical Society and also voiced open criticism of his teacher, Leadbeater.

Sept. 1921

During the passage of the AP over Venus and Jupiter, Krishnamurti spent a very happy and easy time. He led in commanding style the first "Star" World Congress, gave many lectures and travelled a good deal. In the autumn of 1921, he briefly fell in love (AP conjunct Jupiter), but sexual relations, marriage and a family of his own had no further appeal for him.

LP 5

On August 20, 1922, when he was 27, he underwent a complete change of life. As a result of intense meditation and in great physical pain, he experienced Samadhi (absorption in the divine) for the first time. Although the AP was transiting Low Point five (exact in January 1923), it was making no special aspect at this time apart from a weak semi-sextile to Pluto.

MN-AP Oct. 1922

In view of this dearth of radical aspects, I took a look at his moon mode horoscope and found that the MN-AP had reached Saturn and was activating the Saturn-Jupiter trine directed at the 9th house region of religious knowledge. Apparently, that summer, Krishnamurti burst through the bounds of his earthly existence as it was at that time. From then on, under great physical suffering (Saturn) he at last brought to maturity the spiritual fruit (trine) that had been in him from birth.

May 1925 Cusp 6

At the end of 1925 his brother Nityananda died. This loss finally shook his confidence in the Theosophical psychics who had predicted a recovery, and represented a significant stage in Krisnamurti's detachment from the world-view of the Theosophists. In March 1925, the MN-AP formed a quincunx to the Sun, and in March 1926, the radical AP formed a quincunx to the Moon and to the Galactic Centre. This represents the feelings of pain and longing for his dead brother. But the aspect does not explain the inner change that took place in Krishnamurti afterward, a change he expressed in the following words (31):

> *A dream is dead and a new dream is born, like a flower thrusting up through the hard soil. A fresh vision has taken shape and a new consciousness has to unfold with it... My brother and I are one. As Krishnamurti I now possess greater enthusiasm, greater faith, greater compassion and greater love, for in me now is also the body, the being of Nityananda... I can still weep, but that is human. I now know with greater certainty than ever before, that there is real beauty in life, real happiness, which is not capable of being destroyed by physical happenings, that there is great strength which is not weakened by passing events and a great love that is lasting, imperishable and invincible.*

Jun. 1926

A glance at the MN-AP reveals that in June 1926 there was a trine to Neptune – the freeing from limitations of Krishnamurti's ego through this death: there is no aspect more appropriate to the release of transcendental love and boundless compassion.

Feb. 1927

Again, the most crucial action of his life, his public declaration rejecting the teachings of the Theosophists together with the role they had intended for him, is not clearly mirrored by the radical AP: of course, the sign change from Cancer to Leo did give him the inner confidence to go his own way; but this "Plutonic turning point" would not have been sufficiently motivated by the sign change, in my opinion, even allowing for the square to Saturn that is due a little later.

Mar. 1927

But now look at the MN-AP: in the same spring of 1927 it makes an exact trine to the Pluto-Neptune conjunction, at the MC in the moon node horoscope. The spiritual independence that Krishnamurti had always had deep down now completely broke through and from then on he struck out on his own. As a direct result he dissolved the "Star" and left the Theosophical Society at the end of 1929.

Apr. 1929

This move coincided with a sextile of the radical AP to the Pluto-Neptune conjunction. After the great inner change, which culminated with the trine of the MN-AP to Pluto, this sextile gave Krishnamurti the impulse to act positively and take the external consequences.

A comparison of the MN-AP and the AP shows that the milestones in Krishnamurti's progress since the great change, the Samadhi experience, are better represented by the MN-AP. Apparently, the decisive conscious impulses came from stored experiences and led Krishnamurti's spirituality to a very high degree of development.

The following is his felicitous description of the concerted action of inner and outer (nodal chart) (22):

When we see what goes on in the world, we begin to understand that there are no outer and inner processes, but only a single unitary process, an all-embracing motion, whereby the inner motion is exhibited in the outer and the outer reacts in turn on the inner. To my mind, the ability to look is all that is required; for, when we know how to look, everything becomes perfectly clear. And this act of looking needs no philosophy, no teacher. No one has to tell you how to look. You just look.

And the esoteric seed thought of his Sun sign Taurus is: "I see, and when the eye is opened all is illumined." (15)

The Integration Horoscope

Natal and Nodal

Integration usually implies a pulling together, bringing unity out of diversity, and that's the function of the Integration Horoscope. This is a new method we have evolved to investigate the structure of our personality by means of astrology. It shows the interaction of the ego planets (Sun, Moon and Saturn) of the Moon Node Horoscope (MNH) with their positions in the radical horoscope. It is based on our experience that there is a very meaningful connection between the conscious personality as shown in the natal chart and the underlying conscious energies of the shadow personality as shown in the nodal chart. If we can learn to interpret their interactions, we'll gain new insights into just what it is that makes us tick, and also into the way in which our shadow could best be integrated into our personality.

The Threefold Personality

In our system of astrology, the concept of the threefold personality is important, and the rulership by the three main planets is well established. To recap: Saturn rules the physical body, the Moon rules the feelings, and the Sun rules our capacity for independent thought. We think that any aspects between these planets in the natal chart are useful tools for integration. Whenever the ego planets are directly connected by major aspects, our ego tends to be well integrated. We can assert ourselves adequately and live our lives effectively.

Our personality energies can be co-ordinated and goal directed, usually successfully. We know this quality as the "I Am archetype". But more often than not there are no such connections in our natal charts. However, it may be possible that they may be focused by merging our natal with our nodal chart. In this way we can know, albeit often unconsciously, that we possess a strong ego at these deeper levels, but this knowledge is often inaccessible to us until we have found proof, or confirmation. Looking at our Integration Horoscope can bring such realisations into the light of day, and we can ascertain, by examining the interrelationship of our ego planets, whether we do in fact have a weak or strong ego.

Ego Planets in the Nodal Chart

When we examine the aspects and house positions of the ego planets in the MNH we can gain a pretty good idea of where and how the old personality dealt with life, how it asserted and realised itself. Usually we can find valid structures in it which the present ego can now retrieve from the lower strata of our subconscious mind and put to good use. but quite often we actually find that people behave as if the old conditions of the past still prevailed. Together with workers in the field of depth psychology, some astrological research groups have found that a considerable number of people live more in their nodal chart than in their present one. They don't seem to be able to rid themselves of the old deep-rooted patterns and scripts. But we do continue to develop all the time, and the way forward surely implies extricating the potential of our MNH and integrating it with our natal one.

Working on Ourselves

When examining our personality from the point of view of depth psychology it is fascinating to note how, in lots of people, the old scripts from the MNH live on as unconscious urges or even autonomous drives, and how behaviour patterns brought over from the MNH concerning the use of the Will may work out when they are brought together with the present-day ego of the natal chart.

Will the ego be strengthened or weakened by this? Will the old modes of behaviour come in useful in daily life or should they be corrected? It is most fruitful for us if we have an inkling of just what needs developing, transforming, or eliminating. That's one of the reasons for looking at our Integration Horoscope. First we have to acquaint ourselves with the various levels concerned and then try to co-ordinate them. For further details of this process, see *Moon Node Astrology.* (18)

In the Natal Chart we see the Personality on Three Levels

1. From the position of Saturn we note how the physical ego fares in daily life, how it can cope with the demands of daily existence, and how it can face up to the stark realities of living.

2. The position of the Moon shows us the world of our feelings, how we can relate to others, in love and partnerships, and in our relationships in general.

3. From the position of the Sun we find out about the mind, how we think, whether we are aware of the potential of individual freedom or whether we are hidebound by collective notions.

In the Moon Node Chart we see:

1. Our dormant depth potential (the result of previous life experiences).

2.   Karmic components (The Law of Cause and Effect).

3.   Our shadow personality (suppressed parts of the ego residing in the subconscious).

Taken together all these components give us an insight into the obstacles and also the potential for growth of the personality. It is well known that we'll remain unaware of these parts of our Self as long as we don't make the effort to face them consciously.

It is only once we have become consciously aware of their existence that they lose their power to rule us. Only then can we use them effectively in daily life as lessons learned in previous lifetimes, as useful know-how which would otherwise have to remain dormant. Seen in this light the Integration Horoscope can be of inestimable value to our personal growth.

How the Integration Horoscope was Developed

In the beginning, we simply placed both charts (nodal and natal) on top of each other. But this merely resulted in a confusing muddle of aspect lines*.

All aspect lines

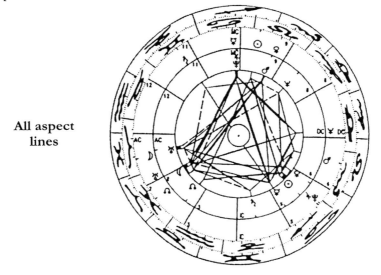

From this multiplicity of lines it was quite impossible to detect points of special interest. So we decided to only use conjunctions and oppositions in the new chart. This gave us the single horoscope which produced a graphic picture of the focal points of a life, especially the oppositions which, as we know, have their own special theme. The very aspects which were challenging in the natal chart also appeared in this particular combination of the two charts, thus pointing out any problem twice over. At first we felt this was a very significant aid to understanding.

Conjunction and opposition only

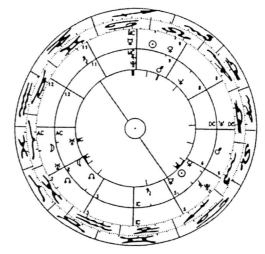

But this method didn't really yield a useful personality profile. So we tried to augment it by adding all the aspects between the three major planets of the two charts, including squares, sextiles, trines. semi-sextiles and quincunxes. In this way, as we have been able to confirm by experience, all the subconscious energies which affect our conscious personality become clear to us. We have termed this chart the Integration Horoscope, because it provides the starting point for successfully accessing our latent aptitudes.

Integration Horoscope
Male, 29.11.30,
12.55, Zurich

Hints for Interpreting the Integration Horoscope

When interpreting the Integration Horoscope we should consider the following combinations:

1. Aspects of an ego planet in the natal chart with the same planet in the nodal chart
   - red aspects (squares and oppositions), potential to achieve
   - blue aspects (sextiles and trines), self-assured
   - green aspects (semi-sextiles and quincunxes), sensitive.

2. Aspects to the three ego planets via an Efficiency Triangle (red aspects only): efficient personality, compulsive activity.

3. Combination with blue aspects: self-assurance, not very sensitive, complacent.

4. Combination with green aspects: heightened sensitivity, vulnerable and gentle inner core.

5. Aspect figures with three colours: great potential for learning and growing. Unpredictable changes of direction.

6. No aspects: insecurity and fragmentation, easily influenced and irritable.

Themes of the Opposition Axes

1-7: Problems between the self and others, relationship issues, dependency on others, personality demands.

2-8: Possession issues, self-protection and defence mechanisms or games, creating enemy figures.

3-9: Thinking axis, open and keen to learn, intelligent, also obstinate and self-opinionated.

4-10: Individuality, wants positions of power and leadership, ambitious, career-oriented, pushy.

5-11: Relationship axis, I am the best, elitist aspirations and disdain of others.

6-12: Existential axis, willing to work, to serve, to sacrifice, Helper syndrome.

Aspects in the Integration Horoscope

Aspects between the Same Major Planets

When we examine the major planets (Sun, Moon and Saturn) we have to bear in mind that we are dealing with 6 planets; 3 in the natal and

3 in the nodal chart. By observing if and how they are connected with each other we can deduce just how we may be able to integrate these energies. For this purpose we had to develop a new approach to interpreting these aspects which we would now like to explain, with the help of a few examples. Obviously these comments should be considered to be suggestions only; they cannot possibly be complete. For this we would also have to take sign and house positions into consideration.

Sun/Sun Trine or Sextile

Frequently we'll find that two Suns (natal and nodal) are trine or sextile to each other, i.e. in harmonious aspect. Therefore, from the subconscious realms, the old Sun with its accumulated know-how (house position) exerts a beneficial influence on the natal Sun. This will have the effect of strengthening the self. It will increase self awareness, self responsibility and self determination. Such people can be very persuasive and influential, they can tell essentials from inessentials, are able to form sane judgements and are discriminating and decisive (obviously these character traits also depend on the signs involved).

Sun/Sun Square or Opposition

With so-called hard aspects, the process of self-realisation finds itself under some kind of pressure. Usually the person reacts by becoming a high achiever. They can cope with a lot more hassle than the average person, consequently special tasks are heaped upon them. They act with unquestioning self-assertion, they don't bother to ask whether other people happen to like it or not, they simply do what they think needs doing. Job satisfaction is most important to them; the knowledge of a job well done increases their feelings of self-worth. Here too we obviously have to consider the quality of the sign.

Sun/Sun Quincunx or Semi-sextile

Green aspects initially bring with them feelings of inner insecurity and self-doubt. The self prefers to assert itself quietly, gently and sensitively. This type of Sun ego is most at ease when it can feel assured of other people's approval. But this of course brings with it phases of self doubt and ego weakness. It would generally be more useful for such people to try and get hold of objective information on which to base their own decisions. With green aspects we have to go through a series of phases of learning and maturing before we can finally find inner stability.

Sun/Sun Not Aspected

If there are no aspects between the two Suns then we'll have to rely for our development solely on abilities indicated in the natal chart. Naturally there may be other planets which are aspected advantageously, and we'll have to study these very closely to determine whether or not they will be useful in the process of self realisation. Some people tend to feel intrinsically helpless, and have no idea just how they might live their lives most effectively.

Saturn/Saturn Trine or Sextile

If the Saturn in the nodal chart forms a trine or sextile with the Saturn in the natal chart, then we tend to be preoccupied with questions of material security and have a highly developed sense of objective reality. We have the ability to cope efficiently with mundane affairs, especially those which promise practical advantages, and we usually concentrate our efforts on those activities which promise to yield the most profit. We avoid or dismiss those activities which appear to us to be useless on the practical level. Caring for others, mothering, and coping with concrete tasks are special gifts conveyed by these blue Saturn positions.

Saturn/Saturn Square or Opposition

With hard aspects between the two Saturns we may find it difficult to cope with the bare necessities of life. Saturn rules all things material, and demands that we conquer all and any obstacles in the way of security. Many people don't even want an easy life, they actually look for difficult tasks and seem to draw them to themselves. They make a meal out of fulfilling their daily needs and complicate matters more than necessary. They make much ado about satisfying Saturn's preoccupation with security needs which rather dampens their ability to relax and enjoy. True to the Saturnian principle of "Work and duty first, pleasure afterwards," they may be dutiful and conscientious to a fault, "work their fingers to the bone," and still feel unsatisfied with their performance.

Saturn/Saturn Not Aspected

If the two Saturns are not aspected there may be a tendency to delegate personal security needs to other people. We may try hard to avoid any direct confrontation with life, we'll leave that to those who are stronger than we are. This of course creates situations of dependency for which Saturn has to pay by accepting obligations and with shows of gratitude. On the other hand, the inability to master the physical demands of daily living can evoke feelings of inferiority, which is a great obstacle to self realisation.

Moon/Moon Trine or Sextile

When the two Moons are connected by the blue aspects we'll find harmonious and well-balanced feelings. Such people radiate understanding and good will. They'll try to avoid conflict on the emotional level and would rather adapt themselves to the feelings of other people than cause them hurt. Such sensitivity, compassion and empathy make them easily popular; they gain many friends and in turn feel supported by those around them. Relationships are very important to them, and the emotional needs are met without much effort on their part. Their wishes are fulfilled comparatively easily. But there might be a slight tendency to be somewhat condescending towards people who don't share their degree of personality skills, and this may alienate them from some people.

Moon/Moon Square or Opposition

Hard aspects between the two lunar positions are frequently a sign of considerable mood swings. Such people somehow don't manage to express their feelings adequately. Often they sound different from the way they intended, and create an effect opposite to the desired one. This makes them feel miserable, misunderstood and at a disadvantage. They'll withdraw at the slightest provocation, tend to feel offended and frustrated – and then suddenly demand that their own wishes be met. And their unpredictable temper tantrums will give them quite a few relationship problems.

Moon/Moon Quincunx or Semi-sextile

Green aspects between the lunar positions indicates insecurity with the semi-sextile and heightened sensitivity and awareness with the quincunx. Such persons can resonate with other people's souls, and understand their needs without the use of words. But they can become victims of people stronger than themselves and then respond to the dictates of their wishes. This makes them dependent on the moods of those around them, and they find it hard to distance themselves from this atmosphere. They'll keep on waiting for something nice to happen; sometimes they'll wait all their lives.

Moon/Moon Not Aspected

Here feelings act independently and aren't easily controlled or directed. Relationships tend to be spontaneous and unplanned, they just happen. Such people are at the mercy of their surroundings, often finding themselves manipulated by all and sundry. Their inchoate feelings can create a state of chaos all around them, unless they can somehow manage to integrate and direct them. This will depend on the Moon's sign and any aspects with other planets.

Connections between different Ego Planets

Up to now we have dealt with the aspects between the same planets. There are, of course, also aspects between the different ego planets.

Sun/Moon

Any connections are a sign that we are fully aware of our own wishes and desires, we know what we want. Whether we can actually have what we want depends on the colour of the aspect. Blue aspects work out harmoniously, red ones give extra energy, green ones bring caution and sensitivity to the process of self assertion.

Sun/Saturn

Any connections here suggest a strong ego which likes to prove its worth in the face of difficulties. We have a serious approach to life, and feel responsible for everything that needs doing. The concepts of duty and security are writ large, Life is lived in accordance with immutable laws, weakness is neither tolerated nor acknowledged. In many people deep-rooted feelings of guilt and shame will drive them to ever greater effort. Much also depends here on the colour of the aspect.

Saturn/Moon

Any connection will strengthen the depth and feeling content of a relationship. Usually security needs will play an important role and any partner may be expected to convey material advantages. At the very least we'll need someone who will belong to us, who believes in us and confirms our hopes that we are OK.

On the other hand, we may like to care for someone who is weaker than we are, whom we can mother. In either case we need the reassurance that we are needed and wanted. Depending on the colour of the aspect involved, when tackling any life task we'll be very dependent on other people's approval of our actions.

Aspect Figures of the Ego Planets

Frequently the three ego planets will form complete aspect figures between each other. These too will strengthen our chance to integrate our personality successfully. If, for instance, we find an Efficiency Triangle formed by the three ego planets, in the Integration Horoscope, then we can see for ourselves that we'll simply have to assess the value of our life by our achievements – we just can't help doing this! It is our chief aim in life and it gives us the highest possible satisfaction in life if we can feel that we have achieved more than anyone else.

If the three ego planets of the Integration Horoscope form a Learning Triangle between them (all three colours involved), then we'll constantly change and adapt, nothing is ever static, we are forever evolving. If we have a blue triangle then we'll enjoy our state of inner peace, be convinced we are on the right path, and nobody can make us do anything unless it feels right for us.

If the ego planets are not connected, then any important life events can cause us insecurity and turmoil, and we just can't decide what to do for the best. Sometimes reason has the upper hand, sometimes our feeling nature, and more often than not we'll only manage to make up our minds when we no longer have the choice.

Connection by Sign in Natal and Nodal Charts

It also leads to interesting discoveries when we place the two charts on top of each other and find out how their zodiacal signs interlink. In example 1, for instance, we have an Aries AC in the natal chart, and a Leo AC in the nodal chart. Therefore we are dealing with a combination of Aries and Leo, a double dose of fire, which makes us expect a strong and fiery ego image with charisma.

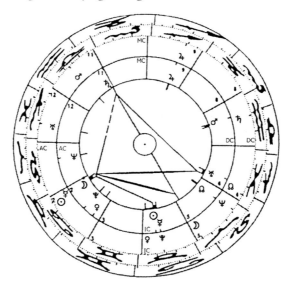

Example 1: Female, 10.5.24, 3.15, Bamberg
Chart with Efficiency Triangle

Combining the placements of the signs of the nodal chart with those of the natal chart throws light on interconnections which explain many a problem and experience that until then was difficult to deduce from the natal chart alone, and which hadn't until then really fitted into the total picture. We can, for instance, suddenly understand why someone isn't totally Taurean although they have a Sun in Taurus in the second house (see again example 1), because the second house is coloured by Cancer from the nodal chart. This Sun therefore shows distinct Cancer characteristics, which is quite apparent to the person concerned and those around her.

Age Progression through Natal and Nodal Signs

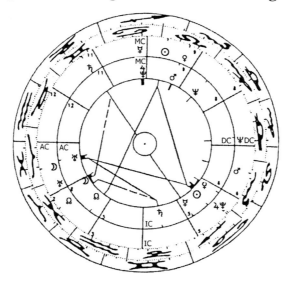

Example 2: Male, 29.11.30, 12.55, Zurich

In Example 2 we see Capricorn in the 11th house with Saturn opposed by Mercury and the Sun in the 5th house of the nodal chart. From the lower chart, the sign Gemini exerts its effect on the 11th house. When the AP reached Saturn, this person had a heart attack with water on the lungs.

It is the Integration Chart which explains this event in its totality. Gemini rules the lungs, the oppositions of the Sun attacks the heart and Saturn narrows the bronchial tubes. Everyone thought he would die.

The two ego planets on the 5/11 axis, which is called the heart axis in medical astrology, produced such a strong pressure simultaneously inward and outward, that normal limits were breached and it caused a collapse.

In actual fact, it took him quite a long time to recover. The trine from Sun/Sun and the sextile from Moon/Saturn came to the rescue; they added energy to the healing process.

We can gain further insights by examining the Age Progression through the individual signs and houses throughout the course of a lifetime.

If you refer back to Example 1 and look at the 12th house, age 66-72, you'll see Pisces in the natal chart and Virgo in the nodal chart. This person therefore experiences not just the qualities of Pisces but also, underlying the nodal chart, the qualities of Virgo. As a matter of fact she accomplished an enormous amount of work whilst going through the 12th house, although everyone assumed that intercepted Pisces would herald a quiet life. But the energy of Virgo could still make its influence felt from her subconscious depths.

These are just a few hints for interpretation. For best results why don't you have the computer work out your own Integration Chart (2). Astrologers are natural researchers, and you too will surely enjoy discovering your own self through this new and fascinating method.

Chapter 10

Low Point Experiences:
Twelve Gates to the Spiritual Life

Today more and more people are influenced by the laws of spiritual progress. Many are taking an interest in esoteric, parapsychological or religious topics: they long for peace, freedom and guidance, for a guru to show them the way. They are fascinated by spiritual questions, even to the extent of neglecting everyday affairs, and so get themselves into great difficulties and developmental crises. Therefore it is necessary for psychologists, astrologers, physicians, educators, and those who want to help others to know something about the laws of spiritual development, in order to be able to understand the needs of those seeking advice and to give them effective support. And here is where Age Progression can give considerable assistance.

The intention of the present chapter is to explain the significance of the twelve Low Point positions in spiritual development. Since this is a wide field, we shall look at it from different angles.

The Five Levels of the Horoscope

The diagram on the next page shows five clearly defined levels in the construction of an API horoscope. These symbolise both the uniqueness and the complexity of the entire human character. The horoscope is drawn up carefully according to specific psychological and aesthetic criteria, for we attach great importance to the appearance of the chart. It is usually calculated and drawn up by computer programme (2).

Bruno Huber describes the five levels as follows in his *Astro Glossarium* (1):

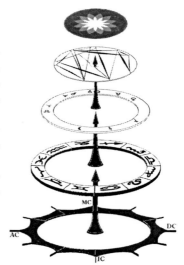

"The art of horoscope interpretation requires that we are not only able to define the individual elements on each level, but also to understand the interaction between levels. For example, an aspect between two planets is a relationship on the same level (two bodies on the 3ʳᵈ level), which are controlled by the next one up. An aspect of a planet to a house cusp (e.g. AC), on the other hand, would be an interaction between two different levels, i.e. a body (3ʳᵈ level) with a place, a sphere of activity (4ᵗʰ level); we do not draw in aspects to house cusps."

The Five Levels

1ˢᵗ level	**the core**	the soul; the connection to the transcendental
2ⁿᵈ level	**the aspects**	the life-motivation; the primal purpose and objective
3ʳᵈ level	**the planets**	the life organs; powers that enable identity experience
4ᵗʰ level	**the signs**	genetic and archetypal influence; innate behaviour
5ᵗʰ level	**the houses**	the connection to the environment; learned behaviour

For a spiritual approach, it is important to distinguish the five levels from each other; we can even see a hierarchical order there. The path goes from the outside inwards and also vice versa, from the inside outwards. These levels make it clear that a relationship on the same level cannot be interpreted in the same way as an interaction between levels. In the interaction of the levels the intrinsic nature can be found, and seen in a meaningfully dynamic and integrating way.

Spiritual Perspective

Insofar as we treat the central core as the centre of being or soul, we enter a religious dimension that gives us the certainty of a spiritual life source within us. We recognise the centre of being as the source of our existence, to which all life experiences flow back. This gives us a more profound understanding of astrological symbolism and automatically causes a transformation of awareness. This very often happens at the Low Points during Age Point transits. In a manner of speaking the soul "awakens" there, we are closer and can experience the change of awareness and learn that in our innermost selves we are in a constant exchange with cosmic forces, which are accessible to us in the centre of being – thereby participating/sharing in the eternal being.

Cycles and Intermissions

The Low Point experience is something of an intermission between two cycles. Technically speaking, this experience has to do with the division of the houses into a cusp region and a Low Point region (peak and valley). The two cycles, descending and ascending, show up clearly on the intensity curve (page 13). The curve changes direction and rises again at the Low Point.

The changeover from one region, or condition, to another involves a brief stop preparatory to moving upward; and this happens every three years and eight months after the crossing of a house cusp. At the passage of the Age Point through the Low Point, we nearly always have a feeling of standstill, and often of stagnation. The spell of external activity and success we enjoyed at and after the cusp has petered out. Nothing seems to be going on, we are just marking time. Also there is a perceptible inward pull, because the Low Point may be seen as the point of ingress to the centre of our being. A phase of introversion begins, usually lasting from eight to twelve months. We call this a Low Point year.

Our own life, like the life of nature, does not solely consist of alternate phases of building up and breaking down; in between come shorter or longer pauses as we go into reverse. We are all familiar with the cycles of ebb and flow, of the passing of active day into inactive night, of breathing in and out, of the many things in life that come and go. These processes are typical of the course of events in nature's three kingdoms. In our conscious experience of these cycles and of the breaks between them, we reach at the Low Point a neutral place that is neither one extreme nor the other, a place from which we can survey and restructure our lives.

At each Low Point we get an opportunity to turn inward, to regain composure, to gather strength for the climb to the next cusp. The time of apparent rest at the Low Point is really a time of reorientation. With any change, something inside us always has to come to an end. New springs from old as the outworn is discarded. What is new is welcome because full of potential. The cycle is one in which no phase is quite like any that went before. Instead it forms a spiral in which crises constantly recur at higher levels. This spiral has its individual rhythm, oscillation or pulse, with intermittent pauses, having a cosmic, and therefore a spiritual, significance. What we are saying can be made clear in *A Treatise on White Magic*, by Alice Bailey (6):

> *"God breathes, and His pulsating life emanates from the divine heart and manifests as the vital energy of all forms. It flows, pulsing in its cycles, throughout all nature. This constitutes the divine inhalation and exhalation. Between breathing out and the breathing in comes a period of silence and the moment for effective work. . . . With the manner in which this One Life of the solar system works in these vast interludes of meditative silence, called technically a pralaya, we need not concern ourselves. . . . What does concern the student of these Instructions however is how he can himself attain a definite constructive activity in his interludes."*

When we learn to make good use of this intermediate time we can achieve great inner freedom.

Spiritual Meaning of Low Point Stations

The Low Point stations have a deep spiritual significance, even for our own small lives. They pull us up short, and present us with an opportunity for spiritual development. During this respite, we become aware of our own depths; we return to base, to a safe retreat where we can relax before pursuing the upward way like one reborn. The Low Point puts us in touch with the soul, the centre of our innermost being, and gives us strength to press onward. These intermissions have much in common with the contemplative state in which the "Light of the Soul" enters our awareness. By cultivating this illumination or intuition, call it what you will, we enable our inner life or pure self – which gradually unfolds during recurrent Low Points – to become a determining factor in our existence and therefore in our environment.

Those who are totally absorbed by the affairs of the busy world, or have few Low Point planets in their charts, almost never appreciate the true nature of intermissions; their psyches could receive an unexpected jolt when braked by the inner self at such times. Judged by our frantic activity, the self is relatively motionless. Not for nothing has it been called the point of absolute stillness and peace. Most people are always in a hurry, they are always doing something, rushing here and there, so preoccupied that they have no time to think of anything else but their duties, their jobs, their money-making and so on. Each Low Point calls a halt, inviting them to come to their senses. Before the Low Point is reached, the fixed region of a house has to be traversed, beginning at the Balance Point. Right here is where a person of sense will consider slowing down instead of stepping up the pace of an already hectic life. Whoever eases off at this stage, ignoring outside pressures, and starts to look within will also be able at the Low Point to hear the inner voice of the true self and, in general, to perceive things not previously experienced.

Those who have given no thought to the inner world would profit from a perusal of the available books on the subject. Because a transformation does occur at the Low Point, whether we know it or not, it is better to turn this to our advantage than to try to fight it with our small egos. The more we baulk, the sharper will be the crisis. Nowadays a growing number of people are concerned with spiritual development and with living in conformity with natural law. And many are professionally active in spiritual and psychological fields as therapists, astro-psychological counsellors, teachers of meditation and the like.

This desire for inner development is none other than the force of evolution directly operating through the will of the self at the Low Points. The universe evolves through us and, at the Low Points, we need to cultivate calm, open the inner ear, and respond cheerfully. By assisting evolution we improve our understanding of the inner self and contribute to progress. Those who are already sensitive to spiritual vibrations, possibly having several planets (especially the personality planets, Sun, Moon and Saturn) at the Low Points, are already alive to these experiences and, when the AP transits a Low Point, will make intense contact with their inner selves and will become the recipients of genuine guidance, insight and knowledge. Many have a vision and inner conviction of immediate goals, experience a new state of consciousness, discover a source of inner strength enabling them, at the next cusp, to achieve the goals that have now become clear. They know that, in the period that is astrologically represented by the climb to the cusp, they will have to put their ideals about themselves and the world into some viable form reflecting their new awareness. By integrating inspirations, concepts, and motivations, they can cooperate with their true will; gaining in the process deep inner satisfaction, more joy of living, better health, and a fresh purpose. They can feel the unity of all life, and can approach the inner self as a copy of the universe and a sacred shrine.

This sense of unity ought to become a permanent feature of our consciousness, and should be treated – not as something to be sampled briefly at the Low Point – but as something that can permanently colour our mental attitudes. When it does so, many problems will vanish of their own accord.

In Low Point experiences, we are essentially coming into contact with the inner self and with live spiritual energies. We experience, perhaps for the first time, the magnitude of the oneness of all life and see ourselves as a reflection of something greater, as a microcosm of the macrocosm. We acknowledge the great law "as above so below" and understand that we are engaged in continual give and take with a larger life of which we form part and from which we derive our being.

It may be a pleasant or, on the other hand, a staggering thought, that our own small parcel of energy shares in the cyclic energy flow of this immense cosmic space or entity. The experience of all-pervading energy and of the synthesis of the One Life is typical of the Low Point at a higher level. Incidentally, the unity of human and God is a ubiquitous religious idea and a ground of ancient astrology.

The Circle in the Centre

Let's look at the horoscope from another perspective. We are familiar with the houses, signs and aspects, and we know of the circle in the centre symbolizing the self. This centre has many names: some call it the soul, psyche, anima or atman; others call it the spirit, higher self, or monad. In fact it does not matter what we call it. What does matter is the realisation that this self, as life-giver and governing factor, is the start and end point of our life, and that we can discover something about it during the Low Point transit.

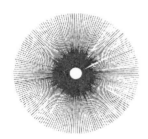

The Circle in the Centre

The self is the creative power that gives birth to the personal I, that sustains it during a lifetime, and then retires into itself. We can think no thought and draw no breath without its aid. The self is the hub of the wheel on which all the spokes of body, mind, and emotions converge. In the horoscope, it is the circle in the centre. When it appears, the native first begins to be. That is to say, it represents the existence of the native and the impulse behind his or her personal development. The problem posed by the Low Point experiences of life is to find and to travel the road back to the self, the circle in the centre; or, in other words, the road back to origin. The urge to go to the point from which we came and to which we return is as old as humanity itself.

We can visualize life energy pouring into the horoscope out of this circle in the centre, and supplying life and strength to the planets that serve us as organs of expression. For their part, the planets receive the cosmic qualities of the sign energies from space that, channeled through the qualities of the individual self, can reach the environment through the house system.

The process is an eternally pulsing exchange – an inbreathing and outbreathing in unison, so to speak, of human and cosmos. This energy exchange is full of mystery, and discloses the riddle of human existence and of creation. The subtle radiations of the self are etheric and stream through all forms of life. It follows that the self comes from the same life substance as the great world in which we live and the nature of which we share.

Experiencing the Horoscope Through Meditation

The simplest approach to the self is to experience the horoscope through meditation. This method is fairly new, and has the character of self-initiation because we identify meditatively with our personal horoscope and thus with our own being.

People who are trained in meditation or who can use their powers of visualization should consciously place themselves at the centre of their own chart. If, then, in the mind's eye, they let the horoscope circle them (after they have studied it well), and imagine that the ascendant is on the left, the descendant on the right, the planets will suddenly light up all round as living forces. See figure.

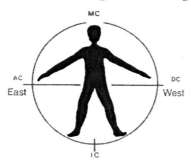

Experiencing the Horoscope through Meditation

Meditation Exercise

In this exercise we withdraw mentally from the outside world of the houses, pass through the zodiac belt, leave behind us the planets or psychic forces and – in the field of consciousness represented by the aspect configuration – locate the still eye in the perpetual whirl of thought, a place of deepest peace and unbroken silence.

When we place our consciousness in the centre of the chart, we see a bright point, shining like the sun. We identify ourselves with this point. Undulatory beams move outward in all directions from this point; and the first thing they fall on is the aspect configuration, since this is something that inwardly preoccupies us. For example, we are well aware of "that square" in our chart and know exactly where to look for it; so, every time it is struck by the inner light, it flashes like an electric filament under high tension. This must surely tell us something about the nature of the aspect.

The blue trines and sextiles are slack, like clotheslines. They sway from side to side under the impact of the imagined inner light, harmoniously following its flow. The quincunx, or long green aspect, is like a thin glass tube in which the inner light is reflected in rainbow colours. It is sometimes called "the yearning aspect," and encourages fantasies, wishes and projections; until, that is, we realize that we come to know something of the light by looking more closely at these reflections of the self. Once we identify a ray of truth, we are in a position to pursue the inner quest. The long green aspect then becomes a decision or will aspect and leads to spiritual growth.

The oppositions are like extended shining iron bars; they are rigid, hard and strong. As they stand like girders in space, the energies of the inner self course along them and make them glow brightly. They conduct these energies very intensely but unidirectionally, according to their polarity. If another planet is present, forming two squares (one to each of the planets in opposition), we get the T-square, which is full of tension and of energies that can make for success.

The aspect configuration should be studied with the inner eye again and again; only then ought we to move on to the planetary influences. When we do, the first thing we notice is that the planets at the Low Points are considerably nearer to us than those at the house cusps. Cuspal planets lie much further away from the centre of consciousness. We have tried to illustrate this in the figure opposite.

There is a direct route from one's innermost being to the Low Points. Any planet standing there is brightly illuminated by the centre and is a vital connecting force. When, for example, Uranus stands at the Low Point of a house, it can be contacted directly; the higher mind has a powerful influence, and the meditative approach to the inner centre is easy to use. And when, to take another example, Saturn is directly reached by the energies of the self, that is to say when it stands at a Low Point, then its transit by the Age Point is usually signalled by a desperate situation along the lines of the house theme. Saturn then acts as the Dweller of the Threshold, and calls for the death of old forms – something often bewildering and very painful.

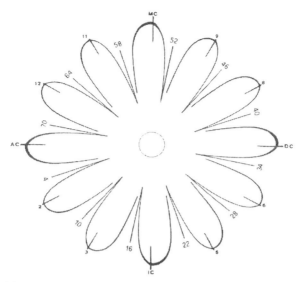

The Low Points – Channels to the Inner Centre

Crystallized behaviour patterns are corrected and made less rigid, and may even be destroyed – all in the interests of clearing the way for further harmonious development.

Since the life centre radiates so powerfully, the aspects need to act as transformers for the inner currents. Their network, as seen by our inner eye during horoscope meditation, vibrates in various colours. The glowing currents that run through it bring about an exchange of vital energy between the planets, and a differentiation in our consciousness. The aspects are thought-structures, by means of which we assimilate our experiences in the outside world and by means of which we can react on the outside world. Conversely, from the standpoint of the self, it is these thought structures and mental processes that the self ingests as experience and stores in the so-called causal body as essence for incarnation.

This visible representation of consciousness is in perpetual motion, and when seen as a medium transmitting the life-energy of the individual, it lies nearest to the self. On the other hand, looked at from the outside, the aspect configuration is furthest removed from human consciousness. Can any of us say that, at this moment, he or she is consciously working on the mental plane? Few indeed; and formerly such activity was reserved for initiates. Although on this mental plane we can now understand and control our thought structure much better, we are still far from building up thought forms consciously and beneficially.

As we have seen, the fierce activity of the living flame is moderated by the aspect structure before it meets the outside world; which is just as well, for the central energy of the life or will is like a consuming fire, to use a Biblical phrase. The more aspects there are, the more differentiated the consciousness, the more intense the thinking, the more suitable the energies that reach the outside world: but also the more laborious the development of thoughts and ideas.

There is always the possibility that there are simply no aspects leading outward from the centre point. We all know horoscopes with lacunae (gaps); in these the environment has direct access to the centre of the being and, when the Age Point passes over such holes, the self is touched on a raw spot [see *LifeClock* (14)].

Frequently an entire half of the chart is untenanted and open. This suggests a sort of uniform consciousness. In a sense, inner and outer are all one; they are not differentiated, are not consciously perceived as separate fields. One could say they exist in a kind of symbiosis in which no personal consciousness is possible. Also, in the sector concerned, there is little sharpness of identity. Thus the free energy flow is not particularly propitious, for the native reacts with less awareness in the given areas of life and fails to apply the forces of the self purposefully.

As already mentioned, it will be found that planets on the house cusps appear to be much further out from the centre. Also they are much less under the control of the central energy, being outward looking and absorbed, influenced and used by the external world. This is in contrast to planets at the Low Point, or even at the Balance Point, which are much nearer to the central force and can convey spiritual energies.

If you will perform the exercise, you will be amazed at what fresh discoveries you can make about your horoscope. This method of visualizing from within is good training for intuition; in fact, we may as well call it "intuitive astrology." Its advantage is the direct experience it gives of what is usually a formal, external, intellectual, mercurial knowledge of the planets, aspects, and signs.

We shall now outline a form of meditation that can be used privately or in self-awareness groups. After the actual meditation, it has been found useful for group members to exchange notes on their mental images and experiences in order to get as much out of them as possible.

Horoscope Meditation

Sit comfortably in a chair with eyes closed and allow yourself to glide into a state of tranquillity and relaxation. Let all your muscles relax until there is no tightness anywhere. Direct your attention to your brow muscles to make sure they are no longer taut. Your forehead should be smooth, your expression friendly, and your tongue should lie in the lower jaw. Breathe quietly and evenly through the nose. As you inhale think, "Breathing is within me," and surrender yourself to the rhythm of the breath – in and out, in and out.

1st Stage: The Circle in the Centre

Concentrate your consciousness in the head and then let it sink slowly in the middle of the body, through the jaw, neck, and upper chest. Allow your consciousness to come to rest in the chest and picture a golden white sun rising in the heart centre. This is the central part of your being; in the horoscope it is the circle in the centre. Install yourself here, and feel yourself securely anchored in this central place.

2nd Stage: Personality Finding

Take a look at your horoscope. On the left is the AC, on the right the DC, below you is the IC, above you the MC. Next visualize the personality planets: the Sun, Moon, and Saturn, arranged exactly as in your birth chart. First turn your attention to the Sun; fetch it in close and examine it in relation to its sign, house and aspects. Then push it slowly back into the outer circle and fetch in the Moon, examining that in relation to its sign, house, and aspects. Slowly restore the Moon to its place in the chart and fetch in Saturn, seeing its symbol in the mind's eye. Examine the planet in relation to its sign, house and aspects before putting it back again.

These three planets are the poles of your personality. Together with the other planets they are the tools of your soul, with which you express yourself in, and impress yourself on, the world. Now let Mercury, Venus, Mars, Jupiter, Moon Node, the rising sign, and the higher planets Uranus, Neptune and Pluto come into mental view. Their positions in the horoscope are an expression of your own self. Recognize your chart and accept it for what it is.

3rd Stage: The Aspect Configuration – Living Consciousness

Bury yourself in your chart, letting it expand and carry the planets over the horizon. You are now left with aspects exhibiting a variety of shining, pulsating, streaming colours.

The oppositions are long, red-hot girders, humming with fiery energy; they are set to point in one direction. The squares are red lines of force, vibrant with electric fire. The trines are light-tubes, in which a dense luminous blue flows quietly and soothingly. The green aspects are thinner and more flexible. A fluorescent green glow flashes swiftly up and down them. The conjunctions are like orange pools of static energy. You should stand at the central point and watch this brilliant play of light.

4th Stage: Self-Awareness

Now retire deeper still inside yourself and see yourself as the source of your life, as the cause of everything. You are a centre of sheer life and will energy. You are the constant, unchanging Self and are in a position to stimulate, heal, guide, and use all the psychological processes in yourself and in your three bodies. Let the light of the golden white sun shine out from your heart on the aspect configuration, the planets, the signs, the houses, and out into your environment. Then contemplate: I am that and that am I.

Slowly withdraw from the state of meditation, breathe deeply in and out, open your eyes, and move your head, hands and feet.

•   •   •

This form of meditation can be altered to suit yourself. We would suggest that, if you are a beginner, you might start with two or three elements and add a few more each time the exercise is repeated. The planets and houses are easiest to visualize – their images spring into view straight away; whereas to see the aspect configuration takes a little practice.

So we have two paths that lead to the self: one is the direct route by which we identify with the circle in the centre through meditation or imagination, the other is the path of life round the twelve houses, unfolding as they do the whole panorama of development from birth to death.

Breathing Rhythms

The way of self-awareness may also be illustrated by the function of breathing in and out. The run up to the house cusp is similar to breathing in. There is a short pause at the cusp; then, like breathing out, comes the glide down to the Low Point, where there is a further pause before the next breath is drawn. Movement ceases at the Low Point, for a moment all is still — then comes another inhalation. The respiratory rhythm (see figure on next page), resembling as it

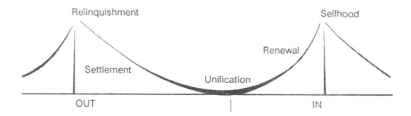

The Breathing Cycle

does the cyclic course of the twelve houses, can tell us something about the meaning of the latter when put in the following terms—relinquishment, settlement, unification, renewal, selfhood.

The house cusp is abandoned in the spirit of letting go. Then, on reaching the Balance Point, it is time for us to settle down, since we are in the fixed region of the house where things are consolidated. At the Low Point, we hold our breath and think of unification. Next comes the indrawn breath of renewal and, finally, self-realisation at the cusp.

Crises of Development and Awareness

As we have just seen, unification has to do with the Low Point. The individual who has experienced mystical union and has come into contact with his or her inner self, or with the divine spark, would like nothing better than to have the experience continue. Unfortunately, for the most part, it quickly comes and goes and is not a permanent state. Therefore this individual sets out to recapture what has been lost, by becoming religious or taking up meditation, and is ready to make any sacrifice for the sake of progress on the path of spiritual improvement. This path is something we must think about if we wish to understand the crises of development and awareness arising at different stages in life. The path of spiritual improvement on which the individual has set out is a long track leading through strange places; it is full of wonderful experiences, but also of obstacles and dangers. It calls for thorough purging, a total transformation of the attitude to life, the awakening of previously inaccessible abilities, the raising of consciousness to new heights, and the acquisition of new motives. These things tend to come to the fore when Low Points are transited; although, obviously, not without trauma.

Someone who has been absorbed in material and social matters may be surprised and alarmed by a sudden eruption of spiritual life as one of the Low Points is passed. Often such experiences are due to disappointments, or mental shock – for example, from the loss of someone close. Those who have been exposed to the forces of change exerted by the self can no longer devote themselves entirely to looking after their physical needs. All the personal details that have so far absorbed their attention lose importance. Getting what they want is no longer a thrill. They begin to ponder over the meaning of life and over the causes of many phenomena they used to take for granted. They ask questions about the sufferings of themselves and others and about the origin and purpose of human existence in general. And this is where misunderstanding and error creep in.

Many do not understand the reason for their new state of mind, worry that they are suffering from morbid fancies and struggle hard to get rid of them. Out of fear that the ground is going to give way beneath them, they do everything imaginable to return to solid reality. They throw themselves with redoubled energy, almost in desperation, into the whirl of life and avidly seek new occupations, fresh attractions, and novel sensations. By these means they succeed in calming their unrest for a time, but seldom in removing it indefinitely. The transforming forces of the soul remain active in the depths of their being, undermining the foundations of their everyday life, and can – even after several years – break out again with renewed violence, usually at the next Low Point.

Frequently, a moral and ethical crisis occurs, and the individual no longer knows what is right or wrong, but gets lost in relative values and is unable to keep a firm grip on absolute standards. What once was good can now be bad. The individual starts living beyond good and evil. Altogether this is a difficult period, esoterically known as "the dark night of the soul." The old order has ended and the new has not yet begun. The inner life matures slowly. The process is long and complicated, consisting of phases of active cleansing to remove hindrances that block the flow and effectiveness of the spiritual forces, of phases when there is a development of inner abilities that formerly were hidden and weak, and of phases when the personality is quiescent, allowing spiritual work to take place while it bears unavoidable suffering with courage and patience. It is a time of change, in which light and darkness, pleasure and pain alternate.

A reaction usually sets in after a period of spiritual growth, because habitual modes of behaviour operate like an automatic mechanism to draw the person back into old routines. Here we have another case of "it always gets worse before it gets better." Everything unwished-for appears en masse, the individual thinks that no progress has been made at all and quickly loses heart. But fresh courage must be taken and renewed efforts made to consolidate the changes. After the first few steps on the path of spiritual development, there is no going back.

Many people nowadays find themselves on the spiritual path and needing help, mostly in the form of understanding, encouragement and reassurance. When we see what the Age Point is doing, and realize that in this position it gives expansion of consciousness and spiritual development, then we can show the inquirer that there is a deeper meaning in his or her experience – however painful it may have been. Only the knowledge that it is part of progress can bring the individual back in unity with the regulatory laws of nature, and put the necessary distance between the self and the problems, so that new positive qualities of life are set free. Often a single astrological consultation is enough to give the native a fresh outlook plus the courage to trust in the inherent forces of development. When shown that progress is a stage-by-stage affair and that crises of consciousness necessarily occur at the Low Points, he or she can adopt a different attitude to problems, and can see the causal connection of the latter so they can be integrated into life. Over the years, as consultants and teachers, we have had the opportunity to observe hundreds of examples of this liberating, neutralizing and healing action.

However, in some cases these crises really unsettle the psyche, often producing the same symptoms as neurosis, schizophrenia or other mental diseases. Roberto Assagioli, the founder of psychosynthesis, made a special study of the relationship between nervous disorders and spiritual development, and from this has come transpersonal psychology. We have incorporated this knowledge in our astrological concept.

In the horoscope, there are many forms of approach to the path of spiritual progress. The most important is Age Progression, as this shows how the I unfolds. The way through the zodiac signs provides another important clue to the inquirer, which is discussed in detail elsewhere (15). Also the position of the North Moon Node in the twelve houses is a point of ascent for the spiritual path. But the twelve Low Point stations place in our hands a real key to the effect of change on the ego and on the spiritual aspirant – especially when they are taken in conjunction with the qualities of the three crosses (cardinal, fixed and mutable).

The Three Crosses
and the Transmutation of the Ego

As we know, the crosses have to do with deep human motivations or, in other words, with why a person behaves in one way and not in another. The ego is closely identified with these motivations, for without them it cannot live: it needs a moving, motivating force to be able to exist. Therefore the qualities of the three crosses are very enlightening when we come to consider the various stages of development and the ego transformations at the Low Points. The qualities of two different crosses will be found to meet at the various Low Points. This can be seen in the following intensity curve.

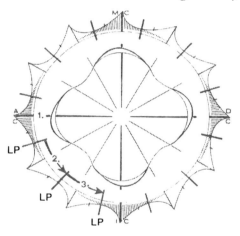

The Intensity Curve

It will be observed that the curve rises from the deepest point to the cusp, then falls again. This means that a house really starts at the Low Point, that the cusp is its strongest region, and that it ends at the next Low Point – the dynamic house system.

As we say, in assessing the transformational qualities of the ego, we have to remember that Low Points are meeting places for different crosses with different qualities. This supplies the key to correct interpretation. When, for example, we wish to assess the transformational quality of the Low Point in the 1st house, we have to start from the fact that a change takes place here from cardinal to fixed, for the 2nd house (fixed) really starts at Low Point one (cardinal). The qualities of the cardinal and fixed crosses meet and produce a motivation here. Again, the cardinal 4th house starts at mutable Low Point three, and so the mutable cross gives way to the cardinal. The same principle applies to the rest of the houses. Where two types of motivation collide, change is bound to occur.

When cardinal gives way to fixed, the will becomes less expansive and self-consciousness is suitably deflated. A clash of fixed and mutable results in a loss of certainty and stability – the disintegration of one's world. The encounter of mutable and fixed means that options can no longer be left open and one has to concentrate on one thing.

This is why decisive changes of motive accompanied by corresponding crises often take place at Low Points. We now describe these more fully in relation to the three crosses and the twelve houses.

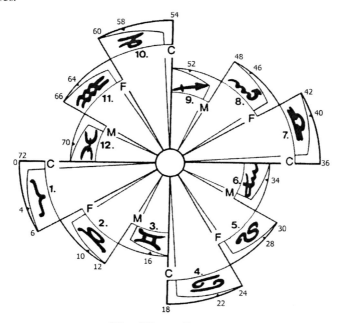

The Three Crosses.
C = cardinal, F = fixed, and M = mutable

In the figure we represent this theme graphically. The signs that project most are the cardinal, the middle signs are the fixed and the innermost signs are mutable. The same applies to the houses, so that the first house begins with the sign Aries. On the outer rims the Low Points are marked by small arrows and the progressed age. Just to remind the reader: on a dynamic view of the houses, each house begins at the Low Point of what would normally be regarded as its predecessor.

The Cardinal Cross

Aries	Cancer	Libra	Capricorn
1st	4th	7th	10th house
4th	22nd	40th	58th year of life Low Point experience

As we all know, the cardinal cross produces an impetus that rises to a point of success or breakthrough, then subsides before gathering strength for a new effort. Its counterpart in the house system is the cusp. From the standpoint of development this cross is typified by mental and spiritual drive, by individualism and the desire for self-realisation, and by shows of strength. It brings the creative power of the will into play. The **Sun** is its ruler.

The cardinal "I" asserts its identity by mastering and controlling forms, objects and people. A person with a majority of cardinal signs and houses is intent on using the will, on proving his or her strength, and impressing it on others, or on getting his or her own way. Everything is measured by will, vigour, and performance. At the cardinal house Low Points, get-up-and-go forsakes him or her and inner powerlessness and ego-loss are suffered. The test comes when he or she fails to achieve some goal. This individual makes plans that will take some time to materialize, but expects to see results right away. Having to wait tries the patience and failure is seen as a bitter personal defeat. It is the crushing realisation, that personal strength is not enough, that begins the inner change. Then comes the surrender to a Higher Power, saying, "Lord, thy will not mine." This makes it possible to be at one with the central will of Being. This person may feel called to work in the interests of making a better world. The personality gains an inspirational quality that points self and others to spiritual goals.

However, if the individual doesn't stand the test but reacts badly at the Low Point, if he or she is excessively proud and arrogant, if the personal "I" is obdurate and imagines it can do everything alone, the individual may become misguided enough to resist the growth of the inner self and to cut away from its vital forces. A barrier is erected between self and life. The energies of the self at the Low Point dash against these stiff walls of the ego. The more the native is wrapped up and encapsulated in the self, the more likely he or she is to suffer the crisis of a mental and physical breakdown. What is required is to recognize that, in the long run, worldly success can never satisfy the inner need; indeed, anxiety, misgivings and emptiness often increase with the growing envy and admiration of others. The sole solution is a drastic reversal – usually possible only when, out of sheer desperation, the individual calls for higher help and guidance, abandons self and becomes open to spiritual things. In transpersonal psychology, this has been given the name of the "Damascus experience" in which a Saul can become a Paul, and lets the personal will fall in line with the Divine Will, applying itself to worthwhile goals that promote progress and abandoning goals that are egotistical.

At the Low Points in the cardinal houses, one reaches one's limits. The correct response is to pull back and to concentrate on doing what is feasible; then success is possible.

The following are brief descriptions of Low Point experiences in the cardinal houses. No more than one or two points can be covered in the space available, so it is necessary to emphasize the importance of the signs in which the Low Points appear. These must be combined with the house qualities, because they can considerably affect, and even alter, the experiences (see page 102 "House/Sign Combinations in the Crosses").

In the 1st cardinal house in the 4th year of life we reach the obstinate or defiant age; the child sets itself against the will of its parents and has to learn that adults are stronger than he or she is. If the child is obedient, all should go well, and he or she will respect the territory of others and will always be able to recognize his or her own.

In the 4th cardinal house in the 22nd year of life the years of childhood and adolescence usually come to a close. The young person wants to live his or her own life and leaves the secure parental home in order to be independent. On becoming self-supporting, he or she discovers that coping alone is not as easy as it looked. It often happens that, for selfish reasons, the young adult declines to leave; however, this can end in family rows that push the reluctant fledgling out of the nest.

In the 7th cardinal house in the 40th year of life the middle of life is already passed. One stands at the parting of the ways. Relationship with the environment and with one's fellow men and women should be harmonious, well ordered and capable of resulting in a genuine partnership. Often, when partnerships are unsatisfactory, this is the age at which they are dissolved. It is also the age when one can be let down by the partner, when one can wait in vain for understanding, sympathy and cooperation, and yet be incapable of escaping from the partner. But whoever is ready for a true partnership or aspires to serve the community can enter a new sphere of activity at the Low Point of the 7th house.

In the 10th cardinal house in the 58th year of life one has passed the peak of life's expectations. Genuine authority in some field must already be ours if we are to work in harmony with the forces of individuation. Anyone who is still locked in competition with others will grimly hang on to the positions already won. But such a person will be lonely and will live in constant dread of being ousted, of being replaced by new blood. Those possessing genuine authority, on the other hand, will help to prepare the way for the young, will lead and guide them and attend to their promotion.

The Fixed Cross

Taurus	Leo	Scorpio	Aquarius	
2nd	5th	8th	11th house	
10th	28th	46th	64th year of life	Low Point experience

This is the cross of fixation, of dogged clinging to gains and guarantees that only have to be given up in the end. The fixed cross causes certain big crises to do with the law of inertia and the process of detachment. Natives with predominantly fixed houses and signs are acutely aware of their identity; therefore they anchor themselves firmly in the world. They stand fast and do not allow themselves to be thrust aside or influenced. They know their limitations, and the stronger the walls they manage to build around themselves, the safer they feel. Their integrity consists in the inviolability of a space in which the I is well established.

The trials that come at the Low Points in the fixed houses have to do with the vanishing of set boundaries and with disillusionment. When the walls that seemed safe are removed, it is as if a protective covering has been destroyed. The result is uncertainty, chaos, and wild anxiety that one will lose everything one has. This fear of loss causes the individual to clutch desperately at whatever has been acquired or is believed to be rightfully theirs.

The paramount influence in the fixed houses is **Saturn**, which plays a significant role as a tester in the processes of change, and as the Dweller of the Threshold. Fixed cross crises are particularly painful and are part and parcel of the eternal dying and becoming. The Low Points are charged with meaning here, since they naturally share the quality of the fixed cross; so, when they are actually in a fixed house, the fixed effect is doubled.

At the Low Points in the fixed houses, a radically new attitude to life needs to be adopted to enable further development to occur harmoniously. These are real crossroads of fate, turning points that make big difference to our lives. In the face of losses of any kind we ought to recognize and accept that life is full of change and is a continual process of growth and development in keeping with natural laws, and that it unfolds according to cosmic order. The belief that all is well, that there is a good reason for everything, and that nothing is accidental, should be encouraged and maintained.

We must continually shake off our fears, break through the walls that threaten to stifle us, renounce the misconceived policy of "safety at all costs" and change our egocentric attitudes, so that we can pass beyond limitations of our own making in order to reach the true self – or, to change the metaphor, in order to vibrate on the same wavelength as the self. Therefore union with the innermost centre at the Low Points implies a letting go, an abandonment, and often a destruction, of whatever binds us to the world. The process of development and the initiatory way require an elastic response to the never-ending changes of life.

Deliverance in the fixed cross lies in continually surmounting barriers until, at last, we are at liberty to make our own decisions. The recognition that what fetters us is unwarranted and arbitrary sets us free to face the new with confidence. Then the new no longer has to pry open our shut fast lives in order to reach us – a painful process – but is welcomed gladly. On our own initiative, and without a qualm, we expand beyond our old limits to find our true measure. No borders can confine the life inside us that knows how to be at one with the Whole.

In reality, this is the middle path, the "razor's edge." The truth is that this path is narrow and quite hard to find. All religions and philosophies refer to it. It is the famous eye of a needle through which one must pass, also the "Noble Middle Path" of the Buddha, the fine line of demarcation between the polarized forces of our being, which can be found and preserved only by passionlessness and by high concentration and powers of discrimination.

Moderation is the characteristic of the fully aware person in the fixed cross. Every deviation from the happy medium, every excess or deficiency, sets in motion the forces of the self, the personal centre of gravity, to restore or preserve the balance. It is the harmonious union of inner and outer, the equilibrium between feeling and understanding, that are depicted in the sage-looking, ever peacefully smiling Buddha.

Of course, this virtue can also land us in a stagnant, apathetic condition, in which we desperately try to stay put purely from fear of loss. Those in particular who are undiscerning need some bad breaks to make them grow up and rouse themselves from their crystallized inactivity. In this case it is fate that produces the inner change – usually at the Low Points of the fixed houses at the corresponding age. Depending on the house and planetary positions, fate may well intervene with the death of a loved one, with the loss of position, career or money, with an illness or brush with death, or with something equally unsettling. In the fixed cross, the native has to adopt the right attitude and make a decisive switch to new goals.

This inner change or reorientation comes from an insight into the futility of all material things, none of which can be taken with us when we go. It involves the calm acceptance that everything is governed by wise laws, that we get what we deserve – neither more nor less. It enables us to put down roots in the deepest part of our soul, having cut material ties in exchange for inner strength and certainty.

Development in the fixed cross comes from respecting the law of economy, by taking, accepting, and giving. In other words, through not trying to grab what we have not earned or what others have got. We must learn to be content. Then we can really appreciate our possessions and can be happy.

At the Low Point in the fixed houses, karma often suddenly comes into play: things to which we have no right are wrenched from our grasp; or equilibrium is restored by privileges being given to some who have never dared to ask for them. At this time, everything is being evened up and Justice is busy with her balance. If we turn a deaf ear to fate and to the voice of conscience telling us to let go and share what we have, if we fail to devote ourselves to a higher order of things, we are bound to suffer for it.

This is where we need to accept that there are others to be considered besides ourselves. A clear understanding of what is meant by equal rights is a great help in fulfilling the requirements of the Low Points. Also the knowledge of what one is, of what one can be, and of what one has to offer the world is an aid to progress. It is no good feeling hard done by, or envying others their status, circumstances and wealth, unless one wants to stand still or run round in circles. True, the testing situations encountered in the fixed cross often tempt us into envy, covetousness and egotism; but a recognition of our own worth, assets and abilities should give us perspective, and enable us to act responsibly toward the greater whole. A liberating and healing power lies hidden in this cheerful self-acceptance. It removes the barriers which false pride and self-defence have erected between our fellow men and women, our inner spiritual forces, and us. Repeated refusals to give and persistent clinging to the past erect a fence that is impenetrable to the true self, and to the new and beautiful things that would come with it. Such negativity not only cuts us off from the forces of life, it is tantamount to tempting fate and opens a chapter of disappointments and reverses.

The thankful acceptance of one's lot is a direct route to those inner regions where the true self dwells. It restores the harmony between us and the higher powers that rule, protect and preserve us all, and so leads to a greater confidence in life.

Low Point experiences in the fixed cross always involve the nonfulfillment of personal aspirations, and often mark a time of disillusionment. What happens in the individual houses depends largely on the native's spiritual development and on the sign on the house cusp. The following are one or two possibilities.

In the 2nd fixed house at age 10, the child realises that material possessions and clinging to parents will give no security in the long run. The child is no longer very interested in these things and turns to other possibilities of self establishment, open to new contacts and the give-and-take with children of the same age. School work may prove burdensome.

In the 5th fixed house at age 28, there are changes affecting love-life and intimate contacts. Disappointments in professional and private life lead to reorientation. It is important to find one's own measure, one's own limitations, and to come to terms with reality. The genuineness of one's attitude is tested. Self overestimation and faulty behaviour are corrected by fate. The reckoning has to be paid.

In the 8th fixed house at age 45, there is a decisive change in lifestyle, usually because of disillusionment. Many a glorious youthful dream finally fades away as we learn to deny ourselves and stick to our bargains. Facing reality and accepting destiny's decrees can be very painful, especially if we have set our sights high. Often our whole world collapses around us and life is forced onto a completely different road. Ties and obligations may feel like hardships from which there is no relief. Nothing seems to happen without a thorough shake-up and a great deal of destruction and reconstruction.

In the 11th fixed house at age 64, we have to slow down and bid farewell to hectic activity. A balance has to be struck, as we reconcile ourselves to the past and cheerfully accept what is still to come. The pensionable age is at the door, and if we do not steel ourselves against the fact that things are going to go on without us, we may suffer from retirement collapse, feeling isolated and thrown on the scrap heap. For many of us, therefore, it is important to forget the claims of the outside world and to prepare peacefully for the evening of life. The way to the Self and to one's inner being is then relatively easy and leads to tranquillity, composure and contentment. Younger folk who see this will come and profit by our experience of life.

The Mutable Cross

Gemini	Virgo	Sagittarius	Pisces
3rd	6th	9th	12th house
16th	34th	52nd	70th year of life Low Point experience

The mutable cross is the cross of love, of regular relationships, and of adaptation to form. It causes ceaseless change and periodic movements in time and space that offer suitable opportunities for the unfolding of the innermost being. The drive or motivation is the urge for love or friendship. In the mutable cross, the native has a continual deep longing for affection, trust, sharing and mutual understanding. Time and again he or she loses love, time and again he or she sets out in search of love. The trek is endless.

In the mutable cross, identity is experienced as a point moving in time and space, free to form relationships with all other things. Any fixation usually results in a loss of identity and of the capacity for love; but these can be regained by letting go. There is a thirst for freedom, an avoidance of commitments and attachments, and an eager waiting for true love. One is ever seeking new contacts in order to make fresh discoveries about oneself and others.

The individual who has many planets (life functions) in mutable signs or houses goes looking for new people, places and situations, in the hope of experiencing love. The steady stream of new relationships helps the conscious mind to develop, and the native identifies with the law of development that he or she recognises, under its many disguises, as the love principle behind evolution. The mutable cross is ruled by the **Moon**.

The tests, or Low Point experiences, typical of the mutable cross, consist of forfeiture of liberty, apparent loss of love, or the feeling of being misunderstood. There is less opportunity for wandering about with no fixed object in view – a decision has to be made in favour of something, even when this will be inhibiting. The restriction on movement is a difficult trial for the mutable cross and requires added depth of personality. One has to concentrate on a single issue, or make a commitment to one person. Limitations may be imposed from without and are experienced as a compulsion or confinement. These are fiercely resisted until it is realised that they are necessary to preserve and protect what has already been achieved and bring stability into life. Voluntary acceptance of sensible rules helps to make the conscious mind less shallow and erratic.

Absorption in some task, or willingness to commit to another person, is a mark of progress in the mutable cross, and produces a greater responsibility towards life and its obligations – the very thing the native wishes to avoid at this stage, believing that love is experienced only in freedom. What awaits discovery is that it is possible when apparently caged, too.

At the Low Points one learns to accept responsibilities and acknowledge the wisdom of laws regulating community life. Social behaviour becomes central, and one is taught by experience how to fit in and contribute to the general good, even at personal cost. The need is for self-control, unremitting effort, and the highest devotion to spiritual ideals, so that love can survive in the daily grind or when an injustice is suffered. Mutual love cannot be taken for granted but must be accepted and cultivated; it needs constant attention. The love that men and women keep seeking through sacrifice, through adoration, through relationships, through sexuality, through every kind of lust, suffering and pleasure, can be found only when the past is entirely forgotten, when enemies are forgiven and one becomes like a child again, newborn and innocent. Then love has no opponent and is without conflict. But before all this, one has to reach the lowest ebb, and, in sheer desperation, surrender oneself with one's hopes and fears. Then one is caught up to another plane, inhabited by the true self. In the final analysis, love is the power that flows from deep within, healing all wounds and restoring us to our centre.

At the Low Points of the mutable houses, love is always the big issue; it is important to give up any selfish demands for understanding, for gratitude, for fair play, for possessions, etc. As soon as such apparently justified claims have been renounced, one is immediately drawn to the centre. What happens is like a sudden revelation from a higher dimension, an act of grace, an initiation, which revitalizes us and relieves us from care and distress. The moment one allows the self, and with it a love for all creatures, to flow out into the world, the world changes. If one can remain in this loving state, even in difficult circumstances, one will make uninterrupted progress and will keep being called to new tasks. The effect will be transforming, and the world and oneself will be seen in a different light. The insight can either catch one alarmingly off guard, or can become a perpetual source of cleansing and renewal.

Low Point experiences in the mutable houses are briefly described as follows. But note, they also depend on the zodiac signs through which the AP is passing.

In the 3rd mutable house at age 16, school days are usually over and professional training begins. The native has to decide what he or she is going to do. The sexual drive increases at the same time, but the desire for more freedom and for a personal love-life is usually misunderstood and curbed by trainers and educators. There are frequent rows with parents and superiors, and the young person is expected to toe the line. At the same time, he or she can start seeing the wider connections of things, and this can lead to a new awareness and to reorientation.

In the 6th mutable house at age 34, professional crises are common. Setbacks and defeats, not to mention health problems, necessitate an adjustment to objective reality, a trimming of plans for expansion, and the abandonment of illusionary dreams of the future. Often one finds at work that someone else is better than oneself; a decision has to be taken to join the community and concentrate on teamwork. Before the desired recognition can be gained, one has to be able to do or produce something. Many realize that they are in the wrong job, and start a fresh course of vocational training or strike out on a new road professionally.

In the 9th mutable house at age 52, there is a crisis of meaning. Everything seems to lose significance. All the experience and knowledge acquired so far now appear to be useless. But if one becomes empty, and admits one's own smallness and lack of power, the guiding impulse of the inner self can centre consciousness and give it a new orientation. One must choose spiritual life, revive youthful ideals, and aim at unselfish goals that will benefit a wider circle. In this way life can take on a new meaning and human love can blossom again.

In the 12th mutable house at age 70, the physical and mental powers decline. Active life wanes. The time has come to think of the permanent side of oneself and to let the world go, in order to be at one with the true Self. People who are unable to cultivate inner detachment will feel lonely and deserted. The fear of death and what comes after can extinguish the joy of living and embitter them. But those who open up to the true Self enter a higher sphere, where it is possible to remain imperturbable. They can peacefully sever earthly ties, and can return serenely to the eternal REALITY from which they came.

Bibliography

(1)   Huber Bruno: *Astro-Glossarium*, Band I, API-Verlag 1995

(2)   Software for Huber-style charts: *AstroCora, MegaStar, Regulus* UK/ Spain/ Argentina. [See "Resources" on page 217 for how to obtain software.]

(3)   Arroyo Stephen: *Astrology, Psychology and the Four Elements*

(4)   Assagioli Roberto: *Psychosynthesis Principles and Methods*

(5)   *Astrolog*, API-Verlag 1981-99 [Magazine of API Switzerland]

(6)   Bailey Alice A.: *Esoteric Astrology* and *A Treatise on White Magic*

(7)   Brunton Paul: *The Wisdom of the Overself*

(8)   Durckheim Karlfried Graf: *Vom doppelten Ursprung des Menschen*, Herder-Verlag, Freiburg, 1973

(9)   Goethe J.W.: *Essays on Art and Literature 2*. See also *Goethe's Colour Theory*, Rupprecht Mattaei, ed., and Herb Aach, ed. and tr.

(10)   Gauquelin Michel: *Cosmic Clocks*

(11)   Huber Bruno: *Astrological Psychosynthesis*

(12)   Huber, Bruno, Louise & Michael: *Aspect Pattern Astrology*

(13)   Huber Bruno and Louise: *The Astrological Houses*

(14)   Huber Bruno and Louise: *LifeClock*

(15)   Huber Louise: *Reflections & Meditations on the Signs of the Zodiac*

(16)   Huber Louise: *Entwicklungsprozesse im Horoskop*, API-Verlag 1980

(17)   Huber Michael A.: *Dynamische Auszahlungen*, API-Verlag 1978 ["Dynamic Calculations" are covered in the API(UK) Diploma Course - see "Resources".]

(18)   Huber Bruno and Louise: *Moon Node Astrology*

(19)   Itten Johannes: *The Art of Colour*

(20)   Jung C.G.: *Memories, Dreams, Reflections*

(21)   Kandinsky Wassily: *Concerning the Spiritual Art*

(22)   Krishnamurti Jiddu: *Freedom from the Known*

(23)   Levinson Daniel J.: *The Seasons of a Man's Life*

(24)   Lüscher Max: *Psychology of Colour*

(25)   Mertz B.A.: *Astrologie als Weg weiser*, Ebertin Verlag 1982

(26)   Müller Aemilius: *Die Moderne Farbenharmonielehre*, Chromos-Verlag 1959

(27)   Newton Isaac: *Opticks, or a Treatise of the Reflections, Refractions, Inflections & Colours of Light.*

(28)   Ostwald Wilhelm: *Die Farbenlehre*, 1912-1923

(29)   Stern Paul J.: *C.G.Jung – The Haunted Prophet*

(30)   Wenk, Sylvia, *Partnership and Relationship Dynamics through 'Click' Horoscopes*, API(UK) publication. 'Click' horoscopes relate the energies of two charts together, and can be drawn by most software generating Huber-style charts.

(31)   Jayakar, Pupul: *Krishnamurti: A Biography* (New York: Harper & Row, 1986).

Contacts and Resources

The Astrological Psychology Institute (UK)

A MODERN APPROACH to SELF-AWARENESS and PERSONAL GROWTH

Astrology has become recognised as a valuable tool for the development of self awareness and human potential. Bruno and Louise Huber researched and developed this approach over many years, combining selective astrology with Roberto Assagioli's psychosynthesis. Our courses are based on their results and inspiration.

PERSONAL GROWTH Most of our Diploma students not only learn astrology, chart interpretation and astrological counselling skills, but find that the course helps develop their own self understanding and personal and spiritual growth.

COURSES We offer Foundation Modules to those new to astrology or to the Huber Method. Our Modular Diploma Course teaches the Hubers' psychological approach to chart interpretation for working with clients. Details are in our prospectus.

EVENTS Our programme of seminars, workshops and conferences includes annual workshops that are an integral part of the Diploma in Astrological Counselling.

CONJUNCTION Our magazine *Conjunction* contains articles, news and supplementary teaching materials.

API (UK) Enquiries and Membership
P.O. Box 29, Upton, Wirral CH49 3BG, England
Tel: 00 44 (0)151 605 0039; Email: api.enquiries@btopenworld.com
Website: www.api-uk.org

API(UK) Bookshop
Books and API(UK) publications related to the Huber Method.
Linda Tinsley, API(UK) Bookshop
70 Kensington Road, Southport PR9 0RY, UK
Tel: 00 44 (0)1704 544652, Email: lucindatinsley@tiscali.co.uk

API Chart Data Service
Provides colour-printed Huber-style charts and chart data.
Richard Llewellyn, API Chart Data Service
PO Box 29, Upton, Wirral CH49 3BG, UK
Tel: 00 44 (0)151 606 8551, Email: r.llewellyn@btinternet.com

Software for Huber-style Charts
AstroCora, MegaStar, Regulus, Regulus Light Special Huber Edition.
On CD: **Elly Gibbs Tel: 00 44 (0)151-605-0039**
              Email: software.api@btinternet.com
Download: **Cathar Software** Website: www.catharsoftware.com

Publications on Astrological Psychology

THE COSMIC EGG TIMER
A practical introduction to Astrological Psychology
by Joyce Hopewell & Richard Llewellyn

An introduction and overview of the Huber approach. Offers a new and exciting way of using astrology, for all interested in finding out more about astrological psychology - and themselves! Using your own birth chart alongside this book you will gain insights into the kind of person you are, what makes you tick, and which areas of life offer you the greatest potential.

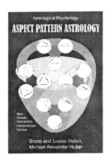

ASPECT PATTERN ASTROLOGY
Understanding motivation through aspect patterns

Essential reference on a key feature of the Huber approach. The pattern of the aspects reveals the structure and basic motivations of an individual's consciousness. Over 45 distinct aspect figures are identified, each with a different meaning. A systematic introduction to the practical use of this method, using many examples. Whether beginner or experienced astrologer, aspect patterns can provide immediate significant revelations about yourself and others.

The Planets
and their Psychological Meaning

Shows how the positions of the planets are fundamental to horoscope interpretation. They represent basic archetypal qualities present in everyone, giving clues to psychological abilities and characteristics, growth and spiritual development. Comprehensive descriptions of each planet, based around fundamental principles aiming to stimulate interpretative abilities. Contains examples plus detailed descriptions of key personality planets Sun, Saturn, Moon in each of the astrological houses or signs.

Books by Bruno & Louise Huber except where authors otherwise indicated.

A Modern Approach to Self Awareness and Personal Growth

MOON NODE ASTROLOGY

Combines psychological understanding with the concept of reincarnation, bringing a new astrological focus on the shadow personality and the individual's evolutionary process. Includes the psychological approach used with the Moon's Nodes, the Nodal Chart and the link with esotericism showing how earlier lives are reflected in the aspect structure and Nodal Chart. Covers the role of three charts in the individual's evolutionary process, the Nodal Chart symbolising the past, the Natal Chart the present, and the House Chart the impetus from the environment for development.

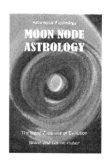

LifeClock

Revised, integrated edition. The horoscope is seen as a clock for the person's lifetime, with the Age Point indicating their age as the 'time' on the clock. Those trying it invariably find significant correspondences between indications in their birth chart and meaningful events in their lives. This deepens self understanding and provides impetus and insight to psychological and spiritual growth. A powerful tool for the helping professions, enabling quick identification of psychological sources of a client's problems.

ASTROLOGICAL PSYCHOSYNTHESIS
Astrology as a Pathway to Growth

Bruno Huber's introduction to this holistic approach to astrology, based on Assagioli's psychosynthesis, following the premise that every human being has a soul which is at the root of all developmental processes. It aims to help people to find their true self and work consciously towards integration and wholeness. The horoscope is used not just as an analytical tool, but also as an instrument to enhance the process of self-realisation and spiritual transformation. Three parts focus on intelligence, personality integration, love/sexuality/ relationships.

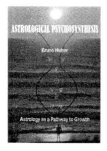

Published by HopeWell, PO Box 118, Knutsford, Cheshire WA16 8TG, UK

Printed in the United Kingdom
by Lightning Source UK Ltd.
133347UK00001B/521/P